WD FARR

WD Farr on horseback, Crystal River Ranch, ca. 1943. Courtesy of the Farr family.

WD Farr

Cowboy in the Boardroom

DANIEL TYLER

Foreword by Senator Hank Brown

For Peter!
Warm regards,
Daniel Tyler
Dec. 2011

University of Oklahoma Press : Norman

Also by Daniel Tyler

*The Last Water Hole in the West: The Colorado–Big Thompson Project and the
Northern Colorado Water Conservancy District* (Niwot, 1992)
Silver Fox of the Rockies: Delphus E. Carpenter and Western Water Compacts
(Norman, 2003)
Love in an Envelope: A Courtship in the American West (Albuquerque, 2009)

Library of Congress Cataloging-in-Publication Data

Tyler, Daniel.
   WD Farr : cowboy in the boardroom / Daniel Tyler ; foreword by Hank Brown.
   p.   cm.
   Includes bibliographical references and index.
   ISBN 978-0-8061-4193-0 (hardcover ; alk. paper)
   1. Farr, W. D. (William Daven), 1910–2007. 2. Businessmen—Colorado—
Greeley—Biography. 3. Bankers—Colorado—Greeley—Biography. 4. Cattle—
Feeding and feeds—Colorado—History—20th century. 5. Beef industry—Colorado—
History—20th century. 6. National Cattlemen's Beef Association (U.S.)—Biography.
7. Water resources development—Colorado—History—20th century. 8. Colo-
rado—Environmental conditions. 9. Greeley (Colo.)—Biography. 10. Colorado—
Biography. I Title. II Title: W.D. Farr.
   F784.G7T95 2011
   978.8'033092—dc22
   [B]

                                                              2010052722

The paper in this book meets the guidelines for permanence and durability of
the Committee on Production Guidelines for Book Longevity of the Council on
Library Resources, Inc. ∞

1 2 3 4 5 6 7 8 9 10

Contents

Illustrations

Foreword

When Horace Greeley visited Colorado after the Civil War, he found a dry and barren plain east of the Rocky Mountains. Previous explorers had described eastern Colorado as part of the Great American Desert. More than a few proclaimed that the area was unfit for human habitation. Greeley foresaw the potential for water storage in the mountains and the promise of irrigated agriculture. He predicted that the desert would be turned into a garden, and he envisioned the development of a prosperous urban corridor along the foothills running from Cheyenne, Wyoming, on the north to New Mexico on the south.

The story of WD Farr and his family is an account of the miracle that transformed the desert into one of the most productive agricultural areas in the world. It is a tale of vision, hard work, triumph, and tragedy, chronicled through the flowering of the eastern plains and the expansion of the farming and livestock industries. It is also a narrative of an extraordinary man whose efforts helped form the basis for commercial and industrial development as the area became more urbanized after World War II.

Readers of *WD Farr: Cowboy in the Boardroom* will comprehend how the eastern Colorado landscape was transformed through WD Farr's leadership. Following in the footsteps of earlier visionaries such as Benjamin Eaton, Elwood Mead, Delphus Carpenter, Charles Hansen, and others, Farr's endeavors in the twentieth century helped define the modern West. From taming flood waters, constructing water storage, and developing year-round cattle feeding to leading the way in water conservation, improved meat grading standards, and environmental partnerships, WD continued the pioneering tradition and adapted it to the dynamics of a post-war world.

Along the way he established a precedent for integrity that garnered recognition and acclaim from many corners. His ability to bring together opposing groups was uncommon. He listened to and learned from everyone with whom he came into contact during his ninety-seven years of life. Tyler paints a portrait of WD's leadership style, demonstrating how his impact extended far beyond the region of northern Colorado. As president of the National Cattlemen's Association, advisor to Congress, and mentor to President Richard Nixon's Environmental Protection Agency, WD had a broad footprint. His election to the Hall of Great Westerners at the National Cowboy and Western Heritage Museum in 2007 recognized the extent of his impact on the West, but without a doubt, his greatest effect was on those who were fortunate enough to have known him and to have witnessed his leadership. As Tyler points out, that unique and effective style was his most enduring legacy.

Senator Hank Brown
Denver, Colorado

Acknowledgments

No work of this extent can be completed without considerable assistance. Betty Henshaw helped me throughout the project, especially with genealogical investigation. She visited the Farr properties in Dorset County, U.K., and worked both with records keepers and with David Stranack, a Devon County resident who helped with connections to the Dorset Family History Society and the Dorset County Council. Information gleaned from this work uncovered data on the livelihood of the Farrs prior to Steven Farr's departure to Canada.

Most of the research in Colorado newspapers was undertaken by Nicolai ("Nick") Kryloff and Carol Lucking. Nick also edited each chapter and provided a stimulating and critical overview of the entire manuscript. Carol also helped with editing as well as with some of the Greeley interviews. To both these individuals I wish to extend my heartfelt gratitude for encouragement and for a candid evaluation of my work. Their participation in this project was invaluable, their friendship a huge bonus.

It would not have been possible to review so many newspapers without the financial assistance of the Northern Colorado Water Conservancy District (NCWCD). Gregory Silkensen of the NCWCD acted as project manager. With the help of Bernice Weber, he oversaw contracts and financial details for three years. To Eric Wilkinson, general manager of the NCWCD, I am most indebted. A great admirer of WD Farr, Wilkinson persuaded the board of directors to authorize the research assistance I requested. Brian Werner, Brad Leach, Julie Stoupa, and Doris Farnham, all from the NCWCD, provided aid on request. Doris, an expert computer guru, saved me on numerous occasions.

At the Greeley Museum, Peggy Ford provided in-depth, unselfish, and detailed assistance. No one knows the history of northern Colorado better than Peggy, and her value as a resource is not limited to research: she is also an astute observer of the community, and she helped me refine several ideas I was exploring over the course of this study. Her contributions were inspiring, and I am pleased to acknowledge the many times she helped me understand complex relationships inherent in the Greeley community.

Many others provided me with provocative thoughts and suggestions. Leslie Farr of Encampment, Wyoming; Sharon Farr of Timnath, Colorado; and Anne Farr of Loveland, Colorado, offered important perspectives on Judy Farr. Beverly Eberle, recording clerk for Garfield County in Glenwood Springs, Colorado; Judy Sappington, water resources engineer for Division 5, Glenwood Springs; Patsy Stark, archivist for the Frontier Historical Society, Glenwood Springs; and Linda Romero Criswell, Mt. Sopris Historical Society in Carbondale, Colorado, helped me understand WD's connection to the Crystal River Ranch. Angie Evans of Meagher County, Montana, clerk for title and escrow records in White Sulphur Springs, Montana, produced documents on the 71 Ranch. Betty Jo Gigot of *Calf News* generously shared her interviews with WD. Barbara Hoskins, information analyst for the St. Thomas Public Library, St. Thomas, Ontario; Jean Bircham, researcher from Aylmer, Ontario; and Gilbert Smith, St. Thomas, Ontario, whose relatives (Willsons) are related to the Farrs, were helpful in searching out evidence of the Farrs' activities in that area. At Colorado State University, I received unstinting support from Linda Meyer, archivist for the Colorado Agricultural Archives, and Patty Rettig, archivist for the Water Resources Archive. Erin McDanal, archivist for the Colorado State Archives in Denver, Colorado, located documentation on the naturalization of WD's grandfather and his brothers. Stephanie DiGiulio of Raleigh, North Carolina, did spectacular detective work for me on the owners of the 71 Ranch in Montana. Susan Wickham, WD's neighbor for the last decade of his life, generously shared her discerning thoughts about the Farrs and helped me visualize a poetic side of WD that could only be provided by a trusted friend.

Finally, I am grateful to those who read all or part of this manuscript and offered their advice: the Farr brothers, Nicolai Kryloff, Carol Lucking, Betty Henshaw, Dr. Robert Ward, Gregory Silkensen, Brian Werner, Dan

Law, and Peggy Ford. Susi Seawald read several chapters and demonstrated a shrewd understanding of WD Farr that helped focus my thoughts. For her insights, I am especially appreciative. Because authors become somewhat mesmerized by their own prose and style, a good copyeditor is essential for improving a manuscript's quality. To this end, I wish to express my profound gratitude to Kimberly Kinne, whose expert eye and skilled judgment forced me to rethink and review much that I had taken for granted.

Introduction

William Daven "WD" Farr used to say his life was just *circumstances*; things just happened, he said, for no particular reason. But he also knew he had accomplished a great deal in ninety-some years by following the lead of his father and grandfather and by pursuing a few simple principles that allowed him to comment in later years that he had never wasted a day in his life. Grandfather Billy and father Harry taught him the dignity of manual labor, the importance of building something of value through hard work, the challenge of having a clear vision of the future, the willingness to accept and accommodate to change, and the obligation to plan for and give back to his own community—local, regional, and national.

Successful individuals like WD owe their accomplishments to many different peoples as well as to *circumstances*. These ingredients for effective leadership, popularized recently by writers such as Canadian-born journalist Malcolm Gladwell, can provide a basic framework for studying WD's life and legacy. Even though Gladwell has been criticized for oversimplifying complex sociological problems, three of his popular works (*The Tipping Point, Blink,* and *Outliers*)[1] convey a common-sense evaluation of the power people have to make meaningful changes in their surroundings through natural intuition and good connections. The sociological and psychological explanations Gladwell uses to explain human nature offer a useful lens for viewing WD's life and understanding why he is worthy of recognition.

Born in 1910, WD lived through a period of major transition, as the West evolved from a region of natural resource exploitation to a more urban, cooperative, and environmentally sensitive community. As he noted in an interview at age ninety, his career was like a bridge between the age of development and the growing interest in a sustainable environment.[2] From his teenage years as a cowboy to his leadership of various livestock organizations, WD studied the stockman's environment with an eye toward erratic markets and ways beef producers could best compete against the lower prices of poultry and pork. Even so, he was not a maverick. In fact, he was loyal to the industry he represented and the cowboy way of life that had meant so much to him as a youth. But he also urged cattlemen to make changes so they could stay in business. Stung by the Dust Bowl and Great Depression and aware of changes and opportunities brought about by World War II, WD learned to study the past in order to conceive a vision of the future that would enable stockmen and farmers to survive roller-coaster markets. As he gained experience, sought connections with knowledgeable people, and amassed information, he increasingly became convinced of the need for a global nexus with farmers and stockmen in other countries. The *circumstances* that brought him such a rich and productive life were a result of this undeviating search for a better way to do things and a determination to seek advice from those who were best informed.

Just as WD lived through major transitions in the cattle industry, so, too, did he live through major transformations in how water was collected, stored, and delivered in the West. Growing up in the semi-arid East Slope of Colorado's Front Range, he knew that irrigated farming was dependent on a reliable water supply. He also knew that the rivers in northern Colorado were in greater demand than the available supply. When the Dust Bowl arrived in the 1930s, he witnessed the fear and hopelessness of neighbors whose productive farmland became worthless as scorching winds and sparse rainfall caused topsoil to dry up and blow away. Because WD had learned to drive a car at an early age and was interested in helping sell the idea of a federal water project for the community, he readily agreed to take his father and others on a tour across the area's farms, promoting the Colorado–Big Thompson project (C-BT). If constructed, the project would bring badly needed water from the western side of the Continental Divide, where snowfall was far greater, to the Front Range, where cities and agriculture were more developed. The experience provided WD with a better understanding of how to unite people, how to respect the views of dissident factions, and how to persevere in a worthy cause.

These encounters convinced him of the value of increased reservoir capacity and the importance of formulating a management system that would make water available when needed—and not just because someone held a proprietary right. As director of the Northern Colorado Water Conservancy District (NCWCD) for forty years, he persuaded stakeholders in Colorado's West Slope that an expansion of the C-BT could benefit everyone. At the same time, his experiences as a consultant with the Environmental Protection Agency (EPA) opened his eyes to the importance of environmental issues and the need to include all stakeholders in complex water negotiations. Ultimately, because of WD's reason, common sense, and breadth of knowledge, even those who opposed him admired him.

As a director of several banks, WD learned about the business infrastructure of his community. He urged modernization of the banks he represented, and he favored cooperation and integration when better service could be provided to borrowers. Because he was smart, always prepared at meetings, thoughtful, and receptive to the views of others, he was asked to serve on many boards and committees in addition to those representing the cattle industry, water development, and banking. From Rotary and the Boy Scouts of America to the Greeley Water Board, WD accepted almost every position he was asked to fill. And because he was so much in demand and so effective as the head of many organizations, his reputation as a leader spread beyond northern Colorado.

It was, for the most part, unsolicited leadership, although WD was pleased to have the power and positions required to implement change. WD led because he was persuaded to lead by those who saw him as having unassailable integrity. He was considered a good person—trustworthy and effective. As Senator Hank Brown has noted in the foreword to this book, WD built on the accomplishments of Benjamin Eaton, Elwood Mead, and Delphus Carpenter. Eaton helped establish the irrigation infrastructure in northern Colorado. Mead focused on water administration and storage and contributed to the advancement of agricultural science. Carpenter recognized the threat to stable water supplies from neighboring states and established a covenant system that served to apportion interstate waters equitably. WD built on their pioneer achievements.

WD used his authority to develop the business side of agriculture, livestock feeding, and water storage. Because he recognized economic movements and social pressures affecting the West in the twentieth century, he used his energy and talent to address societal changes. His curiosity was insatiable. He studied ways to improve techniques and systems—mechanical, procedural, organizational—and he appealed to others for assistance to accomplish benefits for the largest possible number of people. He was willing to take calculated risks, some of which proved costly. Even his own businesses suffered at times from distractions or misguided decisions. But overall, WD was seen as someone who worked for the well-being of his community. Because he was a gentleman, a good listener, a teacher totally lacking in hubris, and one who refused to let disagreement turn into personal conflict, he remained a strong leader even into his ninth decade.

I approached the research and writing of this story with some angst. WD sold the Crystal River Ranch to my father in 1946, and even though I hardly knew him in those years, he was always gracious, supportive, and helpful to me when I began writing books about water many years later. I also knew that WD was beloved by almost everyone I might interview, and I was fearful of sanctifying someone who saw himself as quite ordinary. I wanted to focus on his role in the West's metamorphosis, while fleshing out his personal leadership style. Readers will note that I have included some of what WD said in interviews with Gregory Silkensen, Sally Mier, and myself. I did this because I thought his voice was important in conveying his humanity. He loved to talk, and he told stories. Somewhat folkloric, he had a way of viewing the past in anecdotal terms. His recollections were not always accurate, but his hopes for the future, his desire to live another fifty years, and his humility convinced me that what he said about himself was worthy of inclusion in the biography.

Besides the interviews I did with WD, his family members, business associates, and friends, I had the benefit of two talented researchers, Carol Lucking and Nicolai Kryloff, who helped me scour newspapers, especially the *Greeley Tribune*, for additional tidbits about WD. I sometimes overwhelmed Peggy Ford, the Greeley Museum's accomplished archivist, with questions. I also searched for archival material at the NCWCD, the Colorado State Archives in Denver, the American Heritage Center at the University of Wyoming, the Colorado Agricultural Archives, the Water Resources Archive at Colorado State University (CSU), and the records of the clerk and recorder in the Colorado towns of Greeley, Glenwood Springs, and Fort Collins as well as in Meagher County, Montana. In addition, the Farr family generously made WD's surviving papers available to me before they were archived at CSU. Even though the materials are incomplete—lacking any reference, for example, to the Farr feedlots—I could not have written this biography without them. For the most part, archival research confirmed what I learned in interviews and in the Farr papers.

As I delved into research about WD, it became clear that his activities and travels were so extensive that I had to pick and choose among many themes in order to concentrate on two subjects: (1) WD's life as an interface between the Old West and the New West and (2) his management style in the boardroom as an example of effective leadership. To this end, I decided to include anecdotes that would help describe WD as a vulnerable, sensitive, and warm human being. I wanted to present the likeness of a man who was also an impressive leader. Because he elicited such deep affection in others, it seemed the right thing to do.

Readers will note that I do not extend WD's story into the next generation. Whereas a close bond formed both between WD's grandfather Billy and his (Billy's) son Harry and between Harry and his (Harry's) son WD, that same work relationship developed differently between WD and his children. John, the oldest, left Greeley and went into insurance; Bill (WR) worked the farms and feedlots with WD until he found his real love in banking; Dick invested a career in the feedlot and produced a son, RD, who came the closest to following in WD's footsteps; and Randy, a talented writer who generously provided the title of this book, left Greeley to start his own businesses. John supplied many insights on his father as well as comments on each chapter I wrote. WR and Dick toured me over the farms and feedlots and offered names of people I should interview. More important, all the sons gave me complete freedom to write their father's history—not an easy thing for them to do. I am grateful for their confidence in me.

As historian David McCullough noted in a speech at Miami University on November 9, 2009,[3] there is no such thing as a self-made man. Everyone is shaped by people they know, what they have read, and the *circumstances* of their upbringing. This is certainly true of WD. He had close friends and family who influenced him, and he looked for advisors who were educated and experienced. As much as these individuals impacted his life and accomplishments, WD had a reciprocal impact on those who knew him. He was aware of this ability to influence others. When he reflected on his life in later years, the *circumstances* to which he referred included the reciprocity and collaboration that worked well for him as a leader.

WD FARR

CHAPTER 1

Beginnings

Life is either a daring adventure or nothing.

—Helen Keller

William Daven Farr attacked life with intensity, hopefulness, and tenacity. He succeeded because he communicated a profound interest in the views of others and because be embraced change as opportunity. Whether the task at hand involved farming, cattle feeding, banking, meat grading, water development, or community planning, WD[1] articulated a vision of how things could be better, from the simplest laboring techniques to the nation's role in an increasingly competitive world. And because he listened to others and thought deeply about how his actions might improve life for everyone, he was trusted.

That trust served as the backbone of his leadership. The talents he manifested during his long life (1910–2007) were not formulaic, divinely inspired, or unique to WD alone. They were handed down through several generations of Farrs who believed the essence of a good life included the investment of time and energy in bettering one's own community. Like his predecessors, WD was able to develop and articulate a comprehensible view of what a better future could be, and he demonstrated a willingness to take calculated risks to achieve such goals. In one sense, that willing-ness to take risks was a variant of the pioneering spirit, but the rugged individualism associated with first-generation settlers was replaced in the Farrs by a desire for shared progress and across-the-board community and regional development. These objectives gradually matured in the first generation of Farrs who left England in the mid-nineteenth century in

3

search of a better life in America and became even stronger in the generations that settled in Colorado. The qualities of service, optimism, vision, and willingness to adapt to change that made WD such an effective leader had their genesis in the pioneering attributes of his great grandfather.

Stephen Farr was the third child of Stephen Farr, Sr., and Martha Noakes. He was born on April 12, 1826, in the parish of Beer Hackett, Dorset County, England. His mother died in childbirth. Four months later, his father married Ann Andrews, with whom he had four additional children.[2] According to census data and Stephen Farr, Sr.'s, last will and testament, the family lived comfortably on a small farm of seventy acres that had expanded to 110 acres by 1864. They were assisted by three laborers, who helped with farming and milked a half dozen dairy cows. Stephen's will lists an abundance of farm tools, a milk house, a dairy house, and a main house with kitchen, parlor, and four bedrooms, each amply equipped with feather beds and furniture for every family member. If not abundant, the Farr's assets were comparable to other middle-class households in rural nineteenth-century England.[3]

Stephen Farr, Jr., grew up in this environment until, according to family lore,[4] his father decided to send him to Eton College (King's College of Our Lady of Eton).[5] Eton has no record of his attendance, but the family believes he may have decided to pass up an education for a chance to "sail before the mast" to Australia. Whatever the truth, the father bristled at his only son's demonstration of independence and made it clear that Stephen, Jr., would have to seek his fortune elsewhere. At the age of twenty-five, in a manner that would become familiar to subsequent generations of Farrs, the son dared to imagine opportunity in this setback. With little to keep him home, he married Mary Ellen Dyke from a nearby parish at the Church of St. Peter in Dorchester on May 5, 1851. Shortly thereafter, the newlyweds boarded a ship for Canada.

Crossing the Atlantic in mid-century was an ordeal under the best of circumstances. If Stephen had enough money to purchase a cabin, he was fortunate. But he and Mary were probably forced to ship in steerage, where they could have been exposed to claustrophobia, measles, chicken pox, cholera, dysentery, poor food, and sea sickness. The journey from Liverpool to New York would have lasted two weeks to a month. Some ships were becalmed or subject to pirate attacks, making the journey even longer and more dangerous. Because large numbers of Irish fleeing the potato famine and Germans seeking political refuge were also in search of passage to America in the 1850s, British ship captains often exceeded the legal number of on-board passengers, their vessels referred to as "coffin ships."[6]

The risks to passengers were even greater if ships went to Canada. Canadian authorities rarely challenged British ships, and for the most part, imperial regulations were ignored.[7] Few Canadian records were kept of passenger lists, but if Stephen and Mary came to America via the St. Lawrence River, they would have landed either at Quebec City in the summer or at Halifax, Nova Scotia, a port that remained open all year.

In all likelihood the Farrs ended their sea voyage in Quebec in late summer or early fall. They continued their journey on Canadian soil to Toronto before settling in the town of Port Stanley, Ontario, on the north shore of Lake Erie. Here, Mary Farr gave birth to her first son, John S. Farr, on April 4, 1852.[8] John may have been conceived on the Atlantic crossing. This is, of course, pure speculation, but in consideration of his new bride, Stephen would have wanted to leave England soon after the wedding to avoid crossing the Atlantic during bad weather, and he would have wanted to be at his destination before winter. Consequently, he and Mary were most likely at sea during July and August of 1851, and their Port Stanley destination (Southwold Township) may have been selected because of other Farrs who had preceded them.[9]

Port Stanley was located in Elgin County. Named for James Bruce, the eighth Earl of Elgin, it was separated from Middlesex County in 1852. Seven townships along the lake shore comprised a total population of 25,000 people, most of whom farmed the rich soils within the county. The original land grant awarded in 1803 to Colonel Thomas Talbot was made up of 5,000 acres, but Talbot purchased additional lands in the next two decades. His plan was to encourage British settlement and to build roads for communication and transport of agricultural goods, but he proved to be something of an eccentric and was accused of trying to enrich himself at the expense of the settlers he wooed to Elgin County from Britain and the United States. He returned to England and died in 1853. By that time, a small amount of land was still available for new immigrants, but purchases had to be made from a group of investors called the Canada (Land) Company.[10] These were the lands that Stephen and Mary Ellen eventually farmed after spending their formative years in Port Stanley, but they were renters, not freeholders.

Elgin County was a fertile area. Wheat was the principal crop in Yarmouth and Southwold townships, but within a decade the dairy industry also developed. Some white pine was still harvested in the eastern portion of Elgin County, but toward the end of the 1850s, the lumber industry had moved west into hardwoods, whereas a livestock industry and a small orchard industry were beginning to develop in the east. Port Stanley remained an active outlet for flour, tanned hides, distilled alcohol, woolen goods, and other agricultural products, but when the Farrs arrived, poorly constructed roads inhibited transportation to market. The port also suffered from its location at the mouth of Kettle Creek, which experienced irregular flooding and congested piers that presented dangerous conditions for incoming steamships. Rainfall was ample, with a yearly average of almost thirty-four inches; the growing season averaged 200 days. St. Thomas, Yarmouth Township's largest town, had a population of 1,000, and nearby Sparta attracted a sizeable community of Quakers. Most farm machinery and the amenities needed by the farming community were available as imports or local manufacture.[11]

John Farr's birth in Port Stanley was followed by Mary Jane Farr in 1854 and William Henry "Billy" Farr on August 31, 1855. Lizzie, Emma, Charles, Thomas, Walter, and Anna rounded out the household. For a few years, Stephen garnered income as a teamster, driving a team of horses or mules and getting paid by the load.[12] Even though Port Stanley had a business community that required daily deliveries—a foundry, distilleries, a grist mill, and a railroad connecting to St. Thomas—Stephen's fast-growing family dictated a move to Aylmer, where he leased a hotel as a business venture. The hotel burned, so he contracted as a tenant farmer on land a mile north of Sparta, where he found fertile soil and plenty of work for his young brood.[13]

Stephen continued as tenant on various farms in Elgin and Malahide counties. By the middle of the 1870s, he had accumulated several hundred dollars of personal property and considerable livestock. He and Mary became Methodists. They lived in a stone house and were well accepted in the Sparta community, but their tenant status offered little opportunity

Sparta, Ontario, blacksmith shop, where Billy Farr trained as an apprentice.
Courtesy the Sparta and District Historical Society, Sparta, Ontario, Canada.

for the children. As the oldest, John assisted his father on the rented land.
Eventually, he accumulated enough assets to become a yeoman farmer
with fifty acres of land in Malahide County.[14] But Billy, the second son,
soon recognized the need to prepare himself with a trade. He spent three
years as a blacksmith's apprentice in nearby Sparta and then decided
to try his profession in a relatively unknown and untamed land where
opportunity was believed to be limitless. This time, in contrast to the previous generation, the son traveled with paternal blessings.

Billy was twenty-two years old in 1877 when he headed west. He had
just enough money in his pocket to buy a train ticket on the transcontinental railroad that had been completed eight years earlier in the United
States.[15] The railroad was the major conduit for news and stories about
opportunities in the American West. Billy probably knew about the gold
excitement in the Black Hills and the debacle experienced by Colonel
Custer at Little Big Horn in 1876.[16] It is also possible news had reached

Ontario from the 1876 Centennial Exposition in Philadelphia, where the recently constituted state of Colorado (August 1, 1876) was promoting its assets with the help of Nathan Meeker, one of the founders of the Union Colony of Greeley. Whatever his reasons for selecting Wyoming as his destination, Billy had just enough money for a ticket from Detroit to Cheyenne. When he boarded the westbound train, Billy joined an exodus of Americans looking for ways to strike it rich in a country where American Indian resistance was on the decline and the need for skilled workers was expected to increase rapidly.[17]

For "seven days and nights" he rode various railroads to his destination. He immediately found employment with a big, burly man whose temper and predilection for hard liquor made Billy uncomfortable. Billy was stocky himself and an excellent horseshoer, but when his employer came at him with an axe, he decided to leave Cheyenne for the recently organized settlement of Loveland, Colorado.

Loveland was in need of skilled blacksmiths. Named after A. H. Loveland, president of the Colorado Central Railroad, the town had just been established in 1877 when Billy arrived. He located an employer and once again began to ply his trade. After two months, a stage driver whose horses he had been shoeing told him that Greeley, a more mature farming community, was in need of an additional blacksmith.[18] Billy could hire on right away with a man who hoped to have someone take over his business. Billy demurred. He had not been able to save enough money to pay for the thirty-mile stage ride to Greeley on the Cache la Poudre River. Not a problem, the driver told him. Billy could make the trip for free and could repay the driver when able.

On December 9, 1877, Billy Farr arrived in Greeley. It was the beginning of four generations of Farrs living and prospering in the area. Billy eventually paid his debt to the stage coach driver—with interest![19]

The opportunities for a blacksmith in Greeley were far-reaching. In 1877 the farming community was burgeoning with improvements in irrigated agriculture, requiring the skills of farriers, wheelwrights, and machinery repairmen. New bench lands were being brought under cultivation by the twenty-seven-mile Number 2 ditch from the Cache la Poudre River, and although farmers were still learning how to run water effectively, the potato, alfalfa, oat, barley, and wheat crops benefitted from continuous flows of irrigation water during the entire growing season. A buffalo-robe industry also prospered for a few years. Tanned robes were produced by five tanneries at the rate of twelve a day. According to the 1877 *Colorado Business Directory*, Greeley was expected to become the "robe-opolis of the country." Even Greeley's women participated, making buffalo hide gloves as a cottage industry.[20]

By 1877 the Union Colony had matured in other ways of interest to Billy. Meeker's goal for Greeley was a utopian community populated by educated farmers who would develop schools, churches, spacious residences, libraries, parks, businesses, clubs, and organizations for social and intellectual stimulation and who were prohibited from manufacturing or consuming alcohol.[21] To a great extent he was successful. The Free Masons and Odd Fellows were already established. Baptist, Methodist, and Episcopal churches were building on lots provided by the colony. A controversial smooth-wire fence circumnavigated the colony, keeping out open-range cattle. Although it prompted criticism from outsiders, who sneered about holier-than-thou temperance advocates trying to isolate themselves from the "heathen" around them, the fence was needed to protect Greeley's homes and gardens. Its construction followed the law of the range that required animals to be fenced out where they were not wanted.[22] Greeley residents were mostly farmers for whom a branch of the National Grange (Order of Patrons of Husbandry) had been established to provide some leverage in negotiations with merchants and railroads. Greeley's importance was further enhanced in 1877 by its selection as county seat for Weld County, following several years of competition with nearby Evans for this honor.

However, Billy also noted that Meeker's community was not without financial problems. Residence lots in town had declined in value after the spring of 1871 and would not recover for nine years.[23] Fencing out the "heathen" cattlemen had cost $25,000. The budgetary impact was felt by many farmers who expected the colony to put more resources into constructing dams, reservoirs, ditches, and laterals. Crops suffered when ditch breaks occurred or when upstream users in the newly established Fort Collins Agricultural Colony diverted flows from the Cache la Poudre River during drought years. The pain of loss was exacerbated by four locust plagues (1867, 1872, 1874, 1876), increased salt in the irrigation water, fungi and bugs blighting the potatoes, and the occasional hail storm, all of which reminded Greeley pioneers they had settled in the Great American Desert.[24]

Billy, however, was an optimist. He was making money, and he had a partner to share the work. The blacksmith shop of Farr and [John A.] Taylor was located in a prominent part of downtown Greeley near the railroad station and livery stable. Billy could see opportunities for himself and a family in the long run, but he was impatient to acquire the nest egg he would need to bring the woman he wanted to marry from Canada to Greeley.

Meeker's financial difficulties seemed to offer a solution. As Union Colony president, he had become so involved in the community's growth and development that he ignored his own balance sheet. The *Greeley Tribune*, Meeker's powerful and principal mouthpiece for reminding colonists of their rights and obligations, continued to lose money. Because Meeker had so many other irons in the fire, he found himself out of cash. Horace Greeley was able to oblige with a loan of $1,000 at no interest. Between the two men, it was understood that Meeker would not be expected to pay back the principal until he got his feet under him.

But Horace Greeley died unexpectedly in November 1872. Unaware of the generous terms under which the loan had been made, administrators of Horace Greeley's estate demanded immediate repayment. Meeker protested that his financial circumstances were worse than when the loan was made, but the administrators took him to court. Meeker was able to produce forty acres of land the colony had given him for services rendered, but in order to pay the unsettled remainder of the loan, he accepted the job of agent at the White River Ute Indian Agency in northwest Colorado in 1878.

Removal of the Utes from Colorado had become a battle cry as whites crowded into the mining areas of the San Juan Mountains. In December 1877, the *Ouray Times* was asking why "non-producing, semi-barbarous" people were being allowed to occupy lands which "intelligent and industrious citizens" could develop more productively.[25]

Billy Farr may have asked the same question, but he also saw a chance to use his blacksmithing skills in return for significant remuneration. Without hesitation, he joined Meeker's expedition to the White River in

1879. The group traveled by train to Rawlins. From there to the White River, the route followed government roads and Indian trails. Everyone was expected to provide his own horse and saddle. Billy was forced to turn back, because he lacked the $65 required for these purchases.

Of such seemingly insignificant events is history made. Meeker went on to the White River. Because of his somewhat naive ideological utopian convictions, he immediately got into trouble with Utes, who disdained the farming life and refused to give up their traditional nomadic ways. Well-meaning but determined, Meeker insisted on schools, farms, and other so-called civilizing changes. A last straw for the Utes was Meeker's order to plow up their race track.

The Utes complained to Governor Frederick W. Pitkin and protested Meeker's plans by setting houses on fire, burning the forests, and stealing government cattle. Meeker called for soldiers to enforce his authority. They were ambushed when they arrived. When reinforcements finally quelled the disturbance, a grizzly scene of murder at the agency was revealed. The dead bodies of Meeker and eleven of his cohorts were found disrobed and mutilated. If Billy had been able to produce $65, he most surely would have suffered the same fate.

Instead, he returned to Greeley to focus on business for a while before undertaking another adventure in the spring of 1881. By that time, two younger brothers had come to Greeley to investigate opportunities for their own betterment. Walter J. and Charles A. Farr joined Billy with three other Greeley men to work on the recently organized Oregon Short Line (OSL) Railroad.[26] Incorporated on April 14, 1881, in Wyoming Territory, the OSL planned to construct standard-gauge tracks from Granger, Wyoming (just west of Green River), through Boise, Idaho, to the Oregon border—a route that approximated the Oregon Trail. When it reached the Idaho–Oregon border in 1884, the OSL provided the Central Rockies with a connection to the Northwest that was not possible through the Union Pacific and Central Pacific systems. When the Farrs later became interested in sheep buying in Oregon, this "short line" proved most beneficial.

But none of the brothers remained long with OSL construction crews. They were farmers and stockmen. Walter returned to Colorado to establish himself on a sheep ranch near the Wyoming border, where he was joined by the youngest brother, Thomas. Meanwhile, Billy set out for

Ontario to marry his high school sweetheart, Deborah Jane Willson.[27] A Quaker meeting house had been built in 1865 at the south end of Stephen Farr's property. While Billy was living in Ontario, his route home from the blacksmith shop would have passed close by. Not unexpectedly, he made the acquaintance of a pretty Quaker girl, Deborah Jane Willson, during those trips back and forth. The friendship blossomed, and when Billy decided he had the means to support a wife in Colorado, he returned home to ask for her hand. "Jennie D" accepted.

For the occasion, Billy ordered a new pair of boots. Unfortunately, they did not arrive in time for the ceremony on December 28, 1881. He got married in stockings. Jennie might have been mildly disappointed in his attire, but having been raised in a Quaker family, she had learned tolerance, simplicity, integrity, avoidance of extravagance, and self-discipline. WD later remembered her as gracious and hospitable, always enthusiastic to see him when he stopped by for lunch. Her gentility had no small effect on WD's understanding of how to deal with people. Although she was only twenty-two years old when she left Ontario with Billy and his new boots, Jennie was a model wife in Greeley, devoted to a husband who was determined to establish himself as a productive member of that community.

For a few years, blacksmithing paid the bills, but in 1884 when Jennie became pregnant with their first child, Billy began thinking more seriously about the agricultural potential of a piece of property in the Hillside area, southwest of Greeley city limits. It was dry land on which he had probably been cutting native grasses under the rules of preemption claims since 1878.[28] The property became more valuable in 1884 when a British company extended its irrigation ditch to the Hillside area from the Big Thompson River. Billy's claim was at the tail end of the system, a disadvantage for water users under the best of circumstances, but the British owners of the ditch proved especially inept. They were good businessmen but failed to comprehend the complexities of managing water for irrigated agriculture. Their "inexperience with irrigation and unstable financial backing were handicaps they could not overcome."[29] They recognized the opportunities to be had in building water delivery systems to the parched and unbroken prairie, but their "all or nothing"[30] approach to water delivery resulted in irregular and inadequate supplies during the latter part of the growing season. Nevertheless, they muddled along as owners and administrators of the ditch system until 1900, when a number of frustrated farmers and Greeley businessmen bought out the British so they could run the ditch themselves.

Billy had planted some oats, barley, and wheat; in addition, using occasional waste water, he also harvested grass hay for donkeys and mules working in the silver and gold mines of the nearby mountains. But the most pivotal event on his new property took place before ownership of the ditch changed hands and undoubtedly contributed to his interest in acquiring a reliable water supply for the entire area. That event came about because of an early snow storm in the late fall of 1884.

Brothers Walter and Thomas were trailing a band of 900 sheep to Denver from somewhere in the mountains along the Colorado–Wyoming border, where the sheep had been grazing all summer. About half the band was made up of wethers (castrated males); the rest were lambs.[31] As they crossed into Colorado from the Laramie Plains, a sudden snowstorm took them by surprise. Temperatures dropped, wind velocity increased, and the men had trouble bedding the restless sheep. The weather was so bitter that they had to bring their horses inside an old settler's cabin where they were forced to spend the night. Arising early the next morning, they were greeted by more than a foot of snow on the ground. Sheep had to be urged to their feet, but they muddled on, grazing those spots blown bare by the wind. With lambs fighting to keep up, Tom and Walter struggled to Billy's land in Greeley where they had already planned to rest on their journey to market in Denver. It took them a week to get there, and they had not planned to stay long. But the early onset of winter forced them to remain for several months. The sheep were not driven to market until the spring of 1885. During that cold and snowy winter, Tom Farr had to make many trips from a well every morning with two-and-a-half-gallon pails so the sheep could drink. In the afternoon the Farr brothers fed whatever feed they could beg, borrow, or steal to keep the animals alive.

Such extraordinary efforts expended on this small band of sheep were rewarded by unexpectedly high prices in Denver. Buyers had not seen such extraordinarily fat lambs. The Farrs walked away from the experience with a profit of $1.25 per lamb and with the conviction that the small grains and alfalfa grown in Weld County, which were relatively worthless as market commodities, could be profitably converted to meat in a lamb feeding industry. They were correct. In no time, other farmers in Larimer and Weld counties recognized the opportunity to make money feeding lambs. According to the U.S. Bureau of Agricultural Economics, the number of lambs on feed in northern Colorado continued to rise to record levels up to 1926 and remained a significant source of income to farmers through World War II.[32]

In addition to the availability of good feed, a number of market factors contributed to the success of this industry. East Coast buyers were eager for lamb. In major cities along the Atlantic seaboard, Orthodox Jews would pay a premium price for a shoulder of lamb that could be easily stripped of veins as required under Talmudic law. Lamb feeders in Colorado shipped their fat animals to Chicago, where they were purchased and delivered to Eastern cities for slaughter. Carcass parts undesirable to Orthodox Jews were easily sold to hotels and restaurants. Until this generation of Orthodox Jews began to decline in the 1940s, a strong demand persisted for the shoulders of fattened lambs.

Wool provided a secondary market for sheep owners. Along with cotton, it was the primary source of fiber for clothing until synthetic fibers, such as nylon and rayon, were commercially developed by the nation's principal clothing manufacturers at the end of World War II. Many sheep men had typically kept their animals for two or three years so they could get cash from several wool crops. But the best market for sheep gradually favored younger lambs over those wethers that were two years and older—at least until after the war.[33] By 1945, soldiers returning from overseas duty at war's end were weary of a diet heavy with mutton. They made known their interest in beef at the same time the Orthodox Jewish population was shrinking on the East Coast and stores began stocking clothes made from synthetic fibers. But for the first forty years of the twentieth century, feeding lambs and older wethers in Colorado, Wyoming, and Nebraska proved extremely profitable. Stockmen with a keen business sense were able to accumulate considerable wealth.

Alfalfa was an important reason for this success. With the advent of extensive irrigation in northern Colorado, alfalfa gradually became a dominant crop. At two dollars a ton on the open market, it was relatively worthless until farmers discovered that lambs rapidly converted this protein-rich legume into meat. Although at first the Greeley area lagged behind

Fort Collins in growing alfalfa, the completion of major irrigation projects and the early success of the Farrs with lamb feeding resulted in significant increases in alfalfa production.[34] The price of alfalfa gradually rose, along with corn and other grains, but when sugar beet factories came to the Front Range of the Colorado Rockies, they produced a waste product that proved even more beneficial to livestock feeders. Sugar beet pulp allowed the number of lambs on feed in northern Colorado to top half a million.[35]

The establishment of sugar factories began on Colorado's western slope in the town of Grand Junction in 1899 and proliferated along the Front Range during the next five years. The Greeley and Eaton plants were established in 1902, followed by factories in Fort Collins, Longmont, and Windsor the following year. For the most part, the factories were welcome additions to these communities, although some Greeley residents feared they might turn their community into an "industrial center."[36] Others complained about "sticky streets" as a result of the pulp being hauled from the factories to feedlots in leaky wagons.

But the addition of sugar beets to the agricultural base of northern Colorado was an unqualified success. Farmers who contracted with sugar beet companies had a guaranteed cash crop, and those who fed livestock were able to use the beet tops during harvest and then the pulp residue after the factories had processed the beets for sugar. Farmers also learned that sheep manure dramatically increased the per-acre tonnage of beets.

As WD remembered, however, hauling the pulp was very hard work. It had to be loaded on wagons at the factory with a scoop shovel, each scoop weighing close to fifty pounds. Unloading the pulp into feed troughs required the same effort, and then it was back to the factory for another load. On average, lambs were fed the beet pulp for as long as it lasted, about four months—from early November through February. Toward the end of this period, more alfalfa and grain were added to their diet for proper finishing.

Billy bought and fed his first sheep on the homestead in 1886, and he fed every year after that until his death in 1932.[37] He was also the first of the four Farr brothers to become a naturalized citizen of the United States in 1886.[38] Although his principal home with Jennie was in town, Billy divided his time between the blacksmith shop and the homestead in what is now the southwest part of Greeley. Brother Walter brought in the lambs. His ranch near the Colorado–Wyoming border was large enough for sheep grazing, and because of its location ten miles northeast of Eaton in the Lone Tree Valley, the land also produced feed crops on 400 acres with water from the Larimer and Weld Ditch. Walter delivered lambs to other farmers for feeding, but he encountered problems trying to fulfill contracts. It soon became difficult to locate enough animals to match the enormous gains in feed production that had arisen in northern Colorado with the expansion of irrigation.

For Walter, this problem translated into a unique business opportunity. Lambs weighing forty to fifty pounds could be purchased in the Southwest for around a dollar a head and brought north by rail for distribution to local farms, where they were sold for $1.40 to $1.70. Huddled in double-decker palace stock cars, 225 to the car, lambs and their new owners were at the mercy of whimsical railroads. But if everything worked as expected, and the lambs doubled their weight after arrival on northern farms, profits were impressive.

To capitalize on this opportunity, Walter became a traveler in search of reliable sources of stock. Beginning in 1896 the *Greeley Tribune* noted his departure for New Mexico almost every fall, followed by his return with 10,000 to 50,000 animals. He scoured eastern New Mexico near the Texas border, then Las Vegas, Wagon Mound on the Santa Fe Trail, and Española. He formed a partnership with Jesse Gale and extended his travels into the Navajo Reservation, sometimes purchasing the ancient churros whose ancestry dated back to the sixteenth-century Spanish occupation.[39] When lambs became scarce in New Mexico, he sought contracts in Utah, Arizona, Nevada, Idaho, Montana, Washington, and Oregon. It was a big business, but not without risks.

Weather—too hot, too cold, too rainy, too dry—could bring on sudden sickness: scours, pneumonia, stomach worms, foot rot, pinkeye, scabies, and other conditions resulting from bacteria and stress. As demand and prices increased for lambs, contract buying became hysterical. Operators expressed a willingness to pay a premium for lambs before they were dropped by the ewes. Many of them contracted to deliver lambs but found themselves unable to obtain the stock. Consequently, they lost their entire business when lamb feeders sued for failure to deliver.[40]

But such was the nature of the business. Jesse Gale and Walter Farr knew it was chancy. Risk was inherent in livestock feeding, and they had to be smart enough to learn from sporadic setbacks. Sometimes their lambs were too fat, and they had to take a lower price. On one occasion, they lost 4,000 sheep appropriated by a neighboring rancher with a Winchester who felt the animals were trespassing.

This entanglement involved the Warren Live Stock Company, which had illegally fenced lands they leased from the government, making it almost impossible for other stockmen to reach their own railroad lands. In protest, Walter's herders drove a band of sheep through Warren's fences, resulting in a mixing of two herds. The Warren herders drove the two bands fifteen miles to a corral on their own land and kept Walter away with the threat of violence. Walter went to court. After hearing both sides, as well as Warren's claim to more than $6,000 in damages for the trespass, the judge found Walter guilty but ordered him to pay just one dollar.[41]

Other risks permeated the business. Periodic storms might produce a raging torrent that drowned lambs before they could reach high ground. A few years of drought could easily reduce the supply of alfalfa hay necessary for feed. Although ewes could be expected to produce healthy twins with regularity, on one occasion Walter reported a generic rarity: a "freak of nature in the shape of a lamb with one head, two bodies and six legs" which was alive and doing well.[42]

Walter eventually settled down in Eaton (established in 1883), where he became a town trustee and volunteer fireman. He helped persuade local government to support creation of a school district and to accept bonded indebtedness for the construction of a new school building. And because of his expanding influence in agriculture and his booster spirit, Walter was elected Eaton's mayor for two terms, beginning in 1902. During his administration, Eaton's first water works were completed, lessening the fire danger in this rapidly growing community. After completion of his term, Walter joined with others to incorporate an acetylene gas plant that provided Eaton with its first artificial lights in 1903. Although the plant exploded the following year, Walter's vision of electrical service for northern Colorado was realized in 1906 with the creation of the Eaton Water, Light and Power Company. It became part of a legacy of business success and community betterment matched by his older brother in nearby Greeley.

Billy also expanded his sheep feeding operation. His homestead was well situated, not far from the sugar factory that occupied a fifty-acre site just east of Greeley. The Greeley Sugar Company (later Great Western) began operations in the fall of 1902, and by 1904, even though the feeding of beet pulp was still considered "experimental," the Farrs (Billy and Walter) were listed as having 9,000 sheep on several ranches and were considered the largest feeders of beet pulp in Weld County.[43]

Like his brother, Billy sought ways to improve community assets. The British managers whose ditch extended to Billy's homestead approached various farmers to ascertain if they might be interested in purchasing their New Loveland and Greeley Irrigation and Land Company. Billy was one of seven men selected to hammer out a mutually acceptable purchasing agreement. Early in 1900, the group offered to pay $35,000 "lock, stock, and barrel" for company property, but this bid was far short of what the British owners expected. Negotiations went back and forth for the remainder of the year, finally resulting in an agreed-upon purchase price of $48,750. The Greeley and Loveland Irrigation Company came into existence with ownership of water rights, reservoirs, and a ditch system capable of irrigating 17,000 acres of land between Loveland and Greeley.[44]

To celebrate his success, and to satisfy an ongoing curiosity about the Old World, Billy decided to make a trip to the Paris Universal Exposition in 1900. He had already traveled outside the state to Washington, Oregon, and Idaho to see how others tackled agricultural problems. Now his curiosity about Europe was stimulated by news that the Paris Exposition was a showplace for American technology. He hoped to see for himself what could be learned and what might be of use in Weld County.

Leaving Jennie D. behind with their twelve-year-old son Harry (born August 17, 1887) and nine-year-old son Karl (born October 17, 1890), Billy joined forces with his partner Albert Igo and with Harry C. Watson. Watson may have been the 1877 stage driver who loaned Billy the cost of transportation from Loveland to Greeley in 1877. If so, the $500, eighty-day trip represented Billy's repayment of a thirteen-year-old debt with considerable interest.[45] In May the men sailed out of New York on the *Tartar Prince*, a totally electrified steel-screw steamship whose six water-tight

Billy and Jennie D. Farr with children, Harry (*in back*) and Karl (*in front*). Courtesy of the Farr family.

compartments were supposed to make it one of the safest ships on the Atlantic.[46] During the crossing, Billy wrote letters home, complaining of four days of seasickness and stating emphatically that "the Atlantic has no charms for me."[47]

But once on land, Billy recovered his enthusiasm for the journey. In Paris he saw the much anticipated technological developments: talking films, wireless telegraph machines, diesel engines running on peanut oil, the first line of the Paris subway, and Gustave Eiffel's impressive tower. Continuing their travels into the countryside, the men marveled at orange and lemon groves, vineyards, and farms specializing in figs, olives, and chestnuts. In Italy they enjoyed gondola rides on Venetian waterways, attended stage plays, toured cathedrals, and experienced the splendor of the Alps. They wrote home about all they saw, including the abysmal poverty and congestion of larger cities. Billy complained about "unrelenting thirst," because most people just drank wine. "I drink tea," he wrote, "at twenty cents a cup [because it] is the only thing that will quench my thirst. I would give up my interest in Europe for a bucket of artesian."[48]

Before boarding the ship for New York, Billy visited his grandfather's holdings in Dorset County, England.

Arriving back in Greeley in September, Billy returned to the tasks at hand. The Farr Produce Company was booming. Established in 1891 in partnership with Greeley banker Charles M. Jackson, the company specialized in shipping potatoes. Jackson had noted the size and quality of Billy's potato crop, and he believed money was to be made by contracting for the best potatoes in the county and shipping them to eastern and midwestern markets. Billy's job was to identify the most reliable growers, receive the harvested crop in the fall, sort and sack them by size, and load the spuds on trains for market. Jackson would remain a silent partner. To Billy fell the bulk of the work, not only because of the distance he had to travel between farms, but also because he was responsible for storing the potatoes so deliveries could be made year-round. Billy acquired a warehouse near the railroad station, where he installed a hydraulic elevator for moving the heavy hundred-pound potato sacks into storage or onto rail cars.[49]

Altogether, five Greeley companies bought, sorted, and shipped potatoes. Known as the High Five, these companies met regularly to review railroad tariffs, stock on hand, orders received, and prices to be paid to farmers. Their collusion reduced competition and price wars in hopes of keeping everyone in business and providing fair prices to farmers. Although the practice might appear unfair and monopolistic from today's perspective, it was typical of much of the business that transpired in Weld County. Many of the same families sat on boards together, encouraged their children to intermarry, and socialized in other ways. The Farrs were totally immersed in this system, and their success was to no small extent a result of making the right connections at the right time with the right people.[50]

By 1902, potatoes had become Weld County's main crop. The discovery of chemical synergies that occurred when potatoes were planted in alfalfa ground resulted in more and better harvests.[51] Sugar beets, alfalfa, and onions followed in importance. Some barley and oats were raised for stock feeding, but wheat was deemed unprofitable because of its need for high-priced water.

Billy used the Farr Produce Company to sell various supplies to sheep men, and he constructed potato cellars around the county so he could maintain a reliable supply line to his warehouse. By 1910 the first potato experiment station was located in Greeley as the area became the focal point in the nation for potato shipping. When Billy's son Harry entered the business in 1904, the company gradually shifted its attention away from potatoes to pinto beans. It proved to be another smart business move.

The success of the Farr Produce Company enabled Billy to become more widely involved in the community. Having dissolved his partnership in the blacksmith shop, he had more time to focus on other interests.[52] He became a director of two Greeley banks and ran successfully for the position of alderman on the Greeley City Council. In that capacity, he encouraged the city to look to the mountains for a water system that would meet the needs of future growth.

As of 1902, Greeley's water was provided by two wells that pumped into reservoirs north of the city. The pumps were strained and close to capacity, even though they ran for nineteen hours a day. Securing an ample supply of clean water for the city had been discussed increasingly as citizens concluded that future growth might be stalled by the limitations of the existing system. The higher land in Greeley frequently lacked water pressure, and buildings of more than one story were often unable to provide water to all floors. When H. G. Watson was elected mayor in 1901, his first move was to organize a committee with instructions to investigate the feasibility of securing a supplemental water supply from the Big Thompson River near Loveland.

Billy Farr was selected to serve on this Committee on Water Works. Two years earlier he had been elected to city council from the third ward. During his tenure on the council, he had shown a keen interest in improving Greeley's water supply and delivery system, recognizing in the process that the economic prosperity of Weld County would depend on having an adequate supply of water for ongoing municipal and agricultural growth.

In September 1902, the committee reported to the council that a quantity of water (almost seven cubic feet per second [cfs][53]) could be purchased from W. R. Adams, who owned an early water right on the Big Thompson River. If that water right were purchased, the committee said it would recommend changing the existing point of diversion in order to better funnel the water into a pipeline that would deliver it to Greeley. The council advised further study. When the committee reported back on December 9, the entire council voted in favor of proceeding with the purchase. Billy Farr cast the only negative vote.

His opposition may have reflected concern about the possible impact such a deal might have on his own farming operations at the end of the Greeley–Loveland ditch system. During an extended drought, diversion of water from the Big Thompson River above the Greeley–Loveland headgate could have an effect on water available to Billy and his neighbors in the Hillsborough area southwest of Greeley. Billy probably knew that Adams's seven cfs had an earlier appropriation date than the water in the Greeley–Loveland system. Water removed from the Big Thompson River for Greeley, therefore, would have first priority in the event of shortages. He might also have voted against the project because of its cost, or because he was in competition with Adams for political and economic advantage in the community.

None of these possibilities should be discounted. Billy left the council in 1903, making it difficult to determine his thoughts over the next few years. But there is evidence to suggest that Billy viewed the Adams deal as flawed and not in Greeley's long-term interests. A better arrangement for the city might be attained through negotiation with Fort Collins on the Cache la Poudre River.[54]

Over a two-year period after Billy left the council, Greeley discovered that transferring Adams's water to the city would be problematic. Court proceedings revealed unexpected complications and disputes, requiring employment of a referee. When the referee began showing signs of opposition to the transfer, city council dropped the matter. Meanwhile, Fort Collins offered to sell 7.5 cfs from the Cache la Poudre River for half the price of Adams's water right. Although some Larimer County farmers objected to a pipeline that would permanently remove water to rival Greeley,[55] the district court adjudicated the water right and approved the transfer. Soon thereafter, the city of Greeley approved the issue of bonds in the amount of $350,000 to cover the cost of a twenty-eight-mile woodstave pipeline and a slow sand filtration system to be built in Bellvue northwest of Fort Collins on the Cache la Poudre River. Mayor Watson decided to build the pipeline out of wood because iron was too expensive.[56]

Without additional evidence from primary sources, the rationale behind Billy's opposition to the Big Thompson River deal will remain open to speculation. However, the record left during his four years on city council would suggest he had concrete reasons to oppose the Adams plan, while he continued at the same time to search for alternate supplies of water that would assure Greeley's future. First, if supplemental city water were to come from the Big Thompson River in an open ditch, it would have to pass through fields of cattle and sugar beet waste produced by Great Western. Water quality would be an issue, and Greeley residents were already clamoring for the pure and soft water of the Rocky Mountains. Second, Billy may have believed that Adams's price was too high for a water right whose validity the courts would question. Equally good water could come from the Cache la Poudre River. A committee of physicians had already compared the Poudre and Big Thompson rivers for water quality, and they concluded that with the use of slow sand filtration, either source would be ideal for Greeley.[57]

There is no direct evidence that Billy preferred a Poudre River deal, but he had become influential enough in the community to be outspoken if any plan displeased him. In addition, Billy's interest in procuring an adequate water supply for Weld County was revealed in his early efforts to bring water into the area from the western slope of the Continental Divide. Joined by family and some of the neighbors he most respected, Billy filed a claim in 1902 on a small quantity of the runoff water that naturally flowed into the Grand (Colorado) River.[58] This farsighted interest in transmountain diversion as a means to provide supplemental water to a growing community would mature thirty years later when his grandson WD joined with other Greeley citizens to promote the C-BT Project.

Billy's brothers Charles and Thomas were, perhaps, less civic minded than Billy, but they, too, made noteworthy contributions to Weld County. Charles joined with Bert Huffsmith to establish the first implement dealership in northern Colorado. As representatives for McCormick and Deering (Cyrus McCormick had invented the reaper), they were on the cutting edge of agricultural mechanization for many years. The company did well, eventually becoming the Northern Implement and Produce Company of Eaton.[59]

Thomas was a solid farmer, but he also had a spark of his father's adventurous spirit. In 1899 he joined a group of Cripple Creek miners in San Francisco who made a 1,900-mile journey to Skagway, Alaska.

They were among the fortunate argonauts who successfully negotiated the difficult Chilcoot Pass with 5,000 pounds of food and gear, arriving in Dawson City in June. There they found 50,000 other gold seekers, all looking for easy pickings. Two months were enough to convince them of the futility of staying longer.[60] Thomas was cured of the travel bug, but the rest of his life he moved frequently and never settled into a career.

By this time, Harry Farr, a young, freckle-faced, red-headed adolescent, began showing up regularly as an able hand in the Farr enterprises. He was the oldest of Billy's children after a sister died in infancy. He enjoyed the outdoor life and had a love of farming. He was a good student, graduating from Greeley High School in 1905 and attending the University of Colorado for a year and a half. Restless to make a mark in the family business, he left the university and enrolled in a course of study at the Barnes Commercial School of Business, which he completed in 1907.

More than anything, Harry wanted to work with his father. Billy was happy to have him. At barely twenty years of age, Harry was managing the Farr Produce Company. He traveled the countryside on a bicycle, making deals with potato growers. The trips were long and tiring on a bike. Like his father, Harry was enamored of technology, and he believed he could be more efficient if he had a car.

The first car manufactured in Greeley was built in 1903. It had a top speed of thirty-five miles per hour and appeared capable of speeding up Harry's rounds considerably. But not everyone saw the automobile as a positive invention. In fact, the newspapers described some drivers as having a disease called "ecchymosis." It was a fever said to produce an enlarged cranium, symptoms of "moral anesthesia," and a pronounced aversion to the law. Victims of this disease were seen as threats to women, children, dogs, and small babies. Unfortunately, the medical profession disagreed on the best course of treatment for the afflicted.[61] But as soon as Harry was able to prove to his father that an automobile could go up and down hills, he was given permission to trade in his bicycle for one of the four-wheeled machines. According to family lore, Harry acquired the first Buick sold in Greeley by the Weld County Garage, a company that is still in business.

Harry became more efficient. With the time he saved on potato buying rounds, he could work more actively in the sheep feeding business. He began accompanying his uncles on lamb buying trips to the Southwest. He also accompanied loads of fat lambs to the Chicago market, where he was introduced to the industry's most knowledgeable professionals. One Chicago livestock representative noted that Harry was "a fine young businessman and a royal good fellow."[62]

Harry already had owned a farm west of Greeley, which he sold for one with better water rights. In his dealings with others, he was building on a reputation as a leader, earned at the University of Colorado, which was based on public relations skills and an exceptional organizational ability.[63] At the age of twenty-two, he decided it was time to take a wife. On June 2, 1909, Harry married Hazel Louise Daven. On May 26 the following year, William Daven Farr was born.

The 1910 Greeley into which WD made his appearance was a place in transition. Agricultural opportunities far exceeded what had been available to the original pioneers forty years earlier. Diversification was evident everywhere. Peach and apple orchards had proliferated. A commercial vegetable industry had begun with onions, peas, tomatoes, and cabbage; a canning industry had also started up. Hog raising and bee keeping were in evidence, but water was still the region's Achilles' heel. Harry estimated in 1910 that eighty acres of land required between $4,000 and $6,000 worth of water for crops needing irrigation.[64] The Great Western Sugar Company was adding cash to farmers' bank accounts, but some were suspicious that company seed, which beet growers were forced to use, was designed to produce smaller beets with higher levels of sugar. Because they were paid by the ton, farmers wondered if the company was cheating them out of their fair share of profits.

Some Greeley residents were additionally nervous about changes occurring in the landscape around them. In the past decade, the federal government had extended its control over the West's natural resources. Fourteen new forest reserves were created between 1902 and 1908, and a powerful agency in the Department of Interior—the U.S. Reclamation Service—had been created by a 1902 act of Congress for the purpose of assisting in the management, ownership, and control of western water.[65] Some could already see the potential threat to states' rights.

But others, like Harry Farr, tended to welcome change. Overall, those who celebrated in 1910 the fortieth anniversary of the Union Colony's

Billy Farr with grandson WD, ca 1915. Courtesy of the Farr family.

founding extolled the "conquest" of nature and the "victory" won over the Great American Desert. A Weld County population of 40,000 could boast sixteen reservoirs and 300 miles of irrigation canals. In Greeley, one could count nineteen churches, two daily and two weekly newspapers, four banks, a public library with 4,000 books, ten restaurants, a telephone system with 2,000 telephones, a gas and electric light plant, a mountain water works system owned by the city, an ice plant, eight hotels, a sugar factory, and no saloons. Temperance, although increasingly challenged, was still a fact of life in Greeley, and it was regarded as one of the reasons why the city had been so successful.

As residents celebrated their accomplishments, they gave credit to irrigation as "the most marvelous victory recorded in the peaceful conquest of the great West."[66] From their vantage point in 1910, the challenge for future generations was to accelerate control of water by means of tunnels driven through mountains, reservoir storage, and the establishment of well regulated irrigation districts so that rivers would "cease their useless rush to the sea and be harnessed and driven to do the bidding of thousands of willing, resolute Colorado farmers."[67] This was the world in which WD grew up. Claim to legitimate occupancy of the land was based on a man's ability to make it bloom, to transform it into a capitalistic market to which he was proudly connected. And all bets for a bright future were off if the water was not controlled.

Harry Farr mentored WD along these lines, and WD proved to be an attentive disciple. The western values and goals of his grandfather, great uncles, and father determined the course of his own development and launched him on a path carefully laid out by earlier generations. It might not have been what Helen Keller meant as a "daring adventure," but it was filled with calculated risks, a sense of noblesse oblige in regard to his own community, and an enormous amount of courage and common sense. These were among the characteristics that defined WD's leadership as an adult.

CHAPTER 2

Apprenticeship

One father is more than a hundred schoolmasters.

—George Herbert

Mine was the most unusual life anybody ever had.
—William Daven Farr, December 26, 2006

During the final years of his life, WD would often pause during interviews and hold up his hands, as if to offer an image that communicated better than words the real nature of his youth. Gnarled, calloused, and roughened by time, the crooked fingers conveyed WD's enormous pride in the dignity of labor and the lessons he had learned from his father, Harry. "My father and grandfather and I were all close friends," he recalled wistfully. "The older I got, the more time I spent with him [Harry], usually on weekends, going to the country to sort lambs or to see what was happening on the farms. . . . I grew up in the days when everything was hard. Look at these hands," he would say. "It was all hard work. We didn't do anything easy. Nowadays, with machinery, it is all easy."[1]

An exaggeration, perhaps, but Harry wanted his sons to learn farming from the ground up. WD absorbed every aspect of his mentor's teaching. Harry responded in kind, especially when it became apparent that WD's brother Ralph, born a few years after WD, was not as healthy as WD and was far less interested in the nuts and bolts of irrigated farming. WD's close relationship with his father and grandfather lasted from childhood to maturity and eventually expanded to include his parents' friends and business associates. He related well to older people, and the next generation saw in him a respectful, smart, hard-working, and teachable young man.

WD Farr's hands. Courtesy of the Farr family.

"Mom Hazel" was just as influential in molding WD's character. Two months younger than Harry, Hazel Louise Daven was born to Peter Ferguson Daven and Eva Noel Daven in Jefferson County, Wisconsin, on October 25, 1887.[2] The family moved to South Dakota and then to Greeley, Colorado, around 1895. Peter worked a farm west of Greeley and was a director of the Greeley–Loveland Ditch Company. His daughter Hazel attended the South Ward School and Greeley High School, graduating in 1905 in the same class as Harry. She attended Colorado State Normal School (Colorado State College or Colorado State College of Education, now the University of Northern Colorado), receiving a teaching certificate in 1907. For the next two years, she taught fourth grade in Loveland before marrying Harry in 1909.

Hazel was intelligent, a good socializer, and a committed homemaker. She was perceptive about human nature, outgoing, and deeply interested

Harry and Hazel Daven Farr moved into a new house on 10th Avenue in the 1920s. Courtesy of the Farr family.

in education. She cultivated social relationships with five presidents at Colorado State College and enjoyed watching that institution expand from one building, when she was a student, to more than thirty. She was also the first woman elected to Greeley's school board and was a dedicated benefactor of the First Congregational Church. During both world wars she aided the local Red Cross and was a charter member in 1920 of the Greeley Women's Club, which promoted cultural, educational, scientific, and literary improvement for women. The breadth of her intellectual curiosity was displayed in presentations she made to Greeley's Want to Know Club. She crafted essays on travel, book making, architecture, and the rise of South American republics.[3]

Hazel had an inquiring mind and was committed to making her community a more livable place for established local families and for those less fortunate. The only real disagreements she had with WD related to his obsession with physical activities. The fishing, hunting, football, and bronco busting WD enjoyed did not please her, but the outdoors was WD's church, and she learned to accept what she could not change. Along with her dedication to the value of educating oneself, acceptance of change may have been her greatest legacy.

WD adored her. Although he was unable to complete a college degree at the University of Wisconsin for health reasons,[4] his focus on education underscored every enterprise he undertook. Those who knew him recognized how well prepared he was, and over a lifetime he taught himself many different tasks. Although he was disappointed by his failure to attain a degree in Madison, he accepted his misfortune and moved on. "I've wondered what would have happened," he asked rhetorically, "if I'd went ahead and gotten a university degree? I doubt if I missed an awful lot—practical things. I had my father, and I listened to him an awful lot and I took his advice."[5]

By age twelve, WD was mature enough to help Harry on the farms. He could drive a car, set irrigation water, sort sheep, and sack potatoes. "You could make a dollar or two picking potatoes," he recalled. A digger would lift them to the surface. "Then you went along and picked them up in a wire basket and carried the sacks tied to your belt. A half-sack of potatoes wasn't too heavy to lift into the wagon, and you got paid by the bag."[6] When he was not working, WD hunted ducks on his grandfather's homestead or on the South Platte River when he could wade the shallow waters in late summer and fall. As much as he enjoyed Harry's company, WD's passion for hunting and fishing required connections with other men. Harry lacked sufficient enthusiasm for such sports, so WD struck out on his own.

Uncle Charlie Farr was the one who introduced him to the North Platte River near Encampment, Wyoming. In 1922 they traveled over dirt roads in a Hudson Super Six open touring car. Between flat tires, they managed a speed of twenty miles per hour. It took an entire day just to get to the Charles Sanger Ranch. Bearing fresh vegetables, they were greeted warmly. Camping in the bull pasture, cooking over an open fire, and sleeping in a tent on the ground were pure delight to WD. They fished with three-piece bamboo poles, using cotton line that sank when wet, and they tied on flies that came from England: royal coachmen, grey hackles, and ginger quills. The fishing was spectacular. After three days they had filled several three-gallon crocks, layering fish and salt from the bottom up. They were tired, but WD's appetite for good fishing would last the rest of his life. Their hosts agreed to allow formation of the Sanger Fishing Club. The Farr family's love affair with Encampment has continued to this day.[7]

Back in Greeley's South Ward School, WD was a reliable student— mostly As, a few Bs, and a C+ in deportment.[8] He played football against teams from other junior highs on "old, crude, dirt fields full of stickers and sand burrs."[9] When he attended high school, he owned a Model T Ford his father provided when he promised to refrain from smoking until his sixteenth birthday. WD had no interest in smoking anything. He had watched his father repeatedly strike matches on sandpaper glued to the dashboard of the family car, and he had concluded that pipes and cigars were a waste of time. Owning a car made for an exciting senior year at the new Greeley Central High School. He played center on the football team and remained a better-than-average student, completing some graduation requirements before his last semester. He later recalled having taken classes in Latin, algebra, and geometry and remembered the "good English teachers who made us read a lot of Shakespeare."[10]

An early instinct for leadership found him serving as president of the Hi-Y Club. Composed of twenty students, Hi-Y encouraged its members to plan for college and to focus on extra-curricular activities. WD followed the Hi-Y faculty advisor's counsel by becoming editor in chief of the 1927– 1928 class yearbook, *The Spud*. For reasons not altogether clear, this particular yearbook turned out to be somewhat unorthodox. Filled with cartoons and an impressionistic narrative, the pages contain minimal formatting, featuring instead a disjointed dialog between two students that wraps around photographs and pays little heed to organization.[11] If this was WD's attempt at humor, he may have learned from the experience that, although he would always enjoy a good joke, he would have to solicit help when he wanted to incorporate wit into written speeches or essays. WD was not a natural comic.

Neither was Harry, but the father–son relationship became increasingly secure. By graduation in 1928, WD recognized how successful his father had become and how much he was admired in the agricultural community. Harry was "Mr. Big."[12] He had weathered the difficult years following World War I and had become an active and highly respected representative of sheep feeders. Challenged by a steady decline in lamb sales and the Hershey Company's nickel candy-bar slogan, "More Sustaining than Meat,"[13] Harry concluded it was time to promote the lamb business. He spearheaded a big ad campaign for the Colorado–Nebraska Lamb Feeders Association he helped found in 1922.[14] In his role as president, and as representative of the lamb feeders on the National Livestock and Meat Board, Harry traveled to Chicago to meet with people from the packing industry, trade journals, and retail establishments. Targeting housewives, he spoke on the radio to convey the message that lamb was cheaper than any other meat on the market. Railroads agreed to put stickers on their cars saying, "Now in Season. Lamb. Healthful. Nutritious."[15]

Back home, Harry placed great importance on his membership in Rotary. He was one of its original members in Greeley. At the time of the Greeley Rotary club's founding in 1917, Greeley was the smallest city in which Rotary had ever placed a club. Harry was also active with the local organization of Boy Scouts and with the chamber of commerce, and he served on the board of directors at Great Western Sugar Company, the Denver Union Stockyards, several banks, and the Federal Reserve Board in Denver. WD learned from his father that service to organizations representing farming and related industries was not only good business, but also a crucial aspect of maintaining status and realizing opportunities in a competitive environment. Harry worked well with people and was viewed as a "prime mover" in matters relating to farming and water development.[16] His college roommate, William Kelly, paid Harry a sincere compliment when he said, "Truly it is to be said of Harry W. Farr, as [no other]: He could walk with kings and never lose the common touch."[17]

WD was certain he wanted nothing more than to work full-time as a partner with his father. But he was also beginning to show signs of independence. When his father returned from a Federal Reserve Board meeting with news that Wyoming senator Robert Carey[18] was looking for men to care for a herd of steers on a ranch west of Steamboat Springs, Colorado, WD jumped at the possibility. Neither Hazel nor Harry viewed the summer job as appropriate for a young man trying to learn irrigated farming. Furthermore, they thought his education would be served far better if he joined them on a trip to Europe. But WD persisted. He had no interest in visiting cities, preferring instead to spend vacation time in his beloved

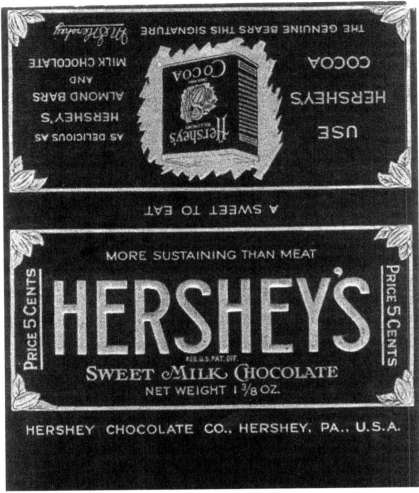

Hershey's five-cent chocolate bar, with the "more sustaining than meat" advertisement that was used from 1906 to 1926. Courtesy of Hershey Community Archives, Hershey, Pennsylvania.

mountains. In the end his parents proved understanding and supportive. For thirty dollars a month and food, WD and a friend signed up to punch cattle during the summers of 1927 and 1928. More than any other experience, the two summers in California Park whetted WD's appetite to become a cattleman.

His first trip to the ranch turned into an adventure. Leaving Greeley on a warm May morning, the boys traveled northwest in WD's Model T toward Rawlins and then to Wamsutter, Wyoming, where they spent the night. Early the next day they were at the railroad depot for breakfast, ordering the standard ham, eggs, and toast. As he recalled many years later, WD realized he was coming to a less urbane region when he bit into the ham and found pig bristles still attached to the locally butchered meat.

But the rugged life of a cowboy was what WD wanted. Continuing their journey through Baggs and down to the Yampa River, the young men arrived at Carey Ranch headquarters[19] in Hayden late in the afternoon of May 21, 1927—the same day "Lucky Lindy" arrived at Le Bourget Field in Paris.

From the grizzled foreman, Frank Hoskins, WD learned they had ten days to become familiar with the area and to make peace with a string of twenty rough-broke horses: ten for each boy, some as wild as the steers expected shortly from Mexico. The "dogies," Hoskins warned, would arrive hungry and thirsty, unaccustomed to the country, nervous, and prone to stampede. They would be the boys' responsibility for three months and would first have to be driven twenty miles north from the railroad to California Park.[20]

To make matters worse, the train carrying the steers and yearling heifers arrived late in the afternoon. It was well after dark when the animals were bedded down, but they remained restless through the night. The next day, led up the trail by a cook with an old-fashioned Studebaker camp wagon carrying grub and bedrolls, the herd was coaxed toward California Park. They spooked and ran every time they encountered a rushing stream: they had never seen running water and were afraid to cross. But they made their destination late in the day, and the herd became calmer in the fresh grass of the park.

Cattle won't stray far from salt deposits, so the boys were instructed to control the cattle with the strategic placement of rock salt and to allow them access to the timber on the edge of the park for shade. Except for a few sheep herders and an old hermit on a nearby creek, they were entirely isolated: no roads, no cars, and no people. They had a cook tent, a Dutch oven, and a sleeping tent where they spent the night rolled up in tarpaulins on the ground. Their horses were rank. WD knew how to ride, but he was not prepared for the feisty animals provided by the ranch. He was bucked off twenty-eight times that summer. Steamboat, one of his more ornery mounts, later became a famous bucking horse for local rodeos. When Hoskins, the ranch foreman, made his monthly visit to California Park, they all enjoyed a respite from the routine of herding. Hoskins liked to fish, so they took gunny sacks to Elkhead Creek and caught a hundred trout, which Hoskins took back to ranch headquarters for his large hay crew. WD and his partner went into Hayden a few times for food and to bathe in a four-legged tub for a dollar, a price that included a haircut. The blue plate special was available for thirty-five cents, and although it was not haute cuisine, the food was a welcome change from the venison, fish, and biscuits to which they had become accustomed.

The second summer was more of the same, except that WD was accompanied by a new partner, Bill Spaulding, who was also his best friend. The ranch sent a log-cabin builder with them. They cut logs at the edge of the green timber, hauled them into the campsite, and peeled off the bark. Logs were notched and placed in the walls one at a time. The builder returned to town for flooring, roofing, and doors. The cabin took six weeks to complete. Its remains are still visible in the park.

Entirely satisfied with himself and his cowboy life in the Rockies, WD remained a source of worry to his mother. She persuaded Harry to drive to the north edge of California Park so she could see for herself what the attraction was. What she saw served only to heighten her fear that her son might be injured, but she did not intervene. WD was clearly doing what he wanted and was determined to learn as much as he could during the short summer vacation. "The experience molded my future," WD recollected. "I took a lot of bruises and lived through heavy rains and hail storms, but [the job] taught me to take care of myself and gave me a burning desire to have a cattle ranch." He learned about cattle, horses, and wild animals. "My love for the cattle business was developed. Necessity taught us to work hard, endure hardship, be self-reliant and to help each other. I felt fortunate to have been part of the Old West."[21]

When the summer ended, it was time to put aside the cowboy life. WD had been accepted to the University of Wisconsin, which was known both for its animal science department and for Professor Frank Kleinheinz, the university's first shepherd, whose book on sheep management

WD Farr (*left*) and Bill Spaulding (*right*) at California Park cow camp, 1928. Courtesy of the Farr family.

had served as a textbook for a decade.[22] Kleinheinz died in the fall of
WD's freshman year, but WD had already decided on a business major
before he arrived in Madison.

The School of Commerce had an outstanding course of study in agricultural economics. WD registered for the pre-commerce degree program
in the faculty of Letters and Science. He enrolled in the mandatory courses:
composition, geography, English history, algebra, foreign language, and
physical education. He chose rowing as his sport. It was something untried,
a challenge, a way to learn a skill he would not encounter in Colorado.
He also pledged Beta Theta Pi, the first fraternity to locate a chapter west
of the Mississippi River. Its mission statement emphasized a principled
life that included "devotion to intellectual excellence, high standards of
moral conduct and responsible citizenship."[23] WD did not take lightly
these guiding principles. A few years later, when he joined Rotary at the
age of twenty-one, he embraced another set of ethical standards that
echoed those of the fraternity.[24]

But principled ethical behavior could not save WD from a nasty infection he contracted at the beginning of his second semester. Used to the
dry cold weather in the West, WD was unable to cope with Wisconsin's
humid winter. Long days of shoveling snow at the fraternity, combined
with allergies to certain foods, produced a sinus blockage followed by
acute headaches severe enough to require hospitalization. WD recalled
what happened:

> I was delirious from the sinus pressure and pain. My mother came
> and after four or five days they decided to operate. [The surgeon]
> drilled into the sinus cavity just behind the eyebrow and put a tube
> in so it would drain. I was in the hospital for five weeks and for a
> week or two I wasn't supposed to make it. Then they straightened
> out my nose for better drainage, and by that time I had lost six
> weeks of school and a lot of weight, so I came home.[25]

The infection worsened. Doctors in Denver decided on another operation. This time they made a larger hole and cleaned out the bone splinters
remaining from the first surgery. The sinuses began to heal, and WD was
able to revert to a normal life. But doctors advised him not to return to
Wisconsin. The head of the university's medical school warned him that

he was going to be a sickly, unhealthy young man who would have a short life. But that scenario was not consistent with WD's self-image. As Harry's health began to deteriorate from intestinal ulcers, perhaps aggravated by the dozen or so cigars he smoked every day, and with the Farr Company showing considerable potential for growth in the pinto bean business, WD was content to remain in Greeley. In a few years Harry would make him an official partner in the Farr Company.[26] Staying home just made sense to WD. "I was doing well and was able to do a lot of things [Harry] couldn't do any more, and I was doing what I had planned on doing all the time. The bean business had replaced the potato business, and it was making money."[27] Besides, WD relished the chance to continue learning from Harry's generation. "I have always associated with older people," he noted "and I have never seemed to have time to get into too much trouble, because there was always so much to do. These older people were teaching you and pushing you a little bit to where you learned to do things on time."[28]

One of the things WD addressed was Harry's reluctance to comprehend and apply mechanical solutions to farming problems. WD taught himself how to survey land so irrigation water would flow evenly over the crops. He also took on the problem of standing water on one of his father's farms near Eaton. There was no place to drain the six inches of water that had accumulated, so a tile drain would be a waste of money. Furthermore, the cause of the standing water needed to be addressed. Ralph Parshall at Colorado Agricultural College in Fort Collins was an expert in solving irrigation problems.[29] WD paid him a visit. Parshall asked if the nearby Larimer and Weld Canal had been cleaned recently. WD replied that it was cleaned the previous year, the first time since construction in 1890. Parshall theorized that cleaning had broken the seal on the canal, allowing water to seep outward under the surface and into Harry's field. Because turbine-driven pumps had just been invented in California, it would be possible to dig a well fifty to sixty feet deep to an impervious shale layer where seepage water could be collected and pumped to the surface for repeated use in the same field. The well was the first of its kind in Weld County, and it saved Harry's farm. Its success also stimulated WD's lifelong interest in water.

He was intrigued by how water could be moved, reused, stored, and shared. On irrigated farms, the basic technique of setting a canvass dam

and cutting breaks to allow the water to follow crop furrows was a labor
that required persistence, skill, and experience. A good irrigator was worth
a lot more than he was paid. In WD's words,

> All irrigation then was with shovels. You made two cuts and set your
> water on ten rows, or forty rows, depending on the stream and what
> you were irrigating. [It] fascinated me to see how those old-time
> men [worked] and how quick they were with the shovel and how they
> could cut just right and basically get the same amount of water in each
> ditch. . . . I loved to watch them, and it just always fascinated me.[30]

But he also learned from the Eaton farm experience that water had a
way of unexpectedly seeking its own level. Concrete lining for ditches
and constant supervision, he discovered, were required for surface water,
reservoirs, and underground pumping. His observations on Harry's farms
would serve as the foundation for more sophisticated projects later on
and would etch in his mind the belief that whatever the task, there was
always a better way to do things.

Those qualities—awareness, keen observation of others, and constant
curiosity about why things were the way they were—defined WD's character.
He asked questions relentlessly and wanted to know from others where
they had been, what they had seen, what they had learned, and what their
thoughts were going forward. It was one of the ways he educated himself, and his behavior convinced people of his genuine interest in their
own stories.

But in 1929 no one could predict the future based on past observations.
Agricultural data for the 1920s were irregular and unpredictable. The
lamb feeding business actually improved after some bad years following
the end of World War I. Weld County fed more lambs in 1929 than any
other county in the nation, and Harry Farr was among the largest operators,
finishing 40,000 to 50,000 lambs a year. In the next six years, he would
double the number of lambs on feed on his six farms. At the same time,
he provided other farmers with lambs to feed all over Weld and Larimer
counties. Even though there had been an upward trend in the quantity
of sheep on feed between 1924 and 1929,[31] the total number of sheep in
the United States averaged just under 43 million head. This was 3.4 million
fewer than were on hand in 1867. In addition, the average farm value of

Left to right: WR, WD, and Dick Farr at the Farr feedlot adjacent to the Great Western Sugar Co. refinery. Courtesy of the Farr family.

lambs had been reduced during the 1920s, and per capita consumption of lamb had dropped nationally to 7.3 pounds per year. In contrast, per capita consumption of beef was on the rise at 53.2 pounds, a number that continued unsteadily upward during subsequent decades.[32]

But Harry continued to have faith in sheep feeding. According to the *Greeley Tribune*, he was the most trusted authority on sheep and livestock production in Weld County.[33] Farm commodity prices had stabilized somewhat during the second half of the twenties, and irrigated land values remained solid. Overall, as of 1929, agricultural returns in Colorado had nearly reached the 1920 highs.[34] Harry had been known to go against the advice of bankers before when he purchased twelve carloads of lambs in a tough 1921 market, and the gamble had paid off.[35] In 1929, even though the business was experiencing difficulties, he saw no reason to change time-honored strategies that had worked well for him and his father.

On October 28, 1929, WD, now a savvy nineteen-year-old, boarded a train with Harry for New Mexico to make the annual purchase of young lambs. It was WD's first lamb buying excursion, one he would never forget. They located several thousand sheep in Las Vegas and Gallup, contracting to buy the animals at twelve cents a pound. On October 29, while riding in the club car, they learned about the stock market crash. Harry and WD discussed the event with others on the train, all of whom agreed that Wall Street's loss would probably have little impact on the West. The Farrs brought the lambs to Greeley and put them on feed just as Harry had always done. In the spring they sold for seven cents a pound, resulting in a loss of three to four dollars a head, but Harry honored each contract he made on that trip.

For WD the learning experience was powerful. Unexpected economic forces could easily decimate one's capital reserves; risks were acceptable but not without resources to protect assets when unpredictable events caused precipitous market declines. More important, WD determined once again that honor and integrity were the essence of successful business dealings. In the last years of his life, he would proudly note that he never consciously cost anyone a dime in any transaction. He not only believed in fairness, he learned from Harry that, in the long run, consideration of others made for solid friendships and better business.

Unfortunately, the Farr enterprises experienced a second unexpected blow when they returned from New Mexico. A series of cold fronts swept through northern Colorado in the late fall. Snow arrived earlier than usual, and freezing temperatures froze the sugar beets in the ground. Harvesting proved next to impossible. The best efforts resulted in broken machinery and a lost crop. Because Weld County was so dependent on the cash Great Western Sugar Company paid farmers for beets, all local businesses and bankers suffered a loss when the annual payments failed to materialize in the hoped-for quantity.[36]

When the final numbers were tallied, only 20 percent of beets planted were harvested for the factory. The Mountain States Beet Growers Association, which represented farmers, pressed Great Western Sugar Company to pay as much per ton in 1930 as they paid in 1929. They were hoping to encourage farmers to plant another crop. Great Western Sugar Company consented, but by April only 75 percent of the 1929 acreage was contracted to be planted. Farmers were feeling vulnerable after what had happened the previous fall. As noted by the Weld County Extension agent H. H. Simpson, they seemed restless, looking for surer ways to make money, and they were willing to upset well-established crop rotations in search of something "easier."[37]

Prices of most farm commodities began to slide during 1930, at the same time the *Weld County News* logged "record production" for the year.[38] A glut of feed and food was developing, but according to Harry the chief obstacle for farmers was cheap foreign imports that undersold America's farmers. He traveled to Washington for a personal audience with President Herbert Hoover, who had promised a modest tariff increase during the 1928 campaign. Harry believed the livestock industry would not survive without a rise in tariffs on agricultural goods. He left the White House to meet with congressmen, whom he urged to pass the Hawley–Smoot Tariff.[39] A weak feeding industry, he argued, would affect irrigated agriculture in general. Feeding, farming, and sugar beets were all integrated. "To maintain the fertility of our farms," he asserted, "we must raise alfalfa and fertilize. Large scale feeding operations are the only feasible method for the Colorado irrigated farmer to obtain a market for his alfalfa and keep up the fertility of the land."[40]

The extreme restrictions imposed by the Hawley–Smoot Tariff, and the timing of its passage when the economies of other countries were experiencing their own problems, served to hasten the onset of a worldwide economic depression. Even though the sugar beet industry actually made $10 million more in 1930 than in 1929, total cash income for Colorado farmers dropped by 14 percent as the higher tariffs triggered reciprocal protectionism in dozens of countries around the world.[41] If there was any lesson in this for WD, it was an incipient awareness that change was inevitable. Sometimes it happened faster than expected, but it was unavoidable in every field of endeavor. Good leaders, he soon learned, had to be able to cope with such forces when they occurred.

Another threat to economic stability arose from Mother Nature. Although indicators of distress proved temporary during the 1930 growing season, the Farrs may have worried as much about changing weather patterns as the vexations of an unsettled agricultural market. Hot winds, a few dust storms, and inadequate spring rains caught farmers by surprise. Those who had just finished planting beets watched in dismay as the razor sharp sand cut away at tender plants just emerging from the ground. By the first week in May, total precipitation for the Greeley area was "far below" the ten-year average of 3.19 inches.[42] The complex network of dams, reservoirs, and irrigation ditches radiated in all directions from the principal streams, but there was far more capacity to irrigate in the system than available water. Seasonal rains were still necessary to get many of the crops started. A radical diminution in snow or rainfall could spell disaster for farmers with junior water rights. Fortunately, rains returned by the end of May, and in July, precipitation was significant. Nevertheless, a seed had been planted in WD's mind as he witnessed Harry's preoccupation: If irrigated agriculture were to succeed with continuity and confidence in the future, an additional water supply would have to be found.

Meanwhile, with crops growing once again, Harry found himself in the enviable position of adding to his liquid assets as a result of the sale of his shares in the Home Gas and Electric Company. Organized in 1886, the Greeley Light Company became the Home Electric Light and Power Company in 1902 when Greeley was a community of 3,000 people. "Solid and sedate citizens" were guaranteed electricity up to ten o'clock at night, when it was believed that respectable people would be off the streets and in bed. Kerosene lanterns were still available for "wild youngsters" and "dissolute elders."[43]

In 1911, the company name was changed to Home Gas and Electric. Expansion of service occurred in 1920 when Walter Farr, Harry's uncle, sold the Farmers Electric and Power Company of Eaton to Home Gas and Electric. Harry soon became a stockholder, and in 1926 he was elected to the board of directors. Over the next four years, the company promoted sales of electrical household appliances. Increasing electricity use by farmers with irrigation pumps along with rising sales of labor-saving devices to Weld County's growing population resulted in improved earnings and dividend reports.[44]

In June 1930, when Harry was one of the "heavier stockholders" and president, the company received a purchase offer from the Nathan L. Jones Investment Group in the amount of $1.6 million.[45] At this time, annual revenue for the company exceeded $400,000 a year. Approximately 40,000 shares were outstanding. According to company minutes, Harry owned 406 shares of stock in 1928 at a par value that may have been as high as $50 per share. Existing company records do not provide data needed to ascertain the exact amount of cash Harry actually received when the sale was consummated. But a windfall in the range of $10,000 to $20,000, at a time when depression and drought were beginning to drain cash from the Weld County economy, is worthy of note.[46] Even more noteworthy, perhaps, is the fact that Harry and a group of four or five men repurchased the company in 1944, with Harry the elected president until 1958. Although fearful that outsiders would make an offer to the Refinance Credit Corporation, which had assumed ownership when Jones's investors failed,[47] the Greeley consortium was able to retain ownership. Harry believed the company would continue to make money, and indeed, Home Gas and Electric proved to be a cash cow.

Having extra funds in a stable bank was a good thing for the Farrs. By 1931, Colorado was beginning to feel the economic woes that other parts of the nation had experienced earlier. As agricultural and precious metal prices fell, lost jobs followed. Denver, which had escaped the problems of more industrialized cities, was suddenly confronted with increasing numbers of unemployed.[48] Without an income or sales tax, and with a "natural inclination to balance its budget and reduce its debts,"[49] Colorado had to rely on private agencies for relief. The money soon ran out. Between 1930 and 1932, the number of hungry people needing relief quadrupled. Urban organizations, such as the Unemployed Citizens League, "scrounged for food and shelter," often bartering with farmers to trade labor "for tons of carrots, cabbage, and potatoes." They renovated old buildings, baked bread, and ran soup kitchens, but by the end of the year, they, too, had drowned in the crisis.[50]

Weld County felt the pain. In the summer of 1931, following a heavy downpour, the South Platte River ran "a brilliant red color."[51] Although residents said they had never seen such a thing before, the metaphorical bloodshed followed months of blowing top soil and little rain. The event seemed to forebode major climate change. In September, beavers were observed building their dams larger and higher, as if the animals could somehow sense the change to drier weather and were planning accordingly.[52] Grasshoppers were everywhere, along with chinch bugs, cut worms, cabbage loopers, bean beatles, melon lice, thrips, and potato beetles.[53]

By the end of 1932, Colorado was "deeply mired in the morass" of economic stagnation, as reports of crop production revealed the unforgiving impact of drought and depression. The $213 million earned by farmers in 1929 had been reduced to $82 million in 1932. Great Western Sugar Company lost $500,000 in 1931 and more the following year, forcing workers out of jobs. For farmers, drought had the same impact on income as layoffs had on wage earners in the cities.[54]

In the midst of the mounting crisis, Harry continued searching for ways to adapt to these unprecedented conditions. As with most farmer–businessmen, he was self-reliant, suspicious of the federal government, and convinced that his talent and resources were sufficient to make the necessary strategy shifts to survive. But he remained committed to sheep feeding and hardly expected the suggestion that came from his oldest son. At the very moment when Colorado was in its worst economic crisis,[55] WD requested permission to start a pen of cattle to feed. With the generally unsavory reputation cattle had experienced since the market glut of the early 1920s and the dismal prospects for marketing any livestock under existing conditions, Harry was reluctant to sanction a project he felt was certain to lose money. But he approved his son's request. This decision not only reflected the great admiration he had for WD, it also made possible the investment WD needed to begin a career that reflected his ability as an innovator in cattle feeding and related fields.

As with many good ideas, this one had begun with a casual conversation. The Farrs shipped their lambs at Lucerne on the Union Pacific Railroad a few miles north of Greeley. They had three feedlots nearby. From February until early in May, WD loaded fed lambs into rail cars. Other farmers were doing the same thing, so they helped each other. Gradually, a friendship developed among WD, Warren Monfort, and Bert Avery. Because the switch engine came late in the afternoon to load cattle, the men had time to settle the affairs of the world while sitting on the top rail of a corral fence. Monfort was Harry's age, a veteran of World War I. He had tried teaching school after the war in Illinois, where he observed the cattle and hog economy of the Corn Belt states. He was unfulfilled as a teacher and believed the weather and quality of feed in Colorado were superior to what he had seen in Illinois, so he returned to an eighty-acre farm north of Greeley and began feeding cattle. He was unable to make much money, because his fat cattle were always being shipped at the same time everyone else shipped. The packing houses had the upper hand. WD and Monfort decided there had to be a better way.

Monfort had a keen eye for cattle and people. He recognized in WD a young man who was open-minded, curious, and enterprising. WD saw in Monfort an older man with whom he was comfortable and who understood the appetite for working cattle that had been whetted in WD during two summers on the Carey Ranch. Together they concluded that Greeley was uniquely located, with ample feed available from irrigated crops and a transportation network capable of carrying fed cattle to all markets: Denver, Omaha, Kansas City, St. Joseph, Sioux City, and Chicago. Most important, they agreed on three venturesome precepts, all of which were rejected as unsound by the rest of the industry. First, they believed that corn and other feeds should be brought to the cattle, not vice versa. Second, they favored lightweight cattle, especially heifers, in order to provide the smaller cuts of meat desired by restaurants serving the tourist industry. And third, in order to take advantage of higher prices from packers when finished beef was in short supply, they would feed year round.[56]

These ideas were anathema to other cattle feeders, and according to WD, they were opposed by experts at Colorado State College, who argued that profits were out of reach if feeders tried to bring corn from the Midwest to cattle. But WD, Monfort, and Avery were certain cattle feeding would be profitable if they had fat animals ready for market at times when the supply of grass-fed beef was depleted. In 1931 and 1932, the availability of corn in Weld County was limited by the short growing season and the lack of scientific experimentation with hybrid varieties, but some farmers had already tried creep-feeding calves with limited supplies of cracked corn. They had discovered significant weight gains in late calves that had access to corn, grass, and milk from their mothers.[57] It was not too much of a reach from creep-feeding a few calves to the feed-lot concept WD wanted to implement, but he needed Harry's approval to launch the plan that he and Monfort had discussed on the corral fence.

Harry was impassive at first. His experience with cattle was unimpressive. For at least fifteen years, he had been running an occasional herd of steers on pasture, feeding them whatever grass and grain might be available through the winter.[58] They were usually purchased in the fall and sold in the spring at 1,100 to 1,200 pounds. He had been unable to make money on these two- and three-year-old steers, even when he fed them molasses. The high-protein content of molasses was supposed to improve weight gain, but profits were still elusive. In addition, the number of cattle in Weld County had increased 25 percent since 1930,[59] and the overall agricultural downturn was increasingly problematic. Harry was averse to unnecessary risk, but he believed in WD and shared his conviction that a better way to feed cattle might result in profits.

Great Western Sugar Company provided the cushion Harry needed to diminish the risk associated with buying more cattle. The company had come to realize that farmers would be unable to use all the wet beet pulp produced during the sugar refining process. They approached Harry with a guarantee of 5,000 tons annually of wet beet pulp if he would lease some Great Western Sugar Company land just east of their factory. Harry was excited by the possibilities and took WD on a tour of other sugar beet factories in the Arkansas Valley and Nebraska. Convinced that the close proximity to feed would be advantageous for lamb feeding, Harry and WD worked fifteen-hour days during the summer of 1930 to build a lamb feeding yard for 7,000 head. The work of feeding pulp and corn brought in from Nebraska and Iowa was enormous, requiring employment of 100 men.[60] With such a large operation dominating activities near the factory, Harry felt comfortable approving the use of one pen for WD to begin feeding 132 cattle.

Except for what Monfort had already accomplished, the concept of feeding cattle in a feedlot was untried. The first year WD was barely able to break even, but he was free to make changes. When he began working with 400-pound heifer calves that were fattened and marketed at 800 hundred pounds, he made money on every lot,[61] even though economic crises in Colorado were increasing exponentially.

By 1933, the depression was threatening everyone. In addition to the sufferings of the unemployed, one-third of Colorado's banks had closed. When Franklin D. Roosevelt (FDR) ordered a bank holiday the day after he was sworn in as president, WD realized how vital a stable banking system was to business and why his father had accepted invitations to serve on the boards of various financial institutions. Greeley's banks closed for the required four days, but they remained financially sound. As director of the Greeley Union National Bank, Harry had earlier approved a newspaper ad providing information on the bank's resources and liabilities. The First National Bank made a similar announcement.[62] They succeeded in avoiding a demand by depositors for their assets, but faith in the financial system and in the state's willingness to provide relief were shaken.

Some people had already resorted to violence. In January 1932, irate Larimer County farm women stormed the courthouse to demand a reduction in taxes and government spending. Two months later, 200 farmers attacked the Sedgwick County courthouse for similar reasons. Shortly thereafter, 1,500 farmers descended on the state capitol in Denver to demand a reduction in the assessed value of their lands.[63] The desperation continued into 1933, when 500 farmers marched into Julesburg to recover a neighbor's tractor.[64] In Denver, the Civil Works Commission predicted that if relief failed to materialize for the 40,000 unemployed in that city, there might be general riots.

Things were not as bad in Weld County, where irrigated agriculture enabled farming to continue during the drought. But throughout the state, the grass roots conservatism of most agricultural people was beginning to buckle as the Great Depression worsened. The traditional view that in a frontier community, anyone worth his salt could find something to do and could make a profit doing it was challenged by the downward spiral of prices farmers received, followed by increased foreclosures and business failures. Hostility to FDR's New Deal programs was led by the new Democrat governor "Big Ed" Johnson, who believed federal relief programs were a "waste of money and an unwarranted interference in state and local affairs." He wanted less government and a curtailment of public services so he could balance the state budget. Placing the burden of relief on counties and municipalities seemed the most sensible solution. But by the summer of 1933, Johnson was forced to recognize that economic conditions could only be ameliorated with the addition of federal funds. Such moneys from Washington, he was told, would be terminated by January 1934 if the state refused to provide matching funds in the form of tax increases. After a citizen protest in the legislature reminded lawmakers of the potential for physical violence if they failed to act, an excise tax was approved on gasoline, and an agreement was reached to buy cattle from farmers to feed the destitute in the cities.[65]

Harry made some concessions to these circumstances. At the request of the local extension agent, he agreed to serve on the Weld County Arbitration Board—another example to WD of his father's commitment to service in the community. Board members were appointed by Governor Johnson, and their job was to arbitrate between debtors and creditors in all Colorado counties. The board had no legal power to enforce its recommendations, but its goal was to save farmers from deficiency judgments. By the end of 1934, ten out of the fifty-two cases presented to the board had been resolved successfully.[66]

Harry was also encouraged to participate in a program to create a wheat cooperative, which he agreed to do. The Federal Farm Board had $500 million available for loans, stabilization of farm prices, and anything else that would aid farmers to help themselves. The wheat cooperative was not promoted as a relief program; instead, it emphasized the need for farmers to organize themselves in order to pool their power and articulate their collective needs.

As noted in a series of guest editorials by Ben King published in the *Weld County News*, Harry Farr emphatically denounced "all farmers' cooperative enterprises, declaring they never had worked, never could work and any scheme of that kind was entirely visionary and impractical." Because the Republican Party had endorsed the co-operatives, and because Harry had always been "enthusiastically addicted" to the GOP, King teased, one would expect him to be an advocate of the plan.[67]

But King was more interested in scoring political points than in understanding one of the county's leading farmers. Harry was fully aware of the difficult circumstances facing his neighbors, and he was no pariah when it came to joining with other people to accomplish goals. He believed the talents of creative people should serve as a source of leadership and energy for the community as a whole. Furthermore, being ready for change and prepared for adaptation required a certain amount of independence. Some might call Harry's philosophy "frontier individualism," but he was not that much of a free spirit. He participated responsibly with banks, water companies, livestock associations, community organizations, and other successful families in Weld County, and he never stopped believing that these connections were crucial to the success of the Farr enterprises. Even though the High Five companies essentially crashed as an informal leadership group during the Depression, the membership continued to believe in itself. The proclivity of small groups to organize certain Weld County businesses was a form of cooperation that Harry endorsed. Their motives were not altruistic, nor did they ask for publicity as heroes for what they did. But they remained convinced that through organization a reasonable profit was more assured, and they believed that their efforts would simultaneously improve the general economic benefits for everyone.[68]

WD learned from his father. Harry was an optimist, a quality his son emulated from an early age. When the two men traveled to Chicago in 1933 following FDR's inauguration, WD came to know R. C. Pollock, the first general manager of the Livestock Meat Board. Pollock gave a pep talk to those who had come to commiserate about falling prices, and he made a persuasive case that things always get better, that cycles inevitably come and go. For WD, "that meeting was probably the most meaningful meeting . . . I ever attended."[69] He had already learned from Harry and others of his generation that change was opportunity, that every day should be lived as fully and as usefully as possible, and that decisions were best made after consultation with the most knowledgeable people in every field of endeavor. He also learned the importance of being flexible, and as he developed a better understanding of the feeding operation he was nursing into success, he came to understand the value of patience in leadership.

As thoughts turned to starting a family of his own, WD had become in many ways an echo of his father and grandfather. But as the next seventy-four years of his life would show, he was also his own man, drawing on the strengths and lessons Harry and Hazel had shown him by example and applying them to his own version of doing things a better way.

CHAPTER 3

Partnership

All who think cannot but see there is a sanction like that of religion which binds us in partnership in the serious work of the world.

—Benjamin Franklin

As he began to root himself in the Weld County community, WD demonstrated an unusual passion for connections with people. His genuine interest in others—especially their ideas and experiences—was a manifestation of his own curiosity about life and his belief that businesses and communities could be improved through individual involvement, interaction, communication, and attentiveness to the variety of issues that concern fellow citizens. From the boardroom to the rodeo arena, from Boy Scouts to Rotary, WD's enthusiasm for engaging with others soon marked him as an aspiring young leader who could be trusted to listen and act without self-interest.

A lingering myth of the American West describes heroes and prominent individuals as loners, or rugged individualists who shunned cooperation and preferred six-gun independence to community rules of law and order. We can thank the first movies, dime novels, newspaper serials, Buffalo Bill Cody, and the art of Charles Russell and Frederic Remington for this image. The myth has endured through two centuries and continues to appear occasionally in the words of contemporary politicians and writers who suggest that moral values of the early Republic were preserved by prospectors, cattle barons, gunfighters, and others who glorified freedom without the limitations associated with government and society.[1]

The truth is that building western communities has always required cooperation. From harvesting crops to barn raising and butchering, early settlers had to depend on one another. The spirit of community sharing and community building has been at least as strong as the right to own and develop one's own property. Even today, although farmers and ranchers tend to eschew organization, they also recognize the benefits they receive when a community grows and prospers. All they need is guidance that is not selfish, fearful of change, or motivated by greed, and when someone demonstrates such qualities by example, that person is sought after as a trustworthy leader.

All three generations of Farrs were recognized as community leaders, but WD used his talents in the greatest diversity of causes. He benefitted from the noteworthy reputations of Billy and Harry as well as from his own associations with an older generation. In addition, WD was able to make his mark as a young leader at a time when some families were driven out of farming by the Depression and young men who stayed were inducted into the military during World War II.

WD's early prominence also resulted from his family's stability during the financial debacle of the 1930s. His enthusiasm for irrigated agriculture, livestock raising, and community activities stood out at a time when many people were despondent and without hope for the future. As of 1932, and on top of his responsibilities as a partner in the Farr Company, WD was secretary of the Colorado–Nebraska Lamb Feeders Association, an officer in the Greeley Chamber of Commerce, an enthusiastic Rotarian (president in 1940), and the man in charge of all arena activities at Greeley's annual Spud Rodeo. He was purposeful and energetic, a community booster who was eager to learn from those with whom he interacted. Far from being the rugged individualist of western myth, WD believed that success was achieved through associations that involved many different interests and voices.

Success, in fact, was not measured by how much wealth one could attain. WD viewed achievement as an outcome of partnerships with other humans and with community institutions. A truly meaningful life for WD was a constant search for ways to better both himself and his community. His commitment to this philosophy became a lifelong pursuit, fulfilling a passion that described the very essence of who he was and what he stood for as a leader.

It was this quality, this energy, that first caught the eye of Gladell M. Judy on a blind date in the spring of 1932. Born in Newell, South Dakota, on May 16, 1912, "Judy"[2] was the granddaughter of George Washington Judy and the daughter of Benjamin Franklin Judy and Amelia Pinuker.[3] Her parents were farmers who had difficulty making a living in South Dakota. When they learned of a coal mining boom in Trinidad, Colorado, they moved first to the home of Colorado Fuel and Iron in Pueblo and then to Colorado Springs, where the Judys ran a small grocery store.

After completing high school in 1930, Judy enrolled at the Colorado State College of Education in Greeley, with plans to earn a teaching certificate. She attended for two years, joined a sorority, took up dancing, performed in several college productions, and earned a teaching certificate.

Shortly before graduation in the spring of 1932, her career plans were interrupted by an unexpected invitation. WD had a friend who was also attending the college. WD inquired if the friend knew any ladies who might accompany him to the country club dance. The friend recommended Judy, whom he had met in class. She was living in a dormitory supervised by the dean of women, and she expressed interest in the date if she could get permission to attend an off-campus dance. Through his connections with the Greeley retail community and his parents' social circle, WD knew the dean and decided to ask her to bend the rules a bit. The dean acquiesced, insisting only that Judy be returned to campus no later than midnight.

Although WD knew "damn little about dancing,"[4] the blind date went well. They enjoyed each other's company and several more dates before WD asked Judy to marry him. She had earned her teaching certificate and an assignment to teach in Maybell, Colorado. Her choice was between marriage and a career. She knew WD was unique, extremely bright, and an excellent conversationalist. In later years, she told her children that on one date in Denver, as they started their return to Greeley, she asked WD what he knew about the function of a train's caboose. An hour later, when they were about to reach their destination, WD was still providing his considered opinion.[5]

They were married at St. John's Episcopal Church in Denver on June 16, 1933. WD was 23 years old, Judy 21. After returning to Greeley to retrieve a new Pontiac coup WD had purchased as a surprise, the couple headed off on their honeymoon to Yellowstone National Park by way of the Plains Hotel in Cheyenne, where WD would later attend his first meeting of the American National Livestock Association in 1938. They fished the Yellowstone River, caught cut-throat trout, and enjoyed a few nights at the Old Faithful Inn, watching the giant geyser explode in spectacular rhythmic bursts. From Old Faithful, they traveled to Jackson and Jenny lakes, where they rode horses and picnicked in the meadows, surrounded by columbines and larkspur.

It was a magical time until WD's sinuses began to plug up from all the spring pollen. His right eye became swollen and soon shut completely. His head ached, and he had difficulty maintaining balance. He had to get home, meaning Judy would have to drive a new car she had never driven. As WD later recalled, "She passed muster. She was scared to death and so was I, but we finally got home."[6] A week later the couple was off again fishing, this time on the Laramie River in Wyoming. WD had found the perfect partner!

He also came to realize he had married a prankster. At a ranch they often frequented while fishing in Wyoming, Judy placed a firecracker in the outhouse and lit it when her mother-in-law was occupied therein. She loved jokes and was known to play tricks on family and friends. April Fool's Day was a special time in the Farr household. She was a fun person, enthusiastic about life, determined to join with WD in the outdoor activities he loved so much, and caring about those less fortunate. She was also a good athlete, a capable rifle shot, an accomplished gardener, and a born teacher. In later years, the Greeley community knew her as "The Orchid Lady," because she gave away her orchids to florists and people who were hospitalized or experiencing tough times. She grew almost a hundred orchid varieties that bloomed all year long in her greenhouse.

In WD's words, "She was a good sport, a fine mother, and everyone loved her."[7] WD recalled that Judy had a way with people; he also recalled

> She rode horseback with me all over the mountains. She loved to travel with me. We went to so many places, and she always participated in those things and came home a lot more knowledgeable. She had a better feel for the world, because she had seen a lot of the good things and a lot of the bad things. . . . She adapted well,

WD and Judy Farr with lamb in front of newly constructed home on 14th Avenue, Greeley, Colorado. Courtesy of the Farr family.

and was fortunate enough to have some athletic ability. . . . But she enjoyed everything. Whatever it was, she liked it; she enjoyed life, and that's the important thing.[8]

For three years, WD and Judy rented a home at 1111 11th Street in Greeley. Their oldest son, John, lived there after being born in the Weld County Hospital. When Judy decided she wanted more children, WD bought a half city block at what was then the southwest end of town, not far from the college. Local architects refused to design the house WD and Judy had in mind, so the two sought advice in Denver and came up with a plan that included a full basement, twelve-inch thick exterior brick walls, steel window frames, cedar shingles on the roof, a twenty-foot-high vaulted ceiling, Texas oak paneling, and a large sandstone fireplace. It was the first house in Greeley to have copper plumbing.[9]

Construction began on May 1, 1937, in the midst of the Depression. Materials and machinery were hard to come by, but men were eager for work. A team of white horses excavated the basement. The foundation was laid using rock hauled from the Cache la Poudre River. Cement was mixed using a little gas engine and hauled by wheelbarrow to the site. In six months, the home at 1914 14th Avenue was completed at a cost of $20,000. It remained the family residence for seventy years.

Farr home at 1914 14th Avenue, Greeley, Colorado. Courtesy of the Farr family

To the *Greeley Tribune*, it was a "commodious English type home" with six rooms, a large sun porch, a full basement, recreation rooms, and a maid's room. And because of its architectural style, location, and landscaping, it became a stop on the "Lovely Greeley Gardens" tour where visitors admired red maple trees, flowers, and a "play yard for children in the Farrs' garden."[10] Indeed, it was a warm and welcoming place. Just as Harry had placed special importance on the comfort of his own home, so did WD. He was aware of his good fortune at a time when men he knew and respected were leaving town or taking their own lives because they saw no way to recover from the severe losses suffered during the Depression.

The year Judy and WD married, one quarter of Colorado's labor force was out of work. In addition, one third of the state's banks were unable to reopen after the Bank Holiday.[11] Opposition to New Deal relief measures began with state and local government officials and extended to farmers themselves, some of whom objected to restrictions imposed on their traditional right to plant what they wanted and to graze livestock on the public domain. And while some farmers received cash for agreeing to have a number of their farm animals killed, the bitterness engendered by this trade-off prompted many to leave the state and abandon agriculture altogether.[12] WD later recalled the despair of those who agreed to the slaughter of their stock. He would see them on Saturday nights when they came into town for groceries and staples, thin and haggard looking, tears in their eyes after losing animals who had been part of their family for years. "I just wanted to buy some hay from them," he recalled, "or some grain, or do something."[13]

For those who continued to farm, pressure came from the Agricultural Adjustment Act to reduce wheat and sugar-beet plantings in order to stabilize prices through a reduction in the quantity of marketable commodities.[14] The decrease in sugar-beet acreage was hard on field workers. When Governor Ed Johnson was told that the influx of Mexicans was adding to unemployment problems in the state, he ordered a group of alleged immigrants to be deported from Colorado and followed this up with a blockade of Raton Pass (the main highway route from New Mexico) by the National Guard. His plans backfired when it was revealed that some of the deported Mexicans were, in fact, U.S. citizens. When New Mexico threatened to boycott goods from Colorado if the National Guard remained on the highway, Johnson backed down. But his actions revealed the desperation with which officials were viewing the growing economic crisis. In addition, some of the state's leaders held a deeply rooted and stubborn conviction that Colorado did not need the federal government to solve its problems.

In spite of such bias, during the last half of the 1930s and the first years of the 1940s, Colorado received $396 million from New Deal programs, ranking the state tenth nationally in federal aid. The undercurrent of hostility toward federal relief gradually gave way to acceptance of the need for aid, however it was offered. For farmers, biting the hand attempting to feed them fell out of fashion, especially as the economic crisis in agriculture worsened with the onset of severe drought. In fact, when the Agricultural Adjustment Act was ruled unconstitutional by the U.S. Supreme Court in 1936, farmers bemoaned the demise of subsidy checks that had netted them more than $15 million in less than three years.[15] Some joined the Farm Credit Administration or went to work on public projects with salaries paid by the Works Progress Administration. Dozens of federal programs aided farmers who were attempting to survive a difficult period.

But while some historians have argued that the New Deal "marked a watershed in American history,"[16] in Colorado the real economic change came with World War II. Until then, the agrarian politics of the state remained fundamentally Republican, having varied little since the 1890s.[17] Historian William Leuchtenburg concluded that Methodist-parsonage morality, individualism, rigid utopianism, and anti-intellectualism in America was wiped out by the New Deal, but in Colorado the ties to frontier origins "persisted beyond the Great Depression as the marrow of the Colorado political personality."[18] Even Governor Johnson concluded in 1944 that, "As I see it, the New Deal has been the worst fraud ever perpetrated on the American people."[19]

The Farrs seem to have been of this mind-set during the Depression. They were committed Republicans. When FDR ran for reelection in 1936, they threw a "President's Party," played games of "Contract," and provided the loser with a portrait of FDR.[20] But they were also practical. The deeper the Depression became, the more Harry was energized to broadcast far and wide the benefits of Colorado lamb. He sent a "fat leg of lamb" to Eleanor Roosevelt, along with lamb chops for Easter breakfast, and mailed other tasty treats to Will Rogers and journalist Arthur Brisbane, both of whom were outspoken proponents of the New Deal.[21] Harry believed that he could be a successful businessman in spite of the economic malaise, and the more connections he had with prospective buyers in Washington, Beverly Hills, and New York, the better chance he would have of achieving his goals.

In addition to their business philosophy, Harry and WD benefited from the diversity and superior capitalization of their businesses during the national economic downturn. They opposed government handouts and focused on ingenuity and Harry's stable financial condition to weather the crises. Harry's strong cash position was further enhanced when his mother's estate emerged from probate in the spring, following her death in May 1935. At that time, WD was managing nine of his father's farms in Greeley, Lucerne, and Eaton. Wheat and sugar beets were the principal crops, along with hay, alfalfa, and feed grains. WD was the largest wheat grower in Weld County, and the quality of seed he produced on Harry's farms earned him first place in the Colorado State Seed Show in 1936 and 1937.[22]

Although livestock prices remained in decline, the Farrs consistently topped the market with fed lambs and steers. Harry continued to support nationwide advertising campaigns that described lamb as the ideal food, putting "the blush of health on the movie belle's cheeks and brawn in the muscles of the day laborer."[23] In 1936 he received the highest prices seen in Denver since 1930 and planned to continue feeding 50,000 lambs annually, unaware that the national lamb market had already peaked. Through county and regional organizations to which he and WD belonged, Harry urged the newly created chain grocery stores to add their voices of encouragement to those of the producers. "If the chains and other distributing outlets can stimulate the sale and consumption of Colorado lamb," he noted, "we will have much to be thankful for."[24]

Unlike so many farmers who retrenched in the 1930s, the Farrs expanded and diversified. They planned a new grain elevator and pinto bean storage facility in 1936 near Gilcrest (eight miles south of Greeley). They also enlarged the capacity of the company's bean warehouse in Greeley with a $6,000 remodeling project.[25] The Farr Company advertised and sold seeds for corn, sweet clover, peas, and barley, and they sponsored their own award (The Farr Company Trophy) for the best pinto beans.[26] For diversification, WD and Harry became officers in the Cunningham Oil Company of Laramie when that company succeeded with its first test well.[27] And they invested in a precious metals mine west of Fort Collins, installing a forty-ton-per-day mill to increase production.[28]

Such affluence and business activity in the midst of economic stagnation was not received well by everyone. Since 1933, thieves had been stealing potatoes from Farr properties near Lucerne. Driving a truck into the center of a field, they would load up in the middle of the night and make their getaway before detection. Harry and WD also faced lawsuits from tenants who claimed the Farrs had overcharged them for improvements made to certain farms.[29] But Harry and Hazel enjoyed a good reputation and a good life, all things considered, and they were comfortable enough to vacation in Hawaii in 1935 and in Europe in 1937.[30]

WD took his own trip, accepting an invitation to travel with Swift and Company from Chicago to the East Coast in order to better understand the complexities of meat packing and distribution. It was a trip that reinforced his belief in the power of good partnerships. Swift and Company was the kind of business Harry Farr admired, and WD's trip with them in 1937 was in part a response to his father's admonition that such connections were necessary for survival in the competitive world of livestock feeding.

Along with Armour, Morris, Cudahy, and Wilson, Swift was one of the five large meat packing companies. Following publication of Upton Sinclair's novel *The Jungle* (1906) and other exposés of the poverty and wage slavery attributable to the power and collusion of the packing industry, the federal government took action. By a 1920 consent decree signed with the Federal Trade Commission, the so-called Big Five were divested of their control of refrigerated storage facilities, stockyards, and railroads. And to prevent the possibility of the packers' return to anti-trust business practices, Congress passed the Packers and Stockyards Act in 1921.[31] Even so, the five large packers still slaughtered 70 percent of all livestock in the United States in the 1930s. The Farrs admired the organizational structure of Swift, but they also foresaw problems if the large packers continued to bully the up-and-coming chain stores.

In 1937, these powerful companies called the shots for those who marketed livestock for slaughter. Their central offices were located in Chicago, where the railroads dominated east–west transportation. They established commission men in stockyards around the country, including Denver, whose job it was to call Chicago headquarters daily with the number and quality of stock ready for slaughter. Given this information, packing companies would determine how many animals to buy and where to send them for slaughter. As WD recalled, "They had a whole desk full of people figuring out what to put in what [railroad] car and where it was going. It was a high stress job that killed people who worked it within a few years."[32]

WD's trip with Swift was the fourth of its kind for the company. It was intended to provide lamb feeders with a better understanding of meat packing, transportation, and retailing. WD was eager to be educated. Already convinced that nothing was ever as good as it could be and that "the right things would happen if you follow your ideals and are patient,"[33] he embarked on the trip with great enthusiasm. A severe blizzard in Nebraska delayed his arrival in Chicago by a day, but when he joined the tour, he was immediately impressed by Swift's telephone and telegraph setup that enabled the company to keep track of potential purchases and markets around the country. He also learned how railroad cars were loaded to capacity with a combination of hanging beef carcasses, lamb, and boxes of hams on the sawdust floor. After three days in Chicago, the tour continued on to Boston, where WD was introduced to the First National Stores, one of the early supermarket chains to be organized on the East Coast. He learned from store officials how they planned to use their own brands and merchandising and how they would tailor retailing to the needs of their customers.[34]

In 1937, and to an even greater extent after World War II, chain stores were beginning to demand uniformity of beef cuts for customers. But no two packers produced the same level of quality. Swift's policy was to use the "premium" label on the best meats they produced on any given day. Armour had its "star" meats; Wilson sold "certified." And Swift's "premium" in Boston was an entirely different piece of meat than that company's "premium" in Denver or any other place. As WD soon learned, the mom-and-pop grocery stores were at the mercy of whatever the packers sent them, but because their volume was so small, they had little impact on how the packing industry responded to their needs.

Packers had resisted federal meat grading since its inception as a voluntary program in the 1920s. The U.S. Department of Agriculture (USDA) published bulletins in which classes and grades of slaughter were defined, and Congress approval federal meat grading standards in 1924.[35] But the packers were uninterested in standardization. Animals were often sent to slaughter without any consideration of the size and quality of meat cuts and often for no other reason than that a bushel of corn could be balanced on their fat backs. "The packers were very proud of what they had done through the years," WD recalled. "They bragged about how they'd buy anything that could walk: an old cancer-eyed cow, or this eighteen-hundred-pound finished steer. They'd buy whatever was offered, and there was a market for everything."[36] The packers scoffed at the idea of standardization and formed the Better Beef Association to protest federal meat grading as unworkable. Unwilling or incapable of recognizing the potential power of the rising supermarket chains, they eventually self-destructed because of their refusal to accept change.

When WD returned to Colorado, he was on good terms with the packing industry. Far from being hostile to their reactionary modus operandi, he felt the packers had been unjustly criticized; that the concentration of power they represented was, in fact, one of the reasons for their success. Their know-how and capital, he believed, made exports possible, and they had developed efficiency in transportation.[37] As a result of the Swift trip, he developed friendships in Chicago, and over the years he returned frequently to reinforce these associations with people whose advice would have considerable impact on his cattle feeding business. He had no idea in 1937 that the packing industry would be so resistant to change. His principal concern at that time was to expand his own operation to take advantage of the connections he had made and the marketing lessons he had learned.

Part of WD's plans for expansion involved having Harry join him in purchasing a half interest in the LF Ranch, situated twenty miles southeast of Greeley between the lines of the Union Pacific and Burlington Northern railroads. As a result of his high school experiences in California Park, WD saw himself as a cowboy cattleman. He liked sheep feeding and farming, but his real love was cattle. The ranch he purchased would give him the flexibility to buy steers, graze them year-round on the blue grama grass of eastern Colorado's sand hills, or channel them to the Greeley feedlots. The ranch was originally owned by John Klug, one of the largest cattlemen in the state until his operation was wiped out by a blizzard in 1917. WD learned about the ranch's availability from Larry Lutz, a commission man in Denver who worked for John Clay and Company, buying and selling feeder cattle. Lutz was willing to put up half the money and provide the Farrs with "stockers" if the Farrs would operate the ranch.[38]

At the time of purchase, the LF Ranch comprised about 3,000 acres. WD eventually expanded the operation to 12,700 acres of deeded land and 4,162 acres of leased land. (Over time, as boundaries were straightened and lands were sold for oil development, the total size was reduced to 16,640 acres—the amount eventually sold in 1984.) He also improved the carrying capacity of the ranch by adding nineteen wells.[39] He never lived on the ranch, but he enjoyed hunting antelope and coyotes. The ranch gave him an opportunity to move cattle into the market during periods of the year when fed cattle were in short supply.

To feed cattle when sugar-beet pulp was in short supply, he would have to import corn, a doomed business decision according to some experts

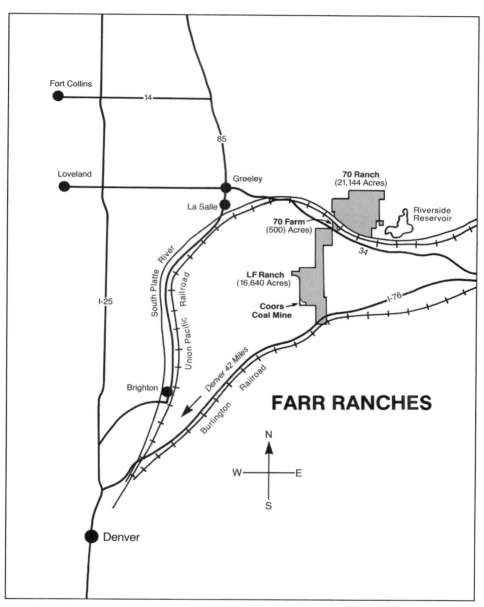

Fort Collins

14

85

Loveland

Greeley

La Salle

70 Ranch
(21,144 Acres)

Riverside
Reservoir

70 Farm
(500) Acres)

34

South Platte River

Union Pacific Railroad

LF Ranch
(16,640 Acres)

**Coors
Coal Mine**

I-76

I-25

Denver 42 Miles

Burlington Railroad

Brighton

FARR RANCHES

N

W——E

S

Denver

LF and 70 ranches. Courtesy of the Farr family.

at Colorado A&M in Fort Collins.[40] Traditionally, mid-western cattle feeders in the Corn Belt (Iowa, Illinois, and northern Nebraska) bought cattle to consume the corn they were unable to sell or feed to hogs. They would go to Kansas City or Omaha, buy a few carloads of feeder cattle, and feed the animals until all the corn was gone, without any thought to carcass grades or standard weights for slaughter. WD wanted to bring this corn to his cattle in Colorado, because the open-pollinated corn raised at that time in Colorado required a long growing season and local supplies were insufficient for WD's year-round feeding plans. A few hybrid varieties had been tried in Colorado, but they were inadequately tested and unavailable in the quantities he would need.

Corn availability and weather were the principal determinants of cycles in the cattle markets, and WD had no control over either. Harry knew the inherent risks in cattle feeding and cautioned his son to develop an operating plan that would reduce the speculative nature of a potentially perilous business. WD's answer was to "buy replacement cattle of suitable type at prices in line with their reasonable value, finish them to the weight and grade that yield[ed] meat of the type most in demand by the largest segment of consumers [the chain stores], and sell every week to get the average price paid through the year."[41] It was a form of dollar cost averaging applied to the feeding business, and it worked. WD had little interest in topping the market with the highest prices or feeding more cattle than anyone else. His objective, as it gradually matured during the first ten years of the business, was to limit the cost of weight gains and to make as much money as possible on each finished animal.

He was intimately involved in developing the business. Box cars from Iowa and Nebraska would arrive loaded with 40,000 pounds of corn. WD helped unload these cars by hand with scoop shovels. It was grueling work. When commission men in Denver called to say that one of the packers had to fill an order, WD would sort finished animals into pens. For years he personally sorted every animal that was shipped, "hundreds of thousands of them, picking them out one at a time and putting them into the car, twenty-five to twenty-eight per car." Mondays and Tuesdays, he brought in the best cattle and watched as Swift and Armour battled to establish a price. The Cudahy man usually sat on the sidelines and watched. When new lots of cattle were brought in on Wednesdays and Thursdays, Cudahy would pay the previously established price, unaware the purchases were for inferior lots. As WD recollected, "It was kind of a poker game all the time."[42]

WD's friend and colleague Warren Monfort was doing the same thing, but he and Farr determined they would sell on different days in order to avoid competing with each other. They made arrangements at the bi-monthly meetings of Greeley's T-Bone Club.

The T-Bone Club demonstrated another dimension of WD's commitment to learning from others and sharing information in local, regional, and national partnerships and associations. The club was started soon after WD and Monfort began feeding cattle and was composed of people whose knowledge would help inform all members about trends and events in the cattle business. At first, membership was limited to twelve: a few feeders, a butcher, the county agent, the owner of the local radio station, an order buyer, a commission man, and others who were invited to join because of a particular expertise.[43] Many who wanted to join were refused membership. Wives were not included until later years. The members met on Friday nights, twice a month. They ate large, sixteen-and-a-half ounce steaks—provided by the cattlemen on a rotating basis—along with salad, vegetables, and dessert with coffee. During the war years, they were sometimes forced to eat stew or corned beef, but the members disdained such fare and returned to steaks as soon as possible.[44]

Discussions were informal at first: no program, no written records. "We just visited," WD reminisced, "as different ones of us would try different things. . . . You had to be involved pretty directly in the business, or you couldn't get in. . . . We were pretty particular in those days."[45]

But as the years passed, speakers were invited to the meetings. They addressed feeding efficiency and nutrition, transportation issues, Congressional actions, breeders' concerns, the role of central markets, prices, and how the feeding industry could be improved.[46] With a variety of new perspectives available from T-Bone members, WD and Monfort could better decide when to sell and how many fed cattle they wanted to place on the market. They supported each other's operations, and WD was able to provide additional points of view by virtue of his being a bona fide rancher.

As of 1938, cattle producers and cattle feeders were organized in separate associations. Ranchers belonged to the American National Livestock Association (ANLSA), which had its annual meeting that year at the Prairie

Hotel in Cheyenne. WD attended. "I did that," he stated, "to learn things—to learn a little more about the cattle business—and I started going to conventions that were close by." In Cheyenne he found the cattlemen "narrow minded; they would not allow railroad men or commission men to join. "If you were staying at the hotel, and a commission man bought you a drink, or lunch, that was fine. You could talk to him out in the hall, but he couldn't come into the meeting."[47]

They were also deeply attached to their conservative, anti-government philosophy. If the Texans had not broken away from the national association to approve the Jones–Connally Act (1934), cattle would not have been designated a "basic commodity," and cattle ranchers would have received none of the relief offered by the New Deal Congress.[48] Even with this succor, the leadership of ANSLA remained hostile to the New Deal. The material comforts on farms and ranches had been measurably improved by 1938. According to the Bureau of the Census, "of every ten farms, seven had automobiles, six had radios, four were lighted with electricity, four had telephones, three had running water in the house, three had tractors, and two had a motor truck." Cattle prices had also improved since passage of the Jones–Connally Act, from $11.40 per head to $24.10. But ANSLA continued to maintain that the "number one public problem" was "economy in government," and at the annual meeting in 1940, resolutions were passed condemning the New Deal.[49]

WD learned much from his first participation in a cattlemen's convention. The reactionary cast of most ANSLA members regarding the New Deal was a pattern WD would see repeated later when, as president of the association, he tried to convince members to focus on efficient beef production rather than on the appearance of cattle they were trying to market.

But when WD returned home in 1938, the principal preoccupation of agriculturalists in northern Colorado was the ongoing drought. Regardless of ANSLA's unprogressive policies regarding the cattle industry, no aspect of agriculture or stock raising could advance without additional water from somewhere.

First recognized in 1931, the drought clearly intensified by 1932. Summers for the next seven years were mostly hot and dry, and when the few rains came they were gully washers, eroding the brittle land and flooding

low-lying areas. Dust storms that shut out the sun and terrified children
in southeastern Colorado were also a fact of life in Greeley. "The dust
was terrible," WD recalled, "and I've seen many a day here when you
couldn't cross the street in the middle of the day because of the dust."[50]
Grasshoppers returned to eat the few crops that survived, and so much
topsoil lifted in the wind that it rained mud in Denver in 1935.[51]

With good reason farmers were discouraged. The ditch and reservoir
system in northern Colorado had been built before World War I. Since
then, the population had grown but the supply of irrigation water remained
constant. When drought conditions developed, the mountain snow melt
ended early, ditch companies incurred water shortages, and row crops
needing late summer water to mature dried up. "No point in planting
potato seed," WD noted, "because water was too short. You couldn't raise
enough hay to feed the lambs. It was disheartening, and that's what
made us go after the C-BT [Colorado–Big Thompson Project]. We didn't
know about conservation or weather patterns or anything else at that time.
There was no knowledge [of weather patterns] and no forecast."[52]

Nor was there a great deal of optimism as to where a new source of
water might be found. The North Platte River seemed a likely candidate.
Its source was in Colorado, and its flow could be diverted into the Cache
la Poudre system if Wyoming would approve. On March 5, 1933, the day
after FDR was inaugurated, Colorado opened negotiations with Wyoming
to suggest exchanging Yampa River water for diversions into Colorado
from the North Platte. The plan appeared to have tentative approval,
but Nebraska cried foul, claiming rights to the same stream and insisting
on being a party to any agreement.[53]

More critical to Colorado's interests on the North Platte was the mood
in Washington in 1933. FDR was determined to fund projects that would
put America's laborers back to work immediately. Because Wyoming had
a project in mind for the North Platte River (Casper–Alcova Project) whose
feasibility had already been determined by the Bureau of Reclamation,
Colorado's efforts to reach an interstate agreement with Wyoming and
Nebraska were doomed to failure. In late July 1933, the government
announced it would fund the Casper–Alcova Project without any consideration of Colorado's needs. The last water hole for drought-stricken Colo-

radans on the eastern side of the Rockies would have to be the Colorado River, but getting that water to farmers would require a costly tunneling project through the Continental Divide.

Optimism soared in August when Weld County attorney Thomas A. Nixon received a telephone call from George M. Bull, executive engineer for the Project Works Administration (PWA) in Colorado. Bull wanted to know if Nixon had any ideas how to spend $200 million approved for the Rocky Mountain region. With encouragement from the Great Western Sugar Company and county commissioners, Nixon responded to Bull that for some time northern Colorado had been considering a trans-mountain diversion project from Grand Lake on the West slope of the Rockies to Estes Park and the Big Thompson River on the East Slope. The route needed to be surveyed, and funds had to be raised to do the initial studies, but a project of this magnitude would accomplish New Deal objectives and solve northern Colorado's long-standing water shortages.

The Greeley Chamber of Commerce organized the Grand Lake Committee to take charge of the project, and Harry Farr was chosen to be one of the committee members. His selection was appropriate. Having served as president of the Colorado–Nebraska Lamb Feeders for many years, he was acquainted with stockmen and farmers throughout the South Platte Valley and all the way to the Nebraska line. If the Grand Lake Project were to be found feasible and the federal government agreed to build it, Harry's connections with landowners in eastern Colorado would be critical. These farmers would have to be persuaded to purchase units of the new water when their finances were already stressed, and they would have to agree to a tax on their property to pay for part of the construction.

The Grand Lake Committee raised the $3,000 required for an initial survey. Completed in the fall of 1933, the survey report concluded that 285,000 acre-feet could be diverted from the Colorado River near its head-waters and sent through a gravity-feed tunnel a distance of 13.1 miles into the Estes Park area, where it would be channeled into the Big Thompson River. But when the PWA received this report, it showed little enthusiasm for investing in transmountain diversion. Moreover, Colorado's senior representative in Congress, Edward T. Taylor[54] of Glenwood Springs, had begun to make clear his opposition to any project that would take water from the West Slope without prior construction of a reservoir to hold an equivalent amount of water for his constituents there. Recognizing the urgency of acting with dispatch to resolve issues in Washington and on the West Slope before additional problems surfaced, the Greeley Chamber of Commerce organized a new committee in April 1934: the Northern Colorado Water Users Association (NCWUA). In January 1935, this organization elected *Greeley Tribune* editor and publisher Charles Hansen as president.

Hansen was already sixty years old. Beloved by his community, he proved to be a patient and skilled negotiator. He had no financial stake in ditch companies or reservoirs, and when he argued locally for the Grand Lake Project, it was because he believed passionately that the Colorado River was northern Colorado's only hope for economic stability and future growth. With consummate patience and political deftness, he guided the Grand Lake Project through the Washington bureaucracy, refusing to be defeated by the growing penury and parochialism of eastern congressmen. Likewise, he transmitted to the West Slope the promise of good-faith dealings and the assurance that Taylor's demand for compensatory storage would be honored.

During his years as president of the NCWUA, Hansen became WD's mentor, urging the younger man to get involved in community projects. The *Greeley Tribune* mailbox was close to the Farrs' box at the post office, so the two men had many chances to converse there. They also had the opportunity to talk at lunch during winter months when they would gather with other community leaders to discuss the project's status. "I sat next to Charlie and ate lunch with him two or three hundred times over a period of years," said WD. "Probably, Charlie Hansen contributed more to the City of Greeley than any other man I have ever known."[55]

He also contributed to the success of what was now being called the Colorado–Big Thompson Project (C-BT). The Bureau of Reclamation had shown an interest in taking on the job if they could be assured that the entity in Colorado with which they would be dealing had the authority to honor contractual obligations. To this end, Hansen persuaded the Colorado legislature to pass a conservancy district law in 1937. It allowed conservancy districts to sign contracts with federal agencies and to impose taxes on residents within the district in order to pay off a loan that would be used to build the C-BT. Late in the year, the boundaries of

the Northern Colorado Water Conservancy District (NCWCD) were hammered out, and a repayment contract was approved for district voters in
May 1938. It then became the job of Harry and WD, with the help of other
proponents, to sell the C-BT to the men whose lands would be mortgaged
and who would ultimately bear the financial burden of a multi-million
dollar water project.

Harry owned a big Buick touring car that held six passengers. WD knew
how to drive it. Congress had approved initial funding for the project in
1937, but not a cent would be spent without approval of residents in the
seven-county district.[56] To contact as many voters as possible, Harry and
WD planned trips to different towns. It was something of a dog and pony
show for WD. "They'd set up a little room and we'd have lunch, and then
we'd talk."[57] WD learned that each group had different areas of concern:

> I was a good chauffeur, but more important, I understood their
> strategy. They were confident enough in me that if I thought they
> ought to talk about something that would appeal to a young person, they
> would do it. Those older men realized that I was going to stay here.
> There wasn't any question about that. . . . As you look back at it, it was
> very obvious that they were glad to have me, because they were depend-
> ing on me when they were gone. . . . Everybody else had either gone
> to the university, or they had left because it was so dry here and
> they couldn't make a living. I was the only young guy around.[58]

But not every audience was receptive. WD soon learned why some of
the large farmers opposed the C-BT: they had loaned money to smaller
farmers during difficult years, taking ditch company water shares as
collateral. When drought hit the already depressed irrigated farms, the
creditor farmers seized control of the collateral and became, somewhat
by accident, water monopolists. They made money renting the surplus
water they owned and viewed the C-BT as an unwanted intrusion on their
good fortune. "I learned about people during these years," WD confessed.
"There's always a few selfish people."[59]

Overall, the efforts of the Farrs, Hansen, and other community leaders
were enormously successful. Harry beat the drum for the C-BT wherever
he went, cashing in on the great respect in which he was held throughout
Colorado. To those who preferred drilling wells, he replied that "by the

time Grand Lake water is delivered, these pumping plants will be worked out or the wells will be dry. This is the opportunity of a lifetime, and if you don't buy this water, you are making a mistake." Even though he was viscerally opposed to federal government assistance, he viewed the C-BT as cooperative, not speculative. It was an enterprise in which the old Union Colony spirit of working together for the betterment of the local community would triumph. To show his own good faith, Harry would subscribe to 800 units of C-BT water, perhaps 1,000 units when the time came to sign on the dotted line.[60]

With such strong leadership from the community, a repayment contract that obligated the NCWCD to pay back $25 million was approved by a vote of 7,510 to 439.[61] The initial estimate of C-BT cost was $44 million, but Hansen correctly anticipated overruns. He negotiated a deal that obligated the NCWCD to $25 million, regardless of the actual tab. As it turned out, with war-related shortages and delays, the C-BT cost $163 million to complete. With a signed repayment contract in hand, the Bureau of Reclamation opened bidding for C-BT construction in 1938. Before the year came to a close, construction work had started on Green Mountain Reservoir on the Blue River. This reservoir represented the acre-foot-for-acre-foot compensation that Representative Taylor had demanded for the West Slope. If the process of wooing East Slope voters had been delayed, or if Hansen had been unsuccessful in his negotiations with the West Slope, the C-BT would never have been built. It squeezed through a small window of opportunity in Washington when money was still available for public works projects, and it was approved only months before the world was turned upside down by Adolf Hitler's invasion of Poland in 1939. Delays for any reason would have killed the C-BT, northern Colorado would have suffered the consequences, and WD's influence on Colorado water struggles would have been far less consequential.[62] Fortunately, significant construction advances at Green Mountain and in the Adams Tunnel were made before the project was shut down because of World War II.

The war years tested WD, but they also provided unexpected opportunities on which he was able to capitalize because of his increasingly useful partnerships and associations. His responsibility in Rotary accelerated in early 1941. An organization that promoted humanitarian service,

encouraged high ethical standards in all vocations, and worked for inter-
national peace and goodwill, Rotary reinforced WD's personal values.
Only thirty at the time he was elected president, WD was the youngest
man chosen for a position he assumed even before his father, also a
Rotarian, was so honored. Two years later, following in the footsteps of
Billy and Harry, he was brought on the board of the Greeley National Bank.
As an officer in the Colorado–Nebraska Lamb Feeders Association and
the Weld County Lamb Feeders Association, he continued as liaison to the
National Livestock and Meat Board in Chicago. And through his committee
work with the ANLSA, he was becoming known nationally as a dependable
representative of the livestock producers. As the war became a worldwide
conflagration and young Americans were called to serve, WD was increasingly viewed as an exemplary spokesman for the livestock industry. The
five sinus operations he had endured since 1929 disqualified him for
military service, but this disappointment was more than compensated for
by his thoughtful and articulate representation of American agriculture
on many boards in Washington at a time when demand for meat was
high and fear of inflation was even higher.

President Roosevelt established the Office of Price Administration and
Civilian Supply in the spring of 1941. The objectives were to prevent price
spiraling, hoarding, rising living costs, and speculation. In August, this
department was divided into the Office of Production Management and
the Office of Price Administration (OPA). In his capacity as secretary of
the Colorado–Nebraska Lamb Feeders Association, WD was selected to the
OPA board. He predicted a ceiling structure that was, in fact, placed in
operation by President Roosevelt in his message to Congress on April 27,
1942. For the war's duration, meat prices would be limited to the highest
levels charged in March of 1942.[63]

Price controls were tough on producers. Demand for lamb and beef
was at an all-time high, but the rising cost of production, combined with
rationing and limited availability of railroad transportation, made livestock raising unprofitable. WD was appointed to a special advisory board
to represent ANLSA's concerns about price controls. "[It was] a high-
powered group of people," WD recalled "including the heads of Jewel
Tea, Coca-Cola, Cox and the president of Armour. To find alternative
sources of protein, they worked at increasing fish production, calling in

the Coast Guard, naval people, oceanographers, etcetera to see how fish production could be increased. But the country still hadn't recovered from World War I; not enough ships. So, they imported cheese. This went on for a couple of years and I was right in the middle of it. It was a fascinating experience."[64]

WD had some success in achieving a price increase, but as he looked back on this period, "no one made much money and there was little push for quality. The price controls and rationing were difficult to work with, and no progress was made in the science of feeding."[65] Even though no progress in livestock feeding was made during the war years,, the Farrs regularly topped the market in lamb and cattle prices, but profits were elusive. The Farrs focused instead on what they could do to support the war effort. Harry served on Governor Ralph Carr's Committee on Defense and put energy into selling defense bonds. The Farr Produce Company provided its employees with stamp albums they could use to purchase bonds.[66] "We who are left here on the home front," Harry declared, "can do no less than to attempt to approach the sacrifices of those brave men out on the fighting fronts to whom the last great measure of sacrifice is but a daily offering. They give their lives. We lend our money. It is not only necessary and right that we should assume this additional participation in the war effort—it is an honor to do so."[67]

In this light, but with the post-war period also in mind, Harry and WD ordered the printing of 25,000 thousand brochures that explained how lamb should be boned and cooked. In cooperation with the National Livestock and Meat Board, they sponsored hundreds of demonstrations at army bases to teach the cooks how to handle lamb. With the armed forces taking over 50 percent of the meat raised in the United States, Harry's instinct for good advertising and the Farrs' ability to look to the future combined to create a program that might have succeeded if the soldiers had not returned home sick and tired of too much mutton. The lamb feeding business had peaked, and whatever slim hope it had to survive the war was eclipsed by the replacement of wool by nylon.

Cattle still appealed to WD. He remained convinced that the American public would insist on more and better cuts of beef when the war ended and price controls were lifted. He had noted the arrogant and domineering approach taken by the large packers, and he was certain beef could be raised, slaughtered, and delivered to the chain stores in large quantities, with a level of quality and consistency yet unknown to the livestock industry. "Never before in the history of the United States," he predicted in 1943, "have people been so conscious of meat—or the lack of it— as they are today. And at no other time in history have the livestock and meat industry meant so much to America."[68] If it were available, WD surmised, Americans could eat five billion pounds more meat annually, and the Allied countries could also eat more. It would make sense, he concluded, to be in a position after the war to raise cattle on his own ranch and feed them at his own feedlots.

With this confidence, he turned to the West Slope in 1943 to find a ranch where he could satisfy his cowboy disposition and raise the beef America would soon demand.

CHAPTER 4

Opportunity

A wise man will make more opportunities than he finds.

—Sir Francis Bacon

Seeing opportunity in hardship is a Farr characteristic.

—*Greeley Tribune,* June 17, 1986

In his search for a place to raise beef cattle, WD was guided by the powerful memories of two summers at a ranch in the northern Rockies. He loved the mountains, with their lush grasses, trout streams, wild game, and breath-taking vistas. He had hunted elk several times in the Flat Tops, no more than twenty-five miles as the crow flies from Glenwood Springs. It was the same country where Teddy Roosevelt pursued bear in 1905 and where, in the late 1920s, Ed Budge had built cabins and a lodge for hunters in search of trophy elk. "Budge's" was hard to get to and rustic, but hunting there was one of WD's great joys. After his first trip in 1934, he returned to the lodge regularly, sharing this passion for hunting with Judy and his sons.[1]

WD's fondness for Budge's may have influenced his decision to purchase the Crystal River Ranch[2] twelve miles south of Glenwood Springs in Carbondale. For several years he had been looking at a lot of "shoestring ranches" in the White River Valley,[3] but they all seemed to be limited by geography, distance from rail lines, and minimal potential for growth and development. As of 1943, Metropolitan Life Insurance Company (MetLife) owned the Crystal River Ranch. The company held title to a lot of property in the West and Midwest, much of it acquired through loan defaults during the Depression. The Crystal River Ranch fell into this category.

The Farrs' purchase of this ranch presented opportunities for WD. It also convinced him of the critical need to plan and develop secure water systems. With greater facility than most, he understood how businesses functioned and how they were interrelated. He comprehended the inter-relationship between economic development and prosperous communities, and his extraordinary commitment to lifelong study molded him into an exceptionally accomplished manager. The Crystal River Ranch experience accentuated these talents.

Located in the Roaring Fork Valley, just west of the confluence of the Crystal and Roaring Fork rivers, the Crystal River Ranch began as a potato farm. When the silver mines were booming in Aspen, the lower altitude of the Crystal River valley proved ideal for growing food for the miners. Because soils in the lower valley were porous in a region of ample sun-shine and clean water, potatoes soon became the farmers' crop of choice. Even when mining declined precipitously following the 1893 Congres-sional repeal of the Sherman Silver Purchase Act, a national market for potatoes continued in the hotel and railroad industries.

One example of someone who saw the almost unlimited opportunities to make money growing potatoes in the region was Eugene H. Grubb.[4] In 1895 he and his brothers purchased a ranch and took out homesteads south of Carbondale, believing they could grow the finest potatoes in the United States. In less than ten years, they convinced experts in the hotel and railroad business of their ability to raise varieties that could be easily processed by mechanical peelers. By 1905 they had won a supply contract with the New York Central Railroad. The Denver and Rio Grande (D&RG) and Midland railroads serving the Roaring Fork valley placed eastern terminals within reach of Colorado potato producers. Growers acquired a far more lucrative market in the East than the one they had experienced locally.

Louis D. ("Lou") Sweet was one more of the many who caught the fever. He first came to Aspen to work for the D&RG, serving as station operator and then treasurer of Pitkin County, but he soon became interested in the potential for farming in the Crystal River valley. In fact, he came to be known in Colorado and the nation as something of a potato expert.[5] To grow potatoes in massive quantities, Sweet needed partners. He found them already living in Carbondale.

Frank E. Sweet (no relation) was working as general manager and bookkeeper at Dinkel's Mercantile Store.[6] Because Dinkel's banking and retail businesses enjoyed a monopoly in the Carbondale area, Frank Sweet was able to accumulate a modest amount of wealth. With Dinkel and W. L. Girdner as partners, Frank Sweet purchased land on the East Mesa, where he was involved in the construction of a large irrigation ditch. This area became known as the Big Four Ranch.[7] Eventually, he sold his interest and bought land on the West Mesa where the Crystal River Ranch is now located.

This land was fertile, but it needed water to be productive. To that end, the partners joined with Henry Clay Jessup, who came to Carbondale from Missouri. Jessup bought the local livery stable, furnished teams of mules that hauled lumber and supplies to the railroads, and graded roads around Redstone where J. C. Osgood was building a planned community for his Colorado Fuel and Iron Company workers. Jessup sold the livery business for $10,000 and purchased land near Frank Sweet's West Mesa homestead. Soon thereafter, Lou Sweet expressed an interest in finding partners who would invest in construction of a sixteen-mile canal from the Crystal River to the West Mesa. His objective was to provide sufficient irrigation water for 2,000 acres of potatoes on the flat top of the mesa, where soil conditions were good but water was extremely limited.

It was a risky venture, and it ultimately cost the three men $50,000 to build.[8] But the canal was also an amazing engineering feat. Without irrigation water through the Sweet–Jessup Canal, crops could not be raised with any consistency on that land. Over time, the canal proved to be both the lifeline and the Achilles' heel of the Crystal River Ranch.

In 1974, F. W. Jessup, son of Henry Clay Jessup, reminisced about the early days of the canal and the land it watered. He recalled that his father, Henry Clay, brought in twenty teams of mules to dig the ditch. The work went well, but they experienced at least one runaway mule every day, and if they missed a day, they were likely to have two runaways the next day. "They always had a barrel of whiskey in camp," Jessup remembered. "The whiskey was measured by the cup full. The men wrote their names on the barrel every time they took a cup . . . When the barrel was empty, they added up the number of cups each man drank and [each] paid his share according to the number of cups [he] used."[9]

Possibly because the daily work was so well lubricated, it took three years to complete the Sweet–Jessup Canal, from 1902 to 1905, and no water was allowed to flow until the entire project was finished.[10] The course of the ditch meandered through a variety of terrains and unstable soil, much of which was little more than loose gravel. When workmen encountered creeks running perpendicular to the ditch, they had to build wooden flumes and trestles to carry water across the gullies. Jessup became frustrated with the slow pace of construction and the unwillingness of his partners and the surveyor to run test flows along the partially completed stretches of the canal. Tired of Jessup's grumbling, the partners bought out his $10,000 investment, increasing thereby their own financial burden. But the project finally terminated in 1905, and when water first ran along the grade, it flowed the entire sixteen miles to the West Mesa, where Sweet's [Potato] Seed Farm was to be established.

Lou Sweet put up most of the money; Frank Sweet managed the farm. Together they formed the Crystal River Land Company, which was incorporated with $150,000 of capital stock. The company's objective was to purchase and consolidate the small pieces of privately owned land on the mesa and to construct the buildings, fences, and storage cellars needed for a potato farm operating on a little over 2,000 acres.[11]

Over the next fifteen years, the business grew slowly. The mesa's dry soil required many years of irrigation before it began to produce good potato crops. But potatoes sold well, especially during the First World War, and by 1920, the Sweets were ready to expand even further.

They decided to take out a loan for $130,000, secured by the 2,084 acres deeded to Sweet's Seed Farm, the water rights of the Sweet–Jessup Canal, and a promissory note payable to the Irrigated Farms Mortgage Company.[12] It was a bold move based on two assumptions: (1) that the eastern railroads and hotels would sustain their interest in the tasty and uniformly sized Peachblow potatoes grown on the mesa, and (2) that Sweet's Russet Burbank seed potatoes would remain in demand.[13] One can only imagine what the loan was for, but in all probability the ditch required major improvements, and Lou Sweet wanted to put more land into production.

Crystal River Ranch house built by Metropolitan Life Insurance Co. Author's collection.

The plan was worthy, but it failed to survive the economic shock waves of the Great Depression. In 1931, the bottom fell out of the potato market. Lou Sweet was unable to pay the promissory note, and in 1932 the farm was taken over by MetLife, which had replaced Irrigated Farms as creditor several years earlier.

MetLife operated the farm for ten years, adding buildings and fences to the property and constructing a modern house for the farm manager. The company's biggest challenge was to rebuild the Sweet–Jessup Canal. As of 1932, only one-third of the ditch's adjudicated capacity was reaching the ranch, and under Colorado water law these water rights would be lost if repairs were not forthcoming immediately. In fact, Sweet's Seed Farm would have been worthless without major reconstruction of flumes, trestles, and concrete lining of the ditch in areas where the gravelly soils simply could not hold water. In addition, as recalled in 1958 by Glenn E. Rogers of MetLife, the company had reason to fear the actions of southern Californians who were attempting to acquire all unused water rights in the upper Colorado River basin while Hoover Dam was under construction.[14]

Therefore, the company put a lot of money into the property and began shifting the farm's focus from potatoes to cattle. By 1942, when WD first visited the area, MetLife was running 1,200 steers and two bands of sheep, while farming several hundred acres of potatoes.

For WD, the quality of the property, improvements made by MetLife, and its location near the mountain ranges he loved offered the ranching opportunity for which he had been searching for several years. Although the ditch still needed much work, Rogers recollected that by 1943 the company had "increased the carrying capacity . . . to a point where the canal system was capable of carrying nearly all of the adjudicated water rights at the time the property was sold."[15] Unfortunately, although the amount of water had been increased, distribution ditches and laterals had been allowed to run without proper supervision. Erosion had occurred, deepening the main channel and making it almost impossible to divert water from the main ditch to farmlands and meadows. At least one ditch break occurred every summer.

WD later admitted he should have paid more attention to the condition of the Sweet–Jessup Canal. But when he and Harry first saw the ranch in the fall of 1942, everything was green, the main house appeared modern and well constructed, fences and gates were maintained, and the new calving shed, barn, and corrals seemed to be substantial for a cattle operation. Harry lacked interest in ranching but liked what he saw. "My father fell in love with the looks of the ranch," WD recalled, "and he knew I knew a lot about water. Plus the fact [there was] a lot of land for farming and grass for grazing."[16] Summer permits for cattle and sheep in the national forest on both sides of the valley added to the attractiveness of the operation. The decision to buy such an enchanting property was not difficult.

The Farrs' offer to MetLife involved an exchange of land and cash. For several years WD had been working a section of land known as the Godfrey Farm east of Eaton. Water rights were excellent, but the soil was heavy with clay and the farm failed to realize a profit. Valued at $72,000, MetLife took title to this farm as partial payment. A balance of $85,000 was paid to MetLife at the closing on April 8, 1943.[17]

Not unexpectedly, WD's family caught the excitement of this new adventure. John Daven Farr had celebrated his eighth birthday in May;

WR was barely four; and Harry Richard (Dick) had just been born in January. Somewhat concerned about Carbondale schools, Judy was planning on acquiring a teacher's certificate so she could home-school the boys if necessary. Everything pointed toward a new life, a new adventure, and a permanent move to the Roaring Fork valley—"if things worked out."[18]

As John later recalled, the first trip to the ranch was memorable. After Greeley schools were dismissed for the summer, the family loaded into the sedan and headed west. The road from Denver into the mountains was narrow. Loveland Pass was a steep climb on a gravel road, but coming down on the west side provided some relief. "We pulled into the old town of Dillon," John wrote, "and got gas at a big old barn of a building which had slot machines . . . into which I plunked a quarter. I got way more than I bargained for, because mom and dad raised hell with me for a couple of days over wasting good money."

The rest of the trip proved easier. Vail Pass had a recently paved road, allowing travelers an easier and more direct route west, one that avoided the climb to Leadville at 10,000 feet. From Vail Pass the road followed the Eagle and Colorado rivers, entering the incomparable Glenwood Canyon about twenty miles from Glenwood Springs, where the Farrs checked into the old Denver Hotel. "I could see the vapor of the hot springs," John reminisced, "and smell the odor of the pools. I thought it was magical. The hotel staff was happy to see dad [while] I was outside watching trains go through every few minutes."

The next day, the Farr family piled back in the car and headed south toward Carbondale. "I was prepared for a long ride," John recalled, "but when we popped out of Glenwood, there was Mt. Sopris. Dad stopped to have us look at the mountain. Mom was thrilled. . . . We drove through Carbondale . . . and up the narrow hill past the old potato cellars, and there was this ranch. When we pulled in front of that big house with the big yard, I was spellbound. Mom wandered in like a child. Later she told me that most of the ranches they had seen had old log homes, and this one [by comparison] was spectacular. People who worked the ranch came over and said hello and helped unload the car. . . . Everyone was happy to have someone in charge."

WD wasted little time addressing the ranch's many needs. About 200 acres of potatoes had been planted. Sprayers were trailered over from

Greeley for use in controlling the Colorado beetle. One of the machines arrived with a long rope extending down into its empty chemical tank. When John inquired what was on the other end, Claude Adams pulled out a saddle for him and WR to use on Buster, their Shetland pony. WD had his favorite cutting horse, Navajo, at the ranch. It was a time of high expectations, great optimism, and endless tasks, all of which required indefatigable innovation by WD just to keep the place running.

He located an old hay baler to bale the alfalfa, which had replaced potatoes on many of the ranch's irrigated fields. It took ten men to operate it: a tractor driver, a man forking hay into the machine, another to force hay down into the baler chamber, someone to insert wooden blocks with notches for baling wire, two men on each side forcing wires through and twisting them to tie the bale, a man at the end pulling out the bales, and one more standing on a towed sled where the bales were stacked. It was a dust-choking, labor-intensive job. The baler itself was subject to frequent mechanical malfunctions, and the irregular-sized bales it produced, weighing between seventy-five and one hundred pounds, had to be manhandled with metal hooks.[19]

Haystacks frequently fell apart, so WD visited Colorado A&M in Fort Collins, where he learned how to engineer a water-tight stack. It was another example of his willingness to seek professional advice to solve complex problems. He was not mechanically minded and was unable to build machinery with his own hands, but he was incredibly good with numbers and with designs and could explain to others what he wanted. With the advice of experts, he could then communicate his ideas to the people who did have mechanical skills. In short order, the men on the ranch developed a technique that permitted two men to load hay on a truck and deliver it to a nearby stack.

Using self-taught surveying skills, WD addressed water delivery problems. The badly washed out main ditch called for construction of check dams to raise the water so it could be diverted to the fields. WD recollected the construction process:

> It was wartime. We couldn't get good help. The young guys were all in the service. All you had was a bunch of old men, who were single men, mostly, that just weren't able to do the hard work, like concrete,

WR (*standing*) and John (*on pony*) Farr with Buster. Courtesy of the Farr family.

so it was a major challenge. [But] we put in those checks one after another, and put a drop under them and let the water down, and the ditch filled back up to a point you could work with it and get the water out [into] the contour ditches.[20]

Next came the potato cellars. Built into the ground, they had partly collapsed from inattention and heavy winters. Cellophane wrappers, cardboard cartons, napkins labeled with Jessup's name, and burlap sacks were reminders of Sweet's Seed Farm. In order to warehouse the crop of early Burbank potatoes already in the ground, WD had to shore up the roof and improve storage conditions. WD described the procedure as follows:

> Potatoes need to go through a curing process for about thirty days. They sweat like grain. . . . We put them in storage and when fall came, and you had the fall work done, you got snow and colder weather. This was the place to work your men in the winter time. We had just an old fashioned sorter, which was nothing more than a frame with wooden sides. On the top of it was wire mesh, bent and twisted to certain sizes. You took a pitchfork full of potatoes and put them up on top—a dull pitchfork, so it wouldn't stick in the potato. You dug under the potatoes, lifted up the pitchfork, rubbed your hand over them so the dirt went out underneath, and then the potatoes fell out, into holes according to size, and into four burlap bags of a hundred pounds underneath. You had a little portable scale to check them. Then you took string and tied them where you had two ears, and that was the way you shipped them. That was standard all over the world for potatoes at that time. Wrapped in napkins saying "Crystal River Ranch," the cured potatoes sold to the railroads for $5 to $6 a sack.[21]

As with any perishable crop, potatoes were a risky business. The price of seed was high, chemicals were required to prevent loss from a variety of pests, and a constant and reliable supply of water was crucial.

In the summer of 1944, WD came to realize just how critical that water really was. Every summer, storms posed a threat to the Sweet–Jessup Canal, especially where the ditch crossed over mountain streams. When major cloudbursts occurred, debris roared down the gullies, wiping out manmade structures and taking down ditch banks. When this happened, it was imperative to get the ditch shut off as quickly as possible. But it took time to stop the flow, and damage to neighbors' property and to the ditch itself was inevitable.

MetLife had constructed a flume over Thompson Creek, hoping to avoid damage from summer gully washers. Big wooden supports held up the three-foot-wide corrugated pipe on either end. On July 15, WD was in Colorado Springs at the wedding of his sister-in-law when he received a call that a storm had dumped a huge amount of rain over the South Thompson drainage. A tree had washed down in a torrent of water and trash that wiped out both sides of the flume and carried the pipe 150 yards downhill. The break occurred so fast that water exiting both sides caused the pipe to implode. "As a kid," John Farr recalled, "I could put up my arms and brace myself, and walk up and down the pipe when it was empty, looking for holes." But after the break, the pipe was sucked flat. "I could not get my hand between the [compressed] metal sheets."[22]

The extent of the disaster was astounding, but WD called on past experiences with well disasters in Weld County, his established connections with the Thompson Pipe and Steel Company in Denver, and his own problem-solving skills to address what was clearly an emergency for the Crystal River Ranch.

Even though Thompson Pipe and Steel was preoccupied with the war effort, an engineer was sent almost immediately to appraise the damage. The Farrs' long-standing relationship with the company made possible this courtesy. Surveying the two sides of the gully, WD calculated that if the appropriate steel pipe could be purchased, a siphon could be installed under Thompson Creek, thus eliminating any possibility of a similar washout in the future. In WD's words,

> The engineer and I climbed around the hills and got the measurements. They designed the pipe and shipped it up on the railroad in sections, and we had to unload it off the rail cars on a little small truck and haul it up to the site section by section. The pieces were numbered, and to show you how rapidly things change, during the war they had developed a portable acetylene welder which was mastered in a few days by my man from Greeley. . . . That was quite an experience to see the pieces of steel pipe welded together, instead of fastening the pipe together with a coupling. It all turned out just fine and worked well, but we were without water for thirty days, so our potatoes . . . quit growing.[23]

Loss of income from the potatoes was only a small part of what WD learned from the ditch episode. Just to build the siphon, he had to pay out over $100,000, doing most of the work himself and with available ranch hands. "We didn't have equipment, didn't have cranes or portable

Flume over Big Thompson Creek. Courtesy of Ruth Brown Perry, Carbondale, Colorado. Author's collection.

anything," he recalled. "We had to jigger [the pipes] around with block and tackles and pull those pieces of pipe up and have them hanging there and swing them into place and weld them. It was a hell of a job. We worked twelve hours a day there for a month. I was there every day working with them. That's why I remember."[24]

The ditch break was a turning point for the Farrs. As much as they all loved the ranch, by the summer of 1945 the world had changed. The war was over, and no one really knew what to expect from the economy. Price ceilings remained in effect, but the pent-up demand for beef and consumer goods unavailable for five years would create opportunities for those who were ready and able to produce food. WD always thought of the Crystal River Ranch as a "marvelous" enterprise that would require "a lot of supervision, because there were so many things that needed to be looked after."[25] But raising steers for feedlots on a property that had proven so dependent on a vulnerable water supply now appeared risky business. Harry had taught him about risk levels. Profits on this ranch were now looking uncertain at best.

In addition, Harry was not well. He had intestinal problems and was unable to get around as he used to. He needed WD in Greeley to help him run Farr Farms, and he urged WD to make a choice between his life in Carbondale and his opportunities in Greeley. Better schooling in Greeley for the children, the uncertainties of travel over Loveland Pass, the benefit of an already established cattle feeding business in Greeley with ten years' experience, and the prospect of having to pour money into the Sweet–Jessup Canal combined to convince WD and Judy that they should sell and return to Greeley.

They never had to advertise the ranch. Because of WD's membership on the board of directors of the U.S. National Bank of Denver, and because of that bank's well-known loans to livestock operations throughout the state, prospective ranch buyers often inquired at the bank about quality properties for sale. This is precisely what Sidney F. Tyler did in the fall and winter of 1945 and 1946 during a terminal leave granted him prior to separation from military service.[26]

Before departing on leave, Tyler engaged his boss, General Hubert R. Harmon,[27] in a conversation about postwar plans. Tyler was concerned about a daughter with severe asthma and was aware that the drier climate

of the West might be a better place for her than the damp air of Philadelphia, where his family was located. He was considering ranching, but
with no farming or livestock raising experience, he wondered if he had
any business venturing into a profession about which he knew practically
nothing. "You have plenty of time to learn," the general commented,
"but what makes you think that beef raising should be a profitable undertaking in the postwar era?" Tyler replied, "Because I have seen right here,
as I am sure you have, the public's insatiable appetite for red meat after
four years of skimpy rations, and there must be some way to capitalize on
that" (*A Joyful Odyssey*, vol. 2, p. 119). In this assessment, Tyler and WD were
on the same page, but they ultimately chose different venues for taking
advantage of the coming demand for beef.

The general urged Tyler to visit Harmon's sister, who had married a
large cattle producer near Sheridan, Wyoming. Over the course of a few
months, Tyler and his wife sojourned through Wyoming, found some
rustic cabins to house five children and friends for the summer of 1946,
and made contact in Denver with attorney Churchill Owen, who promised
to keep his eyes peeled for an appropriate ranch property. Owen was
acquainted with Emmett J. Dignan, vice president of livestock loans at
U.S. National Bank in Denver. At some point in the early summer of
1946, Owen learned that WD was selling the Crystal River Ranch. He
called Tyler, who was using Story, Wyoming, as summer headquarters
while he searched for suitable ranches. Owen offered to meet the Tylers
in Glenwood Springs.

As with the Farr family, the Tylers' first sight of the ranch property was
awe-inspiring. "It was a jewel of diamonds in an emerald setting," Tyler
wrote, "and like the Grand Canyon, it was too stupendous to be appre-
hended in a single glance. . . . From the instant of perception, I knew
that our search for Paradise was ended, that we stood in the presence of
the Holy Grail, and that, come what may, we positively had to have it"
(vol. 3, p. 19).

The perfect host, WD regaled the Tylers with every aspect of the
ranch's past and present operations. With his well-known mastery of
detail, he bewildered Tyler with dozens of facts and elicited a promise
from the Tylers to return in two weeks armed with additional queries.

On the drive back to Wyoming, Tyler pondered the unwelcome news that the Crystal River Ranch was running two bands of sheep. Tyler mused,

> The emphasis on the sheep business gave me great concern, not only because lamb was a luxury product commanding a small and vulnerable market, but also because mutton had never been a household favorite, and the heavy consumption of it by our forces in the Southwest Pacific had led to a surfeit not easily to be overcome. I was concerned, too, by the development of synthetics and the inroads they were making in the demand for natural wool. . . . Nevertheless and notwithstanding, the Crystal River Ranch was indeed the pot of gold at the base of the rainbow, and . . . taking all things into account, the potential rewards outweighed the risks. (vol. 3, p. 21)

Returning as promised, Tyler listened attentively while WD explained additional features of the ranching enterprise. He held nothing back and once again flooded his guest with facts. "Bill Farr went to great lengths," Tyler remembered, "to ensure that all my inquiries were fully answered and that everything pertinent was made available. If the significance of what he disclosed failed to register in my mind with proper perspective, the fault was not his. The fact is that his analysis of the business and the details of its operations were just too vast for me to comprehend" (vol. 3, p. 22).

That analysis included an evaluation of the Sweet–Jessup Canal, the recent summer break in the ditch, and a guarantee that all work on the South Thompson siphon would be completed by WD before he left. Tyler did not pursue further questions related to the operation of the ditch, "because the blizzard of information set before me was so overwhelming. In retrospect, I must further acknowledge that if I had pursued the matter sufficiently, there is at least an even chance that I would have lost my nerve and called off the deal altogether" (vol. 3, p. 25).

But just as the Farrs had been mesmerized by the ranch's beauty, so, too, the Tylers could see only opportunity and a purposeful life for five children in a postwar world in which beef was certain to be in demand. A price was agreed upon, and closing was scheduled for November 1, 1946. "All we really wanted to do was get our money out," WD recollected. "We might have made $10,000 or lost $10,000, and I say that literally. . . . Basically, for the [four] years we had owned the ranch, it was a wash."[28]

Reflecting both his genuine interest in other people and his perceptive sense of what was necessary for people to get along, WD gave Tyler an unsolicited piece of advice when they shook hands after signing the sale documents. Tyler recalled that WD told him

> There is one thing you must do when you settle in over there, and that is to get yourself a deer. Have Homer [White, ranch foreman] take you up to the cabin on Cottonwood [Pass] late some afternoon and spend the night up there. Tell him to take you out before dawn the following morning and hide you in some brush near one of our ponds. The deer will come in to drink at first light, and you will be able to get a good shot at close range. All of Garfield County goes crazy during hunting season, and if you get your deer it will be viewed by the community as a sort of badge of acceptance, marking you as one of them. (vol. 3, p. 32)

The advice was flawless, but Tyler's aim was flawed. The deer appeared on schedule, but several shots failed to find their mark, and the group was forced to return to ranch headquarters in polite silence. Although he eventually turned the Crystal River Ranch into a well recognized cattle operation, Tyler's first few years began with unexpected hostility from the local community.

On one of his last days on the ranch, WD took a trip to Cow Camp in the White River National Forest to make sure all was in order for the change in ownership. A low-lying tree branch knocked him off his horse. He got back on and rode the rest of the day in pain. After a restless night and difficulty getting out of bed, he learned from a doctor that he had injured his back and damaged a knee that would eventually have to be replaced. "[That horse] damned near killed me,"[29] WD later recalled, but in retrospect the incident underscored WD's physical tenacity and perseverance.

It was also testimony to his all-around ruggedness. The sinus problems WD lived with most of his life had improved somewhat since the near fatal attacks that hospitalized him in Wisconsin. He learned enough to avoid mushrooms and some grains, but he was still affected by many pollens and molds that caused severe allergic attacks. One eye drooped as a result of the Wisconsin operation, so doctors lengthened the eye muscle and took fat from his belly to restore equilibrium in his cheek. Sulpha drugs proposed by the Oklahoma Allergy Clinic helped with sinus infections, but when things got bad, Judy would have to boil towels so the moist heat would relieve the pressure in his sinus cavities. He was healthy enough in the late 1940s to take on the many opportunities awaiting him in Greeley, but the most telling progress he made resulted from the commercial availability of penicillin.[30] It proved to be a wonder drug when allergy attacks turned into sinus infections.

With the Crystal River Ranch behind him, and with renewed energy, WD took a leadership role in addressing problems and responsibilities farmers and ranchers faced in the post-war era. The economic machinery of peace was built from odds and ends of free enterprise and the New Deal. Its Washington administrators were hoping to find a way to give free rein to the engine of production without creating runaway inflation in the process. In the beef industry, price ceilings, wage boosts, and strikes had created a black market that was so prevalent it "had almost begun to look white."[31]

Six months before selling the Crystal River Ranch, WD traveled to Washington as a representative of the ANLSA Cattle and Beef Industry Committee. Following in the footsteps of his father,[32] he had testified before the Senate Agriculture Committee in 1943, but this time the issues he needed to address were far more critical. In hearings before the Senate Committee on Agriculture and Forestry, WD outlined the impact of "intolerable OPA regulations."[33] Black market activity was increasing across the board, he noted, because of the insecurity experienced by livestock and feed producers. No one knew how to plan. Producers could not stay in business if present price ceilings were obeyed, so everyone was forced into criminal behavior in order to survive. "There is no question," WD argued, "that the removal of price ceilings and subsidies would be a tremendous shock to our feeders. . . . If the Department of Agriculture is right, and it is necessary for us to take a reduction price for our fat cattle, we are willing and anxious to take our loss now while the industry can stand it, and get back to a free economy based on the law of supply and demand."[34]

At the same time, WD confessed,

> We feeders are getting the advantage of the black market. We know our cattle are bringing about $1 per hundredweight over compliance

prices. [But] we don't like this way of doing business. . . . Everybody buying corn today has to patronize the black market. Either livestock, poultry, dairy products, and so forth, will be liquidated in a very short time . . . or we producers will buy on the black market and the jails won't be big enough to hold producing America. . . . We are tired of being forced to be in violation of the laws in order to feed the country. The farmers' morale is breaking down; his respect for the law is breaking down.[35]

It was an articulate and emotional appeal to troubled lawmakers, who praised WD for his "fine statement."[36] It was also an example of WD's command of data, his persuasive style of discourse, and his broad knowledge of the industries affected by government restrictions on free enterprise. As a citizen, WD wanted to help lawmakers find a better way to increase meat production for the betterment of society as a whole. He disliked the idea of a planned economy, opposed burdening taxpayers with subsidies, detested the intensified gambling brought on by uncertain federal programs, and, more than anything, abhorred the way farmers were losing faith in their own government. He was a proud representative of the agricultural industry who craved nothing less than the satisfaction of feeding the country in a free and open market.[37] And he rapidly learned that high-priced feed would make competitive meats (chicken and pork) more competitive. It was a lesson he would recount frequently to stubborn cattlemen in subsequent years, because the majority of beef producers focused more on preserving breed conformity than on establishing the performance records necessary to improve the quality and consistency of cattle ready for market.

The influence of WD's testimony on Congress's decision to terminate price controls is incalculable,[38] but the OPA did remove most ceilings by October of 1946. The following June, cattle were selling better than ever, and two dollars a bushel was the highest price for corn recorded in the ninety-nine-year history of the Chicago Board of Trade. Demand for beef was "amazing," and frustrated butchers blamed packers for gouging the retailers.[39] Inflation was further stimulated by floods in the Midwest, John L. Lewis's wage increase for miners, and President Harry S. Truman's commitment to the Marshall Plan. Consumer pressure for food and household goods seemed to be out of control. Truman asked producers to voluntarily reduce the prices charged for corn, coal, construction, and commerce. He wanted Americans to save food in order to provide more for Europe, and he asked the country to forego poultry and eggs on Thursdays and meat on Tuesdays.[40] It was a tough sell to a nation that had made considerable sacrifices during five years of war, and it was a form of volunteerism many thought would fail. Truman himself finally urged Congress to restore his authority to impose rationing on important consumer goods and wage ceilings on workers, while the Secretary of Agriculture predicted the inevitability of meat price controls because of the escalating demand for beef.[41]

But the livestock and agricultural markets sought their own levels without interference from the federal government. Not until 1951, a year after the Korean War broke out, were price controls reinstated. By then, Farr businesses had expanded substantially. The high prices received for livestock, beans, potatoes, and other irrigated crops provided additional capital for their growth and diversification.

In the summer of 1946, the Farr Company planned to build a second feed mill and elevator. The one at Lucerne was inadequate to handle the many demands placed on it. The new facility was to be constructed next to the Union Pacific Railroad tracks north of Greeley, in Ault. Its design included large amounts of concrete and steel, which caused delays attributable to labor and material shortages, but the five-floored facility was completed in early 1948. Equipped with grinders and rollers for poultry and livestock feeds, it also served as a cleaning and storage facility for locally produced pinto beans. The Farr Company would eventually manage similar facilities in other parts of Colorado, Wyoming, Texas, Idaho, and Utah. Farr Farms, meanwhile, oversaw feedlots in Greeley and LaSalle while managing as many as ten irrigated farms and ranches in the greater Greeley area.[42]

From an office adjoining the one his father occupied on 7th Street near the train station, WD assumed increasing responsibility for management of the Farr enterprises. Invariably dressed in tie and jacket, well groomed like his father, punctual, and respectful in his dealings with others, WD epitomized the professional businessman. But a change of clothes was always at hand. His greatest love was the hands-on business of farming and feeding cattle. He frequently assisted in the building of additional

WD Farr at old feedlot adjacent to the Great Western Sugar Co. refinery. Courtesy of the Farr family.

pens as the feeding business expanded, sometimes in partnership with others, to 20,000 steers and heifers annually. Some animals still shipped by train to Chicago for slaughter, but with the arrival of smaller packers and the advent of double-axle, eighteen-wheel trucks, it became more cost-effective to ship to Denver.

On the farms, WD's skill with a surveyor's transit found him leveling fields that were planted, irrigated, and harvested mostly by renters.[43] The high standards he pursued to achieve efficient use of water as well as his use of the most up-to-date seeds, fertilizers, and farming methods provided satisfaction for those who lived on and worked the Farr properties. When new hybrid varieties made possible the growing of corn for silage (ensilage), WD provided tenants with free seed and contracted with them to produce as much as 5,000 tons of ensilage for the feedlots. Although he was not a nuts-and-bolts mechanic, he had a clear vision of what was needed to modernize feeding and farming operations. He described his ideas to an employee, Lawrence Hurt, who drew out WD's idea with chalk on the machine shop floor and then built the apparatus as described. Repeated successes reinforced WD's belief that a better way to do things was just a matter of persistence and common sense.[44]

By 1948 the cost of living index had reached an all-time high. Food costs were shattering earlier records, and meat prices were expected to continue climbing for the foreseeable future. Although the number of sheep on feed had declined significantly from highs in the 1930s, the number of cattle on feed was up 300 percent and choice steers in Chicago were selling at almost $40 a hundredweight.[45] "Beef consumption in 1947 was the highest in 40 years at 115 pounds per capita (carcass basis). Prices were 125 percent above 1941 prices, and by 1949 they were 210 percent higher. Cattlemen just could not satisfy the new demand for beef."[46]

These were good days for Farr Farms and the Farr Company. Harry and WD were able to make large donations to the new Greeley Community Center, the local hospital, the Congregational Church, and the Boy Scouts. They represented northern Colorado on bank boards and in an array of organizations: the Denver Stock Yards, Mountain Bell Telephone Company, Home Light and Power Company, the Greeley Chamber of Commerce, Rotary, the National Livestock and Meat Board, the Colorado–Nebraska Lamb Feeders Association, the Weld County Credit Men's Association, and ANLSA. WD also joined the Denver Club to meet other state leaders. He did not play squash, but he soon earned a reputation for good business sense. He preferred staying out of political office, because he felt he was more effective on the outside, providing counsel, and because he disdained the dogfights associated with politics.[47] He rarely got into arguments and was good at determining what organizations required to succeed. Once clear objectives were established, he committed himself to providing the necessary tools. He was able to bend and change, to evolve as circumstances demanded. A good student of people and institutions, WD became an effective member and leader of numerous organizations, mainly through his sheer determination to be productive.[48]

Involvement in so many organizations provided WD with great satisfaction. He enjoyed learning from others and benefitted from the wide variety of contacts. But none of the boards, directorships, or memberships gave him as much enjoyment as experiencing the first Colorado River water flow through the transmountain Adams Tunnel in June 1947.

Anticipation of this moment was keen. Many doubted the C-BT could be built at all because of its many-faceted components and the enormity of the engineering challenges. The visceral question about whether the finished project would even work added to the skepticism. Dams and reservoirs on the West Slope of the Continental Divide would have to store and deliver water through the longest tunnel ever built for irrigation. Power plants on the East Slope had to be located to take advantage of flows in and out of reservoirs, streams, and ditches in a timely manner. The C-BT was one of the largest reclamation projects built in the West, and the ten years of observing its construction heightened the suspense of those who awaited the first water.

It was an emotional experience, "the greatest thrill I have ever had in my life," recalled WD.[49] Northern Colorado's faith in having the equivalent of another Cache la Poudre River entering the Front Range had wavered as wartime demands shut down tunnel construction and postwar inflation raised the estimated cost from $44 million to $163 million. Ever conscious of Congressional penury regarding annual funding of water projects, U.S. Bureau of Reclamation (USBR) officials had made no secret of the fact they wanted to renegotiate the 1938 repayment contract. But the NCWCD, backed by the Colorado Water Conservation Board (CWCB), held firm to its $25 million commitment, forcing the USBR to engage in creative bookkeeping to please Congress. By the end of 1946, the Adams Tunnel had holed through. Dams and reservoirs on the West Slope were nearing completion, and Thompson Pipe and Steel Company had been contracted to build a corrugated steel conduit two miles in length from the east portal of the tunnel to the Big Thompson River.[50]

As of June 1947, less than half the entire C-BT project was complete. But the anticipation of seeing Colorado River water flowing eastward under the Continental Divide caused an immediate morale boost to construction crews, Department of Interior officials, and the farmers and towns that had agreed to place a lien on their lands in return for the promise of future water.

June 23 was a cloudy day with rain and a chilly wind. WD, dressed impeccably in coat and tie, with a fedora settled snugly on his head, restlessly braved the elements with others who had come to witness the first water through the tunnel. President Harry S. Truman was supposed to telephone Governor William Lee Knous at 11:00 A.M. to authorize opening the tunnel's west portal, but USBR officials neglected to inform the governor that they had canceled the president's call. Sixteen minutes late, Knous pushed a button releasing 75 cfs of water into the Adams Tunnel.

WD remembered the scene:

> We had been there about an hour waiting. Here is just the tunnel, and it is blank. Nothing! Very quiet! This group of men . . . we were up there to see what was going to happen. We had no idea. We stood around, fidgeted and talked. All of a sudden we heard a roaring noise, not like water or anything. It sounded like a train coming. We couldn't figure that out. Then the biggest cloud of dust I ever saw came out of that tunnel ahead of the water. You can imagine that. Thirteen miles long. It just covered us with dust. We were just filthy, our hats, our clothes. That dust hit us and we couldn't see anything. As that dust dropped down, then [came] the lighter dust behind it. Here was the water rushing out, and we knew it was going to work. We knew the water was there. I have never seen men as happy in my life. Never expect to [again]. These were grown men. I was the youngest of the group. They hugged each other. They kissed each other. They threw their hats up in the air. They did this for several minutes, because finally you had the water, and you knew it was going to change northern Colorado. You had no idea how, but that was the answer.[51]

The USBR celebration sounded a note of caution. At an evening banquet in Loveland, Commissioner Michael Straus referred to the C-BT as part of the USBR's plan to develop the entire Missouri River basin. But because the House Appropriations Committee continued to demand revision of the 1938 repayment contract in the face of escalating prices, he warned, taxpayers and water users would have to increase their share of construction costs.

It was a message to which WD's mentor, Charlie Hansen, now in his mid-seventies, felt the need to respond. "The federal government would be acting with poor grace," Hansen replied, "if it pressed the District for additional construction funds." Property owners had approved the Repayment Contract nearly a decade earlier after considerable soul searching. They would not appreciate the federal government's breaking faith with them at this time.[52]

WD Farr and others witnessing first water through the Adams Tunnel, 1947. Courtesy of Northern Colorado Water Conservancy District.

This steadfastness from a highly respected leader, and the NCWCD's determination to adhere to its $25 million repayment obligation, prevailed. WD learned from the experience: negotiation in good faith was paramount to one's credibility in business; planning for the future was a prerequisite to good leadership; good leaders needed to be both flexible and attentive to change; and flowing water in the West provided confidence and stability in an area that had been too often victimized by extremes of weather. There was no such thing as too much water. Even though the reasons to rejoice on that cloudy June day outweighed all other concerns, everyone knew the droughts would return. The Dust Bowl days had left a scar. It would still take many years to complete the entire C-BT system.[53] WD wondered if the recent advances in long-range weather forecasting might provide an interim opportunity to protect northern Colorado's future.

Through his association with Thomas Dines, president of the U.S. National Bank, WD learned about the achievements of Dr. Irving P. Krick, whose weather predictions had helped make possible the June 6, 1944, invasion of Normandy. By 1950, Krick had developed a weather concept that challenged the chaos theory embraced by the meteorological community.[54] He believed the universe was orderly, that weather patterns repeated themselves. If scientists could determine the rhythm of past weather events, they stood a good chance of being able to make more accurate forecasts.

One of the larger livestock loans made by the U.S. National Bank was to Albert K. Mitchell, a leading cattleman in New Mexico.[55] Dines referred Mitchell to Krick, with the expectation that better weather forecasts might enable Mitchell to increase cattle numbers on his arid lands. For the most part, Krick succeeded. Intermittently over the course of twenty-one years, he provided Mitchell with useful information. For WD, whose friendship with Mitchell would last a lifetime, the promise of understanding weather patterns offered the possibility of an additional level of security for northern Colorado.

Furthermore, by 1950 Krick had begun to promote "artificial nucleation," a process better known as cloud seeding. Discovered by General Electric in 1946, the theory resulted from the recognition that every raindrop and snowflake has a nucleus whose origin comes from a wide variety of different sources. Scientists learned that when moisture molecules collect on the bits of nuclei picked up by wind action, they form a droplet or an ice crystal, depending on temperature. The objective of artificial nucleation was to cause millions of moisture molecules to form on the nuclei, causing a raindrop or snowflake that would increase in weight until gravity forced it to descend from the cloud in the form of moisture.

Seeding storms from the air had proven hazardous and unreliable. Krick found a way to seed from the ground by using portable generators, or furnaces, that worked by burning marble-sized bits of coke coated with silver iodide (dry ice). This process created a vapor that drifted upwards into moisture-laden clouds. In theory, when clouds lacked sufficient bits of dust, salt spray, auto emissions, or other nuclei, moisture would not be released: no rain, no snow. But when artificial silver iodide nuclei were launched into these same clouds at the right time, billions of particles would combine to create the droplets or flakes that fall from the sky as rain or snow.

This possibility fascinated WD and encouraged him to invite Krick's firm to Colorado in December 1950. "I was young," he recalled, "and willing to look at anything that was new, you know, whereas some of the older people pooh-poohed something like that."[56] In addition, he felt a kinship with Krick, who had been vilified by the National Weather Service as a loose cannon and who was regarded by some in the established weather community as a snake oil salesman, not a true scientist. What WD admired was Krick's persistence and his willingness to absorb criticism while taking his convictions to the people who would benefit from his nonconformist ideas. His approach resonated with WD. It inspired him to engage in the same kind of organizing and cheerleading with which he had been so successful when the C-BT idea was considered outrageous by large segments of the northern Colorado community.

Finding the funds necessary to bring Krick to Colorado proved difficult. Farmers were skeptical. But with characteristic determination, WD raised $4,000 from several irrigation companies, Great Western Sugar Company, Coors Brewing Company, and private donors to pay for a survey that would determine the value of artificial nucleation in northern Colorado.[57]

Krick's Water Resources Development Corporation, represented by T. R. Gillenwater, arrived in Fort Collins in the fall of 1950 to make a proposal. WD presided as chairman of a citizens' committee convened to evaluate Krick's proposals. To farmers, ditch company officials, and representatives of northern Colorado cities, Gillenwater offered to double the amount of runoff the following spring through cloud seeding for a price of $100,000. If he failed, there would be no charge for his services.[58]

WD and Warren Monfort were intrigued. The cloud seeding plan, they agreed, might change "the entire agricultural outlook for the whole northern Colorado area."[59] At the same time, WD pondered the plan's potential for disrupting operations of cattle feeders and ranchers, possibly turning some of the rivers into roaring torrents and the land into marshy bogs. From Estes Park he faced criticism that cloud seeding would destroy tourism, that it would be a "costly menace" and would result in lawsuits.[60] But WD assured skeptics that the objective was to increase the snow pack above 9,500 feet, and if the process was successful, moisture from cloud seeding would flow into the reservoirs and enter the rivers gradually.[61]

In January 1951, WD was elected president of the Northern Colorado Natural Resources Association. Composed of representatives of each northern Colorado watershed, the wheat growing area northeast of Greeley, and the foothills ranchers, the association incorporated for the purpose of signing contracts with Krick's Pasadena firm. Entities that contributed funds would receive predictive forecasts by mail as well as a guarantee, underwritten by Lloyds of London, that unexpected damage from excessive moisture would be compensated.[62]

WD's weather-making activities caught the interest of Colorado governor Dan Thornton. A rancher himself, Thornton appointed a five-man board "to supervise all weather modifications efforts and experiments in the state."[63] WD was selected chairman.[64] The board's primary focus was to exercise vigilance over Krick's activities and to receive complaints.

Protests soon arrived. Summit County citizens signed a petition against cloud seeding, claiming economic loss from heavy moisture. Arkansas Valley residents railed about damage from hail and demanded that Krick's generators be shut down.[65] Governor Thornton heard additional grievances and referred them all to WD.

In retrospect, it was hard to evaluate results from Krick's actions. WD thought enough of him to sign a contract with Farr Farms for five years, but as he candidly admitted, "We found that he was right part of the time and not right part of the time."[66] Krick did not have enough data to know how much additional moisture was produced by his generators. But by the fall of 1951, the West was experiencing a serious drought, and any rainfall resulting from natural or artificial stimulation was appreciated by farmers. As with his role in promoting the C-BT, WD had rallied local support and diffused skepticism about a new idea. Long-range weather forecasting was still in an experimental stage, but it would continue to play a major role in WD's thinking for years to come. He had sold a new concept to conservative thinkers with the backing of the *Greeley Tribune*. But as the foreboding signs of drought became increasingly manifest, WD seized on another opportunity made known to him by his banking connections. A large grass ranch about one hundred miles northwest of Billings, Montana, was available for purchase and the U.S. National Bank of Denver was interested in providing financing.

Possessing a working ranch that could furnish steers to his feedlots remained a seductive prospect to WD. Even before owning the Crystal River Ranch, he had been looking at places in the Saratoga–Encampment area along the North Platte River. Unfortunately, the two properties that captured his attention were bought by others.[67] Hence, when Thomas Dines of the U.S. National Bank in Denver mentioned the availability of the old Smith Ranch west of Martinsdale, Montana, WD expressed interest.

This was real cattle country. The rolling grasslands of the Little Crazy Mountains were ideal for livestock grazing: low in altitude, with good moisture, and far enough east to avoid the howling blizzards of the high country. The transcontinental Chicago, Milwaukee, St. Paul and Pacific Railroad (The Milwaukee Road) provided a connection to markets via an electrified line that began fifty miles east of the ranch in Harlowton and continued west to the coast through Idaho.[68] The Milwaukee Road owned alternate sections of land on either side of its tracks. When these lands were sold to ranchers, large spreads developed with the capability of controlling the deeded land as well as the public domain in between. The property secured by WD and his partners included well over a hundred sections of deeded land.

Harry was not interested in another ranch. When the purchase was consummated in March of 1951, the deed listed William Farr, Thomas Dines, and William Magelssen of Billings.[69] Magelssen dabbled in real estate and had served seven months in the Montana State Penitentiary in 1930 for his involvement in a cattle stealing operation.[70] But he had served his time and was considered a solid citizen by the time WD and Dines decided to include him in a partnership to run a steer operation. The partners cleaned up the ranch, began stocking it with cattle, and incorporated it in Colorado as the 71 Ranch Company. WD's boyhood connection to the 70 Ranch east of Greeley, where he hunted ducks and pheasants on weekends, was the basis for renaming the property.

But the 71 Ranch enterprise was short lived. The cattle market collapsed in 1953 from a variety of causes. A deepening drought was exacerbated by cyclical oversupply of livestock, the return of price controls as a result of the Korean War, and the escalation of feed costs due to lower-than-expected grain harvests. In the fall of 1953, WD sold the 71 Ranch to Wellington Rankin, older brother of Montana's history making congresswoman Jeannette Rankin.[71]

Wellington Rankin was not loved in Montana. He tended to be abrasive, egocentric, and a bully. But he was also shrewd and perceptive. He admired WD's honesty and business ethics.[72] Purchase of the 71 Ranch was consistent with his belief that land was the only wise investment. By the mid-1950s, he had become "not only the largest individual land owner in Montana, but in the entire United States. His ranch holdings sprawled across central Montana, and at one point, he could claim 27,000 head of cattle."[73] Unfortunately, he allowed his properties to be overgrazed, failed to maintain fences and buildings, and condoned trespassing on other properties. His management style was a sad commentary on what the 71 Ranch might have been under WD's management.

But WD had to sell. Although it was difficult to part with the 71 Ranch, he had his hands full with farming and cattle feeding at home. Two years of extensive losses, irregular government policies, higher taxes, a record U.S. cattle population of almost 100 million, increased costs of feed and equipment, drought, and radically higher labor costs were enough to demoralize anyone in the business. At a briefing of legislators in January 1954, spokesmen representing key segments of the economy informed the Colorado General Assembly that Colorado's farm marketing had dropped "about 80 million dollars from the 1952 level. Measured in dollars and cents, this price slump mean[t] that, on the average, every Colorado farm family suffered a loss of about $2,000 during the past year."[74] Cattle and potatoes were selling for one-half of what they had been, onions were selling for only one-third, and milk was "badly hurt." Most feedlot operators conducted business at a loss, and all signs appeared to indicate the total demise of the sheep and wool industries.[75] Remembered as the "Great Cattle Bust of 1953" by the National Cattlemen's Beef Association, and as a time when Colorado cattlemen almost came to blows over the efficacy of price supports,[76] this was a moment in agricultural history when cattlemen could choose either to complain about their predicament or find opportunities in existing conditions.

WD chose the latter course. He saw opportunity in change. He always claimed he was a "fatalist," by which he meant that things happened for reasons he might not comprehend and over which he had no control. Actually, he was far more of a realist and optimist, because he was convinced that humans had the power to adapt to and make the most of all kinds of circumstances. In his view, the cattle depression was not so much attributable to an excessive supply of animals, the misguided but well-intentioned government price supports, or the "disgraceful" Korean War;[77]

rather, it was more a result of producers' failure to adapt their businesses to changing times and to understand the role of chain stores, such as Safeway, as the real power in determining the future of beef in American homes.

What was needed, he argued, was more common sense on the part of producers. They would have to feed cattle year round and market animals with attention to holidays, weather patterns, and seasonal demands from retailers. They would need to consider buying lighter steers and heifers, whose smaller carcasses and rapid rate of maturity would better suit the retail market. And they were obligated to account for how their animals would grade.[78] The producers would also have to band together, WD declared, to raise a war chest in order to

> advertise, advertise, advertise. Beef is the greatest food we have. That fact should be shouted from newspapers, radios, television sets, bill boards. . . . In the fall we ought to sell the housewife on the value of hamburger when the grass cattle come to slaughter in large numbers. Steaks and prime ribs will pretty much take care of themselves in any season. In the winter we ought to speak out about the nutritional value of front quarter cuts. It's the season of pot roasts and brown gravy.[79]

He was not alone in touting the need to promote beef, but he may have been one of the industry's best examples of how to take a deflated business and seize on the opportunities at hand to make it better. He spoke publicly about Weld County's underlying economic strength and how success by cattle feeders would help Denver businesses. He encouraged tours of his feedlots by out-of-state livestock men, supported catchy roadside slogans such as "Watch Your Curves: Eat Beef" and "Mmmmm Beef," and he endorsed formation of the National Beef Council.[80] He believed in free enterprise and minimal interference from government, but he also asserted the need for cattlemen to take charge of their livelihood by actively promoting its benefits. He abhorred laziness and apathy; acting as a victim of circumstances was not a part of his temperament.

Perhaps his greatest triumph occurred when the American National Cattlemen's Association (ANCA) finally voted to include cattle feeders as equal members. A motion to this end had failed previously in Phoenix, but WD's patient appeal to the membership about the importance of unity and the power of organization led to success in 1954. As a rancher and feeder, he took pride in this accomplishment. The vote was a measure of the respect in which he was now held by many segments of the cattle industry.

In like manner, the water community had begun to recognize his leadership ability. In 1955, with agriculture still struggling and the C-BT two years away from completion, WD was appointed to the board of the Northern Colorado Water Conservancy District (NCWCD). It was a position he held for more than forty years and one that earned him additional accolades from local, regional, and national organizations. A month before his death in 2007, when asked for what he wanted most to be remembered, WD replied, "Tell them I knew water."[81]

CHAPTER 5

Foresight

The very essence of leadership is [that] you have a vision. It's got to be a vision you articulate clearly and forcefully on every occasion. You can't blow an uncertain trumpet.

Theodore Hesburgh, University of Notre Dame

I agree that I am forward thinking. I'm always thinking about tomorrow and next year and ten years down the road and what is likely to be around and how we're going to cope with it.

WD Farr to Sue Lenthe, *Today's Business* (May 1988)

WD's appointment in 1955 to the board of the NCWCD by Judge William E. Buck launched a lifetime commitment to the CB-T. The C-BT was still two years from completion, but WD embraced the challenges it posed with enthusiasm. He served forty years as NCWCD director, followed by almost ten more as director emeritus. His skills as a facilitator were vital. The escalating struggles between environmental activists, water resource managers, and land developers—partly a response to unprecedented population growth in the West—required imagination and creativity to resolve. With his ability to make people feel important and his faculty for looking beyond present circumstances to the projected needs of diverse communities, WD was able to play a meaningful role in determining water policies and procedures at a time when the simple goal of increasing supply was complicated by a powerfully organized effort to protect nature. The environmental movement caught him by surprise, but a serendipitous acquaintance with Canadian Andy Russell helped him comprehend the need to coordinate water resource development with the goals of those who sought ecological balance in the West.

Russell was a hunter and an environmentalist. He and WD first met in 1949 on a hunting trip in the southeast corner of British Columbia, near the Flathead River. In 1946 Russell had written a successful article for *Outdoor Life* magazine about a giant black bear that had been killing cattle.[1] The story caught the eye of *Outdoor Life*'s editor, Jack O'Connor, who was already familiar with Bert Riggall's Skyline Pack Train and its hunting expeditions in the Canadian Rockies. Russell was Bert's son-in-law and quite involved in the business.

O'Connor engaged Skyline and Andy Russell for a hunt in 1949. Coincidentally, WD had been cultivating an interest in hunting trophy animals. The two men were scheduled to be Russell's clients, but O'Connor had to back out at the last minute, a decision that proved fortuitous for WD. The two-week excursion into the mountains of British Columbia went ahead as planned but with WD as Russell's only client. That experience created an intense friendship between the men that lasted until Russell's death in 2005.[2]

The 1949 hunt was also intense. WD remembered it as "the highlight of my hunting experiences."[3] He wanted to bag a moose and a grizzly. Russell guided him up and down the mountains, through all kinds of weather and into areas so remote that the only people they saw were those connected with the Skyline Pack Train. Forced to hole up in camp during a two-day snow storm, Russell and WD became well acquainted. When the storm passed, they sighted, pursued, and killed a grizzly. "What an unforgettable day!" WD recalled. "Then there was the day we went to the top of the ridge and saw the moose feeding in the valley below. We gradually worked our way down through the heavy timber and killed the moose which still hangs over my fireplace. That was another tremendous day. . . . Other days of [mountain] goat hunting, lying on the side of the mountain, waiting for the moisture to dry out of the telescope site [*sic*]" were also powerful memories. That sighting occurred late one evening. Because goats are known to move fast and never in a straight line, Russell urged WD not to wait too long to shoot. "Take your time," he cautioned, "but hurry!"[4]

WD's marksmanship and fortitude on these occasions earned Russell's respect. Retrieving the downed moose proved especially difficult. Without

WD Farr with moose from 1949 hunt with Andy Russell. Courtesy of the Farr family.

pack horses, they were forced to butcher by moonlight and start back to camp under terrible conditions. "It was pure Hell," Russell later recalled in a letter to WD. "But you just grinned."[5] Slipping and sliding on the talus, horses, riders, and the quartered moose finally made camp at three o'clock in the morning. WD had enjoyed himself immensely, and Russell appreciated the toughness and zeal of his companion.

The two men shared much in common. Russell was WD's junior by five years, but they had both grown up admiring the cowboy way of life. They were good in the saddle and keen shots, and they revered the natural environment. Neither had a college education. Both dropped out of school for medical reasons. Russell educated himself in the library of a neighbor who provided volumes of Dickens and Kipling. By the age of nine, he was familiar with many of the classics and attuned to quality literature and his own zest for writing.

WD was less interested in literature, but he saw in Russell a man who appreciated wilderness and wildlife from a scientific point of view. Although he never completely understood Russell's environmental activism, WD

WD Farr with grizzly bear from 1949 hunt with Andy Russell. Courtesy of the Farr family.

reviewed and revised his own views as a result of the Canadian's tangles with corporations and dam builders. In letters the two men exchanged in later years, Russell raged against the nefarious tactics of the oil and gas industry and narrated his forty-year fight against construction of the Oldman Dam in Alberta. In retrospect, WD thought Russell went too far, that he was too extreme, "too rabid; he got off on the wrong track. He was wrong."[6] But he also learned a crucial lesson: in the struggle between water development and wilderness preservation, the need for moderation, patience, and compromise was paramount. He was impressed by Russell's great knowledge of rivers, especially his notion of how they represented the essential history of a particular area. But he was also cognizant of the West's need to maximize natural resources for man's benefit. As a result, he rejected what he perceived to be Russell's narrow views. In a general sense, WD was more like professional forester and conservationist Gifford Pinchot, whereas Russell embodied the principles of preservationists John Muir and Aldo Leopold, for whom the destruction of anything in nature was profane.[7]

Despite these philosophical differences, the two men felt a strong mutual respect. Their friendship became increasingly intimate, minor disagreements notwithstanding. John Farr described the two men "reveling in each other's recognition," aspiring in some indefinable way to the talents possessed by the other.[8] Each sensed a commonality of instincts and values, making possible a level of vulnerability not easily shared between men. They prized each other's capacity for courage. Russell told WD he admired his "guts," that few men have real courage, and "fewer yet can deal with [adversity] without cracking up."[9] He was praising WD for qualities rarely seen in other clients, and WD acknowledged with pride that Russell viewed him as the "best hunter companion he ever had."[10] "We were young and tough," Russell recalled. "We're still tough, but in a different way."[11]

In addition to sharing similar values and qualities, Russell and WD also shared an ability to view environmental problems and challenges in a broad, big-picture context. Writing to WD in the spring of 1988, Russell noted that he was still fighting the Oldman River dam,[12] but he was getting tired and taking time off. His frustration was related to the fact that so many people were specialists. "There are way too few people," he protested, "who can see the whole picture." The time had come, he decided, to make an educational film that would be shown in schools across the nation.[13] It would portray the complex interaction between man and nature.

"You are a very energetic, capable person," WD replied. "You positively want the world to be a better place when you leave it than it was when you arrived. . . . The same thing has always motivated me . . . trying to do something better. New things and new experiences have always been a challenge. I am sure that this common feeling is what has bonded us together through the years."[14]

The friends embraced hard work, especially work they did with their hands. They viewed life as relatively meaningless unless it aimed in some way at amelioration of the human condition. With their passion for life, they inspired others, teaching values as exemplary leaders and setting a pattern for other generations to follow. Russell wrote books and told stories;[15] WD participated on boards, accepted leadership positions in countless organizations, and welcomed invitations to speak across the country. Russell was a raconteur and a passionate preservationist; WD was at heart a conservative businessman who gloried in the challenge of change. But both were equally transformed by their love of nature, and as their long relationship came to a close, memories of the emotional attachment developed on the talus slopes of British Columbia became a source of solace for both men.

In the 1980s when WD was faced with the need to sell almost everything he owned during a downward cycle in the cattle market, Russell advised WD to "take heed and rest until your batteries are recharged. It is too easy to push yourself beyond the safety line, and at our age that can be dangerous. . . . You have always worked hard and have enjoyed some great successes. What has happened is not something to give too much importance. . . . Your family is in good shape; your real friends think you are one Hell of a man. We all have a deep love and respect for you that nothing can shake."[16]

"As I sit in my trophy room in the evening," WD replied, "and look at my various trophies, I remember the details of each day very vividly. The long day following the grizzly; locating the moose from the top of the mountain. . . . They were all great [experiences] and our sincere friend-ship runs deep."[17]

Significantly, that friendship with Russell, based as it was on a visceral perception of man's relationship to the natural world, fortified WD's self-confidence when confronted by complex matters of cattle feeding and water policy. Russell's example played a role in how WD viewed the future and how he influenced peers in the many cattle associations and water organizations to which he was elected. His love of fishing on the North Platte River at the Sanger Ranch—a place son John referred to as the family

"Mecca"—extended beyond Wyoming to many rivers and different parts of the country. His elk hunting continued at Budge's, and he regularly shot ducks and geese at the Beebe Draw Gun Club.[18] But none of these adventures proved as influential in transforming WD's philosophical approach to his vision of the future as his fifty-five-year friendship with Andy Russell. He never joined the environmentalists' ranks and sometimes faulted them for extremism. But he learned from Russell that to get projects functioning in a way that would satisfy diverse communities, he would have to be a good listener and an active petitioner of all points of view. His effort to comprehend the territorial nature of people engaged in water conflicts, and his success in acquiring adequate supplies for northern Colorado's future, speak to his remarkable understanding of the need to balance economic growth and environmental preservation. "Of all that I've done," WD told a *Rocky Mountain News* reporter, "I'm still proudest of the water. It's here in perpetuity. In 500 years people will still benefit from it."[19]

"We surely can't take anything with us [when we die]," he wrote to Russell. "We had better make the country better for future generations."[20] To WD, "better" implied an obligation on the part of leaders to recognize and respect as many interests as possible, but when he began his forty-year service with the NCWCD, the C-BT system was only delivering water to some of the ditch companies that had signed up twenty years earlier. The others were impatient. Discontent was in the air.

On the NCWCD board, policy making was in a formative stage. Regulations related to delivery, maintenance, and transfer of the new water supply occupied WD's focus for the first few years. The USBR was slow to complete power facilities they had decided to add to the project for the revenue they would generate, and when WD attended his first board meetings, a major drought was still hanging on. "1956 was a dry year," WD recalled, "and we needed some [additional] water. Folks were looking forward to it, but nobody knew anything about how the hell they were going to run it [or] how they were going to fit it with the [existing water delivery] system."[21] In addition, the district was dealing with limited income from the partial mill levy being collected from property owners, a small and inexperienced staff in a new facility in Loveland, and no case law for reference when decisions had to be made about water transfers. "The manager, legal counsel, and the board had to consider everything pretty thoughtfully as to what was right and what wasn't," WD remembered. "You kind of had to make the laws as you went."[22]

But WD enjoyed the challenge. He saw this period as an "exciting time, the beginning of a very proud period,"[23] but it was not so joyful for farmers dealing with limited water, sand-storms, and dry soil. The 1953–1956 drought lingered and was complicated by animosities between upstream farmers who had taken water from South Platte tributaries when they did not need it versus downstream farmers who had to deal with low flows and empty reservoirs. In addition, state-appointed river commissioners complained of new responsibilities they would incur when C-BT water was added to the streams. They demanded larger salaries for the increased work load and expected the NCWCD board to support them. Meanwhile, West Slope officials suspected the NCWCD was in league with the Denver Water Board to steal their water; while from the Denver Water Board came allegations that the C-BT might impact its rights on the Fraser River.

In truth, no one really knew what the impact would be of bringing the equivalent of an entire Poudre River through the Adams Tunnel to the Front Range. But for WD, it was a good time to begin his service on the NCWCD board:

> This was the first conservancy district in the United States, so there were no laws. There was nothing to govern [the] diversion of water to the eastern slope, except the Blue River cases[24] . . . where we'd been challenged and Denver challenged us. . . . But everything the board did, they'd have to look at it, whether it was the right thing for *the total good of everybody* . . . . That made it more interesting than something that had been going for fifty years and was just operating routinely.[25]

The "total good" to which WD referred was his own homegrown version of utilitarianism, strongly influenced by his father and grandfather and nurtured through his association with Andy Russell and his commitment to Rotary. In all likelihood, WD had never read the early nineteenth-century works of Jeremy Bentham or John Stuart Mill (Bentham's student), but his determination to craft a water policy that would benefit the greatest number of people echoed utilitarianism's general principles. As with the

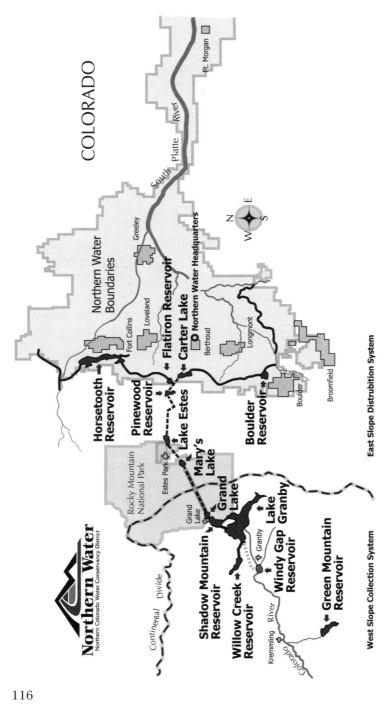

Water Systems of the Northern Colorado Water Conservancy District (NCWCD), ca. 2000, showing the Colorado–Big Thompson Project as originally constructed and the later addition of the Windy Gap Reservoir. Courtesy NCWCD.

English philosophers, WD favored individualism and economic freedom, and he thought that a decision's ethical value was best determined by its results. Leadership required making choices, and that meant some decisions would result in minority interests not being represented. But given the overall objective of promoting growth and providing as many people as possible with the security that comes from opportunity, he was able to judge the moral worth of his actions by the number of people who benefitted.

As a young engineer employed by the city of Greeley, Eric Wilkinson came to know WD when WD was chairman of the Greeley Water Board. Until he transferred to the NCWCD in 1987, Wilkinson had many opportunities to witness WD's unique leadership strengths. He recalled,

> Ideologically, WD's destination was always the greater public good. . . . My interpretation of his attitude toward that was, if you have to sacrifice something, such as part of the environment, or whatever, that was acceptable if you were doing the greater public good. . . . In other words, things should be multipurpose; [ones' actions] should solve more than one problem. . . . To me his whole target, long distance, far down the road, was [to ask] "Where are we going as a community, a ditch company, a city, a region, a water district, whatever? Where are we going and what's best for the constituents of that group?" He was constantly weighing those things. I think his visionary gift really helped him.[26]

That vision was a visceral component of WD's utilitarianism. Compared with other would-be leaders, WD seemed better able to anticipate future circumstances. Wilkinson explained,

> Sometimes you didn't agree with what he said, but he sure had a good reason for saying it when he explained it to you. . . . Many people articulate a future, but it's based on a dream. . . . I think he was [deeply] grounded in the practicality of the world. . . . It was his heritage; his people were all booted and standing on the soil, and they made their lives from scratch. He did, too. I never got the impression he rested on his laurels or his ancestors' laurels. When they couldn't pull the wagon any longer, he got in the harness and he pulled the wagon . . . everything he did was grounded in practicality as he looked to the future. Most people who claim to be visionaries are more esoteric, basing their drive on making the world

into what [they] want to make it. But WD was driven by the knowledge of human character, an understanding of existing resources.

In short, he was motivated by a comprehension of what people really
wanted, not what he wanted to impose on them.

To this end, WD encouraged colleagues on the NCWCD board to think
ahead and plan comprehensively. The NCWCD was operating in new
territory. Its organizational structure combined elements of municipal
government, a private corporation, and singular characteristics unlike
any other system.[27] But WD's understanding of finance, administration,
and management allowed him to guide the board toward broad-based
decisions that would, in his view, benefit as many people as possible for
the present and future.

Water transfer and reallocation policies were developed to create an
open market for C-BT water within NCWCD boundaries. Delivery quotas
were established yearly with the needs of farmers in mind. But from WD's
conservative perspective, the C-BT system also had to be viewed as a bank
account that should regularly augment its holdings in anticipation of inevitable drought. Additional water storage would be needed as the project
matured. WD led that search for a functional reservoir site on the Poudre
River that could store water for farms and fast-growing cities. Because
the USBR was occupied with other projects, and because several years of
ample rainfall had contributed to a diminution in interest, the Idylwilde
(upper Poudre) and Grey Mountain (lower Poudre) reservoir sites were
not pursued to the point of feasibility. However, WD's commitment to
maximize the C-BT's authorized delivery of 310,000 acre-feet and his passion
to provide greater storage capacity resurfaced in other ways during his
tenure on the board.[28]

Because of rampant regional growth in the 1950s and 1960s, flexibility,
storage, and public education were essential ingredients of WD's approach
to water planning. Along with statistics that showed agriculture booming
in Weld County,[29] exponential population increases up and down the
Front Range were causing great concern.[30] Newcomers, mostly urban or
suburban residents, were ignorant of Colorado water law and the fact
that 85 percent of Colorado's water was used in agriculture. They were

also confused about the roles of the USBR and the NCWCD. WD hoped everyone would benefit from public meetings that explained how the C-BT worked, why the USBR had to generate power to raise revenue, and what the role of the directors was in distributing supplemental water from the C-BT to its share-holder allottees. He spoke to service and community groups about project operations, underscoring the importance of keeping politics out of the selection of board members by having them appointed by district judges. Because all property owners residing within NCWCD boundaries were required to pay a mill levy under the terms of the 1938 repayment contract, increasing numbers of new residents complained vociferously about taxation without representation. In response, WD pointed out that public boards functioned best when directors were chosen for their talent and not because they represented a special cause or political agenda. Not everyone agreed with him, but he fought hard in defense of this position, believing it was for the long-term benefit of both the NCWCD and the Greeley Water Board, to which he was appointed in 1958.

Many of WD's opinions about Greeley's future water needs were shaped during round-trips between Greeley and Loveland with Carl Mossberg, NCWCD director and president of the Greeley–Loveland Irrigation Company. Although the C-BT had been designed to serve primarily agricultural interests, WD began to see demographic changes taking place west of Greeley, as urban expansion reached into farmland served by Greeley–Loveland and the C-BT. It seemed to him that the overlapping and competing urban and agricultural interests in this area would result in chaos and inefficiency. He and Mossberg agreed to find a way Greeley could acquire the water rights serving the land that was about to be developed.

The grid system plan that emerged was WD's "brainchild."[31] He knew from his own experience as a Greeley–Loveland Irrigation Company (also referred to as the G-L Ditch Company) board member (1947–1955) and Farr Farms shareholder that Greeley–Loveland had experienced severe water shortages during the drought of the 1950s. The ditch company was conservatively managed and would be interested in a cooperative arrangement that would furnish additional capital. He wanted the city of Greeley to provide small diameter, dead-end lines into the farmland being developed, and he wanted the city to acquire shares of Greeley–Loveland water when annexation occurred. The end result would be additional water for Greeley, a healthier Greeley–Loveland Irrigation Company, and a single supplier of water to developing lands bordering the city.

Convincing all parties to enter into contracts (signed in 1961 and 1963) was the kind of challenge WD savored. He spoke to Rotary, wrote letters to the newspaper, and convinced Greeley's water board and city council that it was the right thing to do. The obstacles must have seemed formidable, but "in his astute and courteous manner," noted Professor Bill Hartman, WD "listened to other viewpoints, recognized the merits of some negative arguments, and realized citizen concern was well founded" if water users ultimately had to pay higher fees.[32] In the end, he overcame detractors with the argument that municipalities must look fifty years ahead in obtaining supplies of water. This was William Kelly's contention when he served as attorney for Greeley–Loveland and the NCWCD. It became WD's mantra and part of the vision he formulated for long-range growth and economic opportunity in Weld County.

The Greeley Water Board was also WD's creation. It was modeled on the Denver Water Board (DWB), because WD had great respect for that institution. The DWB was "more or less hated a little bit," WD stated, "because of their strong-arm tactics and use of water law. Everything they did was legal . . . it was sometimes kind of brutal, but very intelligently done."[33] No taxes were involved in forming the Greeley Water Board, and it was set up to be self-sustaining and out of politics. Five members, each having a five-year term, would be appointed on a rotating basis by the city council, with one new member being appointed or reappointed each year. "It was our responsibility to see that funds were balanced, to set [water rates]," WD said, which the city council could not lower. "If they wanted to charge customers more, we said that was their business. But they had to set the minimum rate at whatever we told them we had to have to operate the system."[34]

For the Greeley Water Board, it meant having to wear the black hats, but because they rarely had disagreements with the city council, they were asked to take over responsibility for Greeley's sewer system in 1973. For all they did, board members received no compensation and no reimbursement of expenses, and in WD's view, they consistently went "overboard to work with the [city] council and not catch them by surprise. . . . We [had] no axe to grind," WD recalled, "and that [made] a difference."[35]

As Weld County's demographics changed in the 1960s, WD's function as director for both the NCWCD and the Greeley Water Board placed him in position to respond to a mysterious visitation from two men who identified themselves as "Bob" and "Bruce." The strangers first appeared in the spring of 1968 in the office of J. Robert Barkley, the NCWCD's secretary–manager for the past ten years. They said they represented a major company looking for land and acre-feet of clean and reliable water to use over a forty- to fifty-year period.[36] They preferred not to identify the company, because they knew their interests could have an impact on land and water values. They had scouted the West from Canada to Mexico and had their eye on land owned by the Great Western Sugar Company in nearby Windsor. Great Western had just shut down its beet processing factory and was wondering what to do with 3,000 unused acres.

Barkley sent the men to see Colorado governor John Love. Love referred them to WD, who was familiar with the land in which they were interested. He also knew that Greeley's main water line ran through the property and could provide the visitors with the clean and reliable water they desired. It took some effort to persuade the Greeley Water Board and city council, but when they learned that Kodak was behind the request, approval came quickly. WD's plan was to have Kodak begin leasing water from the city for ten years. Over a decade, they would gradually purchase their own water, most probably from the open market established for buying and selling C-BT units. WD went back to Rochester to help sell the plan, but company officials were somewhat skeptical. When they returned to Colorado for another look, WD escorted them to Grand Lake, one of the major links through which C-BT water flowed to the East Slope. When Kodak executives saw the quality of this water, they agreed to the deal. "I am not trying to brag about it," WD recalled, "but fundamentally I carried the load and got the [city] council and everybody to approve it."[37]

Great Western Sugar Company's decision to shut down its Windsor plant was based to a great extent on the estimated cost of cleaning up pollution the company had been discharging into the South Platte River. Since the 1962 publication of Rachel Carson's *Silent Spring*, the concepts behind the words "environmentalism" and "ecology" had become more than topics of conversation across the country. In 1963 the U.S. Public Health Service took an active role by identifying "severe pollution and serious degradation of water quality in the South Platte basin, with the biggest pollution source being the waste products of sugar beet processors."[38] From WD's perspective, it was not a pretty picture. "I was a director at Great Western Sugar Company," he recalled, "and they were just pumping from the mills into the rivers. In the fall, the rivers were just terrible from beet processing. Wet pulp, everything just went into the rivers, and they were just a stinking mess."[39] The state lacked regulatory authority to force change, and federal laws requiring industries to address pollution were still in their infancy. Great Western estimated a cost of $30 million to clean up the ten Colorado factories responsible for polluting the South Platte. Company officials came to the conclusion that such an expenditure would result in a "profitless industry."[40] Selling the properties made more sense.

Under President Richard M. Nixon, Congress began passing laws that gave Capitol Hill responsibility for cleaning up the nation's polluted environment. On New Year's Day, 1970, Nixon signed into law the National Environmental Policy Act, and a few months later he approved the Clean Air Act. This was not the first time Congress had addressed environmental issues with legislation, but because it had become increasingly apparent that pollution was not neatly contained within state boundaries, lawmakers decided to amend and strengthen earlier acts by creating federal agencies with the budgets and power to address pollution as a national problem.

Nixon made clear his expectation that environmental pollution would be addressed holistically. He insisted upon the importance of viewing the natural and man-made environments as an integrated unit, and he charged the first EPA director, William D. Ruckelshaus, with the task of amalgamating air, water, and solid waste pollution problems in an inter-mingled study. This broad-based approach was consistent with WD's view of how water projects, industry, and environmental responsibility should coexist, but he was surprised in the spring of 1970 to receive a request from Washington to serve on President Nixon's Water Pollution Control Advisory Board. The experience contributed immeasurably to the breadth and clarity of WD's own long-range plans.

WD's selection as one of the board's nine members was a result of his many years of representing the National Livestock and Meat Board in the capital, appearances before Senate and House committees, and his connections with banks and water boards. Four months prior to this appointment, WD was selected president of ANCA, whose membership was more than casually interested in how the government's recently created environmental agencies might restrict grazing and feedlot operations.[41] Serving on the Water Pollution Control Advisory Board over the next three years, WD learned a great deal about environmental degradation taking place in the United States—knowledge that caused him to reflect on the complex issues he had discussed with Andy Russell. As he noted in a speech to the Greeley Social Science Club, his comprehension of environmental concerns was profoundly impacted by his experience on the Water Pollution Control Advisory Board.

With Ruckelshaus as group leader, the board members traveled to polluted areas of the country four times a year. On government charted passenger jets, the board members visited many of the nation's most polluted areas: Lake Michigan, Chesapeake Bay, Cape Hatteras, California's Central Valley, Sacramento's tidelands, Lake Tahoe, Los Angeles, New York City, Honolulu, and the South Platte basin. WD came to realize that restoration of the environment would be a lengthy process, that urban sprawl—a nationwide cancer—was especially harmful on Colorado's East Slope, and that the logistics of having clean water in the United States in accordance with the proposed federally mandated date of 1985 were "overwhelming."[42] He recognized that drinking water might have to be recycled and that land use planning was inevitable, but he feared a rush toward untried policies and rules based on emotion and irrational thinking. If effective changes were going to be made, two things were necessary: scientific studies of the ecological system and a planning approach that included federal, state, and local considerations. "I believe it is evident," WD wrote, "that good environmental planning must be done on at least a regional basis."[43] He was already anticipating the tension between federal and state laws, the rivalry of states and counties, and the desire of cities to have an impact on enforcement decisions. His ability to consider challenges broadly and to process them in terms of what appeared best for the nation's future paralleled his approach to community and regional problems at home.

Although all travels with the advisory board were memorable for WD, he seems to have been most affected by what he saw in Hawaii and in his own backyard. On the island of Oahu, he witnessed how coastal sugar companies dumped their refuse (bagasse), how the city of Honolulu pumped millions of gallons of raw sewage into the ocean daily, and how U.S. naval vessels in Pearl Harbor got rid of wastes without treatment. He learned firsthand how defensive and emotional people can be when they are told to respect the environment. "Honolulu was the toughest confrontation [the board] ever had," WD recalled. "They had one water treatment facility at Pearl Harbor, but the city had grown so fast, it couldn't keep up. . . . The sugar cane mills . . . were polluting the beaches and killing fish, because the waste got into their gills," and neither the state of Hawaii nor the sugar industry was very cooperative. "They didn't like us! It was a pretty heated meeting."[44]

When the advisory board flew over the South Platte basin, WD saw fecal matter draining out of feedlots into the river. He saw how cattle drank from the river; how floods and snowmelt emptied waste materials, fertilizer, and pesticides into the stream; and how a healthy South Platte River would play a vital role in cleaning up the Missouri and Mississippi rivers. It was a pivotal experience for WD, and it determined not only how he thought about future water projects, but also how he would design his own new feedlot east of Greeley when that opportunity presented itself a few years later.

One should not, however, place too heavy an environmental mantle on WD's shoulders. He was still first and foremost a businessman. Anyone who tried to convince him to support unscientific or single-purpose measures with the intention of returning the land to its so-called pristine condition failed to get his serious attention. He was alarmed by those who advocated removing Glen Canyon Dam and draining Lake Powell. "A perfectly ridiculous idea," he called it. He said,

> It can't happen, and it's just proof that [some] environmental people don't understand, or don't want to understand [the need for water storage]. We have to [have] some of those [dams if we're going to] live and let live. Water in the streams for fish is important, and we have to expect that. It didn't used to be a beneficial use [of water], but today it is. . . . [However], every reservoir you breach, you just take that much value out of the state, whatever state it may be. . . . The pure environmentalists want to have it back like when the Indians

were here, and that's fine. But that's not modern civilization. . . .
When you start removing dams, you remove your food supply. Sure,
you may be [able to] import your food supply from South America
or somewhere, but you won't be able to live in any of those western
states. You absolutely can't.[45]

At heart, he believed that agriculture and nature worked together, and
he was critical of environmental advocates whose objectives seemed more
political than pragmatic. He was uncomfortable with extremists and with
the political deals that produced unfeasible water projects. He became
disenchanted with those who supported such projects or who advocated
against the use of chemicals and hormones in farming without considering
the potential loss of food for the general population. As an agriculturalist
he was accustomed to seasonal and harmonious cycles in nature, but he
also understood that attempts to produce more food for an expanding
population would inevitably cause unexpected reactions in nature. What he
did not know prior to his work with the advisory board was how extensive
those reactions had become in the form of national pollution and how
important environmental issues would be in the future. But over a sixteen-
year period—1970 to 1986—he learned firsthand how rapidly environmental issues had moved to the center of water project debates.

In the summer of 1970, two months after being selected to the president's Water Pollution Control Advisory Board, WD was named chairman
of the newly formed NCWCD Municipal Subdistrict . Its task was to plan
and construct a collection system (Windy Gap) that would enable the C-BT
to deliver through the Adams Tunnel the entire 310,000 acre-feet of water
for which the project had been originally approved. Although he knew at
the time such an undertaking would be difficult because of anticipated
opposition from Colorado's West Slope, WD was enthusiastic about the
challenge. It fit perfectly with his wide-ranging vision regarding the need
to increase water supplies for the growing population of northern Colorado. But he was unprepared for the delays and increased costs caused by
recently approved federal legislation.[46] Although the resulting struggles
were far greater than he anticipated, in retrospect he viewed Windy Gap as
"the single thing I'm most proud of. . . . Fifty years from now," he predicted
in 1997, "Windy Gap will be used—every bit of it, every year, and that will

WD Farr signing the Windy Gap contract, January 1970. Courtesy of Northern Colorado Water Conservancy District.

be the best water the city [of Greeley] will own."[47] It was a visceral commitment that occasionally blinded him to the rising crescendo of concern about water projects. During those sixteen years he labored to satisfy all the stakeholders, there were times when even his renowned patience was sorely tested.

The idea for Windy Gap existed in the USBR's original plan for the C-BT project. Water from two Fraser River tributaries was to be collected in a small reservoir and pumped uphill to another reservoir, from which it would flow into Lake Granby. This arrangement was abandoned during construction of the C-BT, because the USBR determined to place more emphasis on power production and because the cities of Denver and Englewood had filed on water rights in the same area.

NCWCD concerns regarding the C-BT's inability to produce the authorized 310,000 acre-feet resulted in a 1957 study by the USBR. It concluded that excess annual flood-waters from the Fraser River—about 31,500 acre-feet—could be captured in a reservoir adjacent to the Colorado River and pumped up to Lake Granby by way of Willow Creek

Reservoir.[48] As population growth on the Front Range continued to worry elected officials and municipal interest in C-BT water became increasingly evident, the cities of Boulder, Longmont, Loveland, Fort Collins, and Greeley joined together as the Northern Conference Water Committee to discuss the possibility of funding a Windy Gap project. Estes Park joined later. The cities were also fearful of an accelerated conversion of agricultural water allotments to municipal use. They hoped to sustain agriculture as a source of income and wanted to satisfy urban demands through construction of an additional collection system on the West Slope. They did not wish to see the health of their agricultural base eclipsed by future urban water demands.

A trip to Washington to confer with bureau officials convinced city representatives of the need to make a legal claim to the Fraser River tributaries as soon as possible. In July 1967, Longmont mayor Ralph Price filed for a conditional decree of 30,000 acre-feet of Colorado River water at Windy Gap.[49] Because the six cities all had different needs and because their elected officials were being replaced frequently, the best way to advance the Windy Gap project was through a provision in the 1937 Conservancy District Act that anticipated formation of subdistricts. Strongly recommended by NCWCD attorney John Sayre, this organizational scheme proved workable. After all requirements were met, district court judge Donald Carpenter signed a decree creating the NCWCD Municipal Subdistrict in July 1970. The board of directors of the NCWCD, the so-called parent district, became directors of the subdistrict. As the designated head of this new organization, WD served in two capacities: NCWCD director and chairman of the NCWCD Municipal Subdistrict.

"The Six Cities' representatives met every month or two," WD recalled, "everyone agreeing they wanted to protect agriculture along the Front Range. They knew Windy Gap water could cost as much as fifty dollars per acre-foot . . . but they all felt the cities could afford it."[50] Early problems between the cities demanded Sayre's constant attention to keep the organization intact. In addition to his full-time job as NCWCD attorney, he was forced to meet at night with water boards, city councils, and other organizations just to keep the Six Cities Committee from breaking apart. "It was probably the hardest work I ever did," Sayre recalled,[51] and even with all his effort and patience, Fort Collins decided to transfer its shares in the project to the Platte River Power Authority, while focusing on the enlargement of Joe Wright Reservoir on the upper Poudre River. This transfer was a disappointment to WD, but he kept a tight rein on Greeley and offered encouragement to the remaining municipalities to stay the course and look to the future.

More discouraging to him than the occasional obduracy of the Six Cities were the environmental requirements that caused delays, frustration, and, at times, incredulity.[52] In 1976, after paying an environmental consulting firm to conduct federally required studies, the subdistrict was informed by the government that an environmental impact statement would be required for the entire C-BT, not just for Windy Gap. The anticipated labor associated with performing additional hydrology studies, submitting water conservation plans, and doing rewrites of environmental impact disheartened WD. When he felt the subdistrict had finally jumped through all the hoops, the reworked studies languished in the Washington office of the USBR for another six months. During this delay, the estimated cost of construction was escalating at a yearly rate of $2.8 million. Land use permits for construction could not be issued without approval of the environmental impact statements, and the work on designing appropriate pumps for the project had to be postponed until engineers knew with certainty how much water they would pump.[53] Furthermore, mandatory public-comment meetings necessitated written responses, thus delaying construction even further.

But perhaps the most surprising obstacle appeared when the humpback chub and Colorado squawfish were designated endangered species under the terms of the 1973 Endangered Species Act. Windy Gap was seen by the U.S. Fish and Wildlife Service as a threat to these fish because the diversion of water to the East Slope would permanently remove water from the Colorado River basin. Official concerns threatened to derail the entire project. "We can do all we can," WD complained, "but there has to be reason." The federal government eventually admitted they were uncertain where the threatened fish were located, what had caused their population to decline, and where they spawned. "We gave them about $100,000 to do studies," WD remarked, "and then found we could raise them in hatcheries . . . [but] we also discovered they might bring disease to the native fish. All kinds of controversies and problems."[54]

For the most part, WD agreed with the underlying objectives of the Endangered Species Act. He was, after all, a dedicated fisherman who understood the need to preserve balance in nature. He and Andy Russell had been active members of Ducks Unlimited, and both believed in the importance of preserving wetlands. But when it appeared to him that logic, common sense, and science were lacking in the execution of environmental laws, WD balked. How could the USBR require the NCWCD Municipal Subdistrict to take responsibility for protecting species the government had once poisoned? And where was the logic in demanding preservation of a minnow that already had been devastated by the Department of Fish and Wildlife's introduction of hungry sport fish into the river? "We just can't do anything anymore," WD lamented, "because we don't have certainty. We don't know what the Endangered Species Act is going to do to us."[55]

Nor could he have anticipated the potpourri of delays that came next. The Environmental Defense Fund joined with Trout Unlimited and the Wilderness Society to file suit against the federal government, requesting an injunction against the operation or construction of any existing or proposed water project in the Colorado River basin. The suit alleged that removal of water from the river violated federal salinity standards and exposed the nation to litigation as the result of a 1944 treaty with Mexico.[56] The U.S. district court ruled against the plaintiffs, but Windy Gap opponents continued to raise the issue of salinization throughout negotiations with the subdistrict.

The toughest negotiations occurred with the Colorado River Water Conservation District, whose leaders insisted the subdistrict had an obligation to build a compensatory storage reservoir for the West Slope. For years the subdistrict tried negotiations, but they ended first in stalemate and ultimately in lawsuits. During this period, inflation reached 13 percent, judges had to be replaced, and some of the case records required reconstruction after they were mysteriously lost in a Glenwood Springs water court.[57]

WD counseled continuing negotiations with the West Slope. For five months beginning in December 1979, discussions occurred almost daily, not just with the River District, but with the Middle Park Water Conservancy District, Grand County, the towns of Granby and Hot Sulphur Springs, the Northwest Colorado Council of Governments, and interested citizens.

Compared with the negotiations with the West Slope in the 1930s that resulted in construction of Green Mountain Reservoir, Windy Gap discussions proved far more contentious and difficult.[58] A major challenge came from the West Slope ranching community, which opposed on principle any attempt by the Front Range to remove additional water from their lands, regardless of the reason. But WD could talk their language. Through arguments that connected his opponents to the shared concerns of other ranchers and farmers, he was able to soften their opposition. Additional frustrations occurred when the River District ignored correspondence.[59] Although WD wanted to shake sense into his opponents at times, he remained patient and professional. He believed the Windy Gap project was in the best interests of the communities he served, and he refused to allow his vision to be derailed after so much work had been done with so many different stakeholders.

An accord was reached in April 1980. WD was able to persuade the River District's board president, Chris Jouflas, to sit down at a table at a hotel in Kremmling to see if they could work out an agreement. Jouflas recalled,

> For a lot of years the lawyers had been making money off of us. WD decided we could work out our differences face to face, so we decided how much money we needed to abandon the lawsuit [and construct a storage reservoir], but in the final analysis, it came down to WD who wanted to get something done. We were sick and tired of the lawyers making their living on us, so we ended up with an agreement, settled the lawsuit for $10.2 million, and we eventually built the Wolford Mountain Reservoir with the help of Denver. It was a far reaching decision, really; one of the best things that the River District and Northern had ever done, because they got what they wanted and we got what we wanted, and it was strictly Mr. Farr, I think, whose influence made that happen. . . . I had known about him for some time. His reputation preceded him. You knew he was straight-forward, wasn't trying to catch you on anything, and just wanted to get something done. We all did![60]

In retrospect, the Endangered Species Act created as many problems for the subdistrict and for water developers in general as did disagreements with the West Slope. Some opponents of environmental regulations openly scoffed at the need to protect minnows, birds, and rare mice. But

WD recognized the overarching value of a healthy ecosystem, and because he believed so resolutely that Windy Gap could benefit both East and West slopes, he was inspired to forge a compromise with all concerned. He believed such an accord was right and beneficial for the greatest number of people involved. It cost a lot more money than the Six Cities originally planned to spend, but the end result was a water project for the benefit of northern Colorado that WD viewed as even more significant than the C-BT.[61]

Part of WD's sense of achievement in this project was due to the legal status of the water itself. Under Colorado law, water from Windy Gap was considered "foreign water," which did not have to be returned to East Slope rivers after first use. Instead, it could be used and reused by its owners, in contrast to C-BT water, which was allowed only a one-time use because its collection and delivery systems were in essence part of a federally constructed project. Windy Gap, by contrast, was built with money raised by the Six Cities Committee (Greeley, Longmont, Loveland, Estes Park, Boulder, and Platte River Power Authority).[62] Consequently, the project's water had a higher asset value, because it could be resold repeatedly. From WD's perspective, the struggle to build another West Slope collection system was ultimately worth the frustration of almost constant conflict. The inescapable lesson, however, was that future water projects were going to be expensive and would entail more careful and advanced planning with all stakeholders. Rivers now had rights; flora and fauna were represented at the negotiating table. Without some common sense, WD reflected, the Endangered Species Act could become potentially "a vicious thing," possibly more of an enemy than competing interests between the East Slope and West Slope.[63] At the same time, he concluded that those who were fortunate enough to have water rights were obligated to spend money to preserve the environment in which they operated. Speaking specifically in regard to Nebraska's sandhill crane population, WD noted that providing adequate flows in the river for the cranes represented "the price we will have to pay for future society so they can have and see some of these birds."[64]

If the Endangered Species Act had frustrated WD in his efforts to provide East Slope farms and cities with additional water, the years of struggle also signaled a shift in how the West's natural resources were going to be apportioned in the future. He may not have realized it at the time, but WD was engaged in a water battle at a time when the nation was becoming sensitive to the loss of species and what such losses might mean for the future of mankind. Somewhat reluctantly, WD was being forced to adjust from Old West endorsement of unbridled resource exploitation to a New West in which the natural environment would have equal rights at the bargaining table. Given his upbringing and his experience during the Great Depression, it was difficult to make the transition, but WD learned from the Windy Gap experience, accepted the practical value of environmental protection, and eventually applied the lessons learned to the cattle business.

His own cattle feeding operation grew considerably in the 1950s and 1960s. With 26,000 steers and lambs in the feedlot, 2,000 acres of farmland to supervise, and a sand-hill grass ranch with 1,500 steers, he managed a sizeable operation.[65] Before most businessmen, he began using computers. Located in the Greeley National Bank where WD was a director, the machines were dormant at night. WD put them to work computing feeding formulas, recording cash flow, and maintaining employee records. Focusing on the mass market rather than market toppers, he believed the future of cattle feeding lay in direct marketing to the growing number of chain stores and fast-food businesses. Purchasing good quality cattle that could be fed to 1,200 pounds in 125 days and graded choice or good was the objective.[66] The old centralized arrangement in Chicago—dominated for generations by the big packers, an east–west railroad system, and commission men— was unraveling. WD was the principal force behind the beef industry's establishment of a meat grading system that appealed to retailers. Because of the wartime invention of eighteen-wheel trucks that could go almost anywhere, and coupled with the large packers' unwillingness to recognize the significance of consumer demands for consistency and standardization in meat packaging, an entirely new market evolved.[67]

WD was determined to make the most of it. Farr Farms took advantage of scientific gains in hybrid corn development. Renters were encouraged to grow new varieties and to harvest the entire plant for high-moisture silage. They experimented with concrete-lined, open-pit silos and fed a precise balance of dry matter, silage, and a protein supplement to the cattle.[68] WD expected weight gains of more than three pounds a day, and during the course of a year, he planned to move two or three sets of cattle through his pens. Some finished cattle were being moved to market at the same time a pen of recently weaned stocker cattle was starting the feeding process. The variety in age and weight of thousands of cattle moving through the system required an exacting commitment to nutrition, disease control, and marketing.

Alert to Purdue University's work with growth hormones and disease prevention, WD began feeding diethylstilbestrol (DES) to cattle within a year of its availability in January 1955. To prevent Red Nose infection (infectious rhinotracheitis), he introduced antibiotics (aureomycin), and for parasite control, he used phenothiazine in daily rations. The hormones and antibiotics increased weight gains and reduced feedlot sickness, but they also provoked criticism. In 1971, Wisconsin senator William Proxmire asked the Food and Drug Administration to halt the use of DES, which he described as a "cancer causing hormone in cattle feeds." He based his request on studies that appeared in the highly respected *New England Journal of Medicine* and statements by the World Health Organization. In reply, WD noted that DES and other animal drugs were important production tools for healthy cattle, that their use was monitored by a committee endorsed by the Food and Drug Administration, and that in response to Senator Proxmire's suggestion regarding the use of "other growth promoting drugs," the cattle industry was unaware of anything as healthy and productive as DES.[69]

It was a tough sell at a time meat prices were escalating and consumers were becoming disenchanted with beef. With an inflation-sparked consumer rebellion against beef prices, a growing anti-business attitude across the country, and a general suspicion of chain-store green stamp programs, the beef industry found itself on the defensive.[70] WD knew all too well that the cattle industry was also falling behind poultry and pork in the use of science and genetics for product improvement. Too many cattlemen were unwilling to change. They followed traditional guidelines of conformity rather than basing decisions on performance, and they were slow as an industry to use the latest research to improve their product.

In comparison, WD was never content to rely on a single feeding formula. As circumstances changed and new theories were tested, he was ready to modify the approach he used in the feedlot. If the industry expected to compete with poultry and pork on a per-pound retail cost basis, cattlemen would have to get out of the rut they were in. A great deal more feed was required for a pound of beef than for a pound of pork or chicken. Even though the taste of beef might be preferred, a shrewd consumer on a budget would always find the most protein available for a dollar spent. A competitive cattle industry required a pipeline for animals with a guaranteed rate of gain from cow-calf ranches to the feedlot. WD disliked what he referred to as the "mongrelization" of the nation's cattle herds. Too many breeds were too often crossed for the wrong reasons. Good genetics had been lost. He wanted to see ranchers abandon the goal of conformity, focusing instead on three to seven breeds whose genetics were known to produce tender cuts of beef in the shortest time possible. He encouraged "alliances" between ranchers, feeders, packers, and retailers, although he warned that this concentration might result in small producers being edged out. Beef could still be affordable, he concluded, if the industry would agree on its goals, openly recognize its competition, and concentrate its resources on effective marketing. Consumers had the upper hand, and cattlemen would have to march to the consumers' drum if they hoped to survive.[71]

The large, vertically integrated Monfort feeding operation in Greeley pursued some of these same goals. Warren Monfort and WD had developed a close friendship in the 1930s. When Warren's son Kenny took over the family feeding business, he added a packing plant. By 1970, the Monfort Company was feeding and slaughtering 275,000 cattle annually, with 1,200 employees.[72]

Kenny and WD were never close, but they had much in common, respected each other, and shared a vision of how the industry could become more viable. Both wanted meat grading improved by the elimination of "conformation" as a grading factor. Both viewed the international market for beef as the wave of the future. Both believed in the importance of science and research. They treated their employees exceptionally well, prepared studiously for all meetings, had unusual ability with numbers, worked very hard physically, and developed business relations based on trust, respect, and honor. Both believed in the environmental movement and the new laws but only to the extent it made sense for people who actually worked the land. Kenny, for example, deplored the rules that prevented a rancher from killing the wolves that were decimating his livestock.[73]

WD was invited to merge with the Monforts, but he declined. WD thought the Montfort Company had gotten too big too fast and that Farr Farms would lose flexibility and marketing options by joining such a large operation. He believed in preserving competition. If the only market for fed cattle was the Greeley plant, he contended, "we'd have had no choice and would have had to take what we could get."[74] In 1967, he told the Nebraska Stockgrowers Association they would have to stay abreast of research if they wanted to remain competitive. In addition to competition from poultry and pork, the industry faced challenges from the domestic fish industry. To keep pace with the competition, cattle would have to be bred and sold on a performance basis, antibiotics and growth stimulants would be required, and hybrid animals with known backgrounds and genetic propensity for rapid growth would have to be raised, fed, and slaughtered.[75] Somewhat like the Monfort model, he noted, the cattle business would have to be vertically integrated from cow-calf ranchers to feeders, packers, and retailers. Purebred operations, auction markets, and traders would have to be eliminated. "If we're going to have a cattle industry," WD surmised, "we need a type of value-based marketing. If we don't, the industry will quietly go away like the lamb industry. . . . Sheep are a thing of the past, because there is no market. . . . Lambs are great animals and wonderful meat, but there is no sponsorship and no chance for the lamb industry to ever amount to anything."[76]

What WD said to fellow cattlemen was not always what they wanted to hear, but he had a knack for convincing doubters with his reasoned foresight. He shared his vision of the future at dozens of speaking engagements, at committee meetings in Congress, and with the membership of ANCA. As recalled by ANCA economist Topper Thorpe in 1995, WD was able to bring his ideas into the open because he asked a lot of questions and caused a lot of research to be done. He made ANCA into a more effective organization. "His leadership capitalized on a gift for consensus building," Thorpe noted. "He had a keen understanding of people [and] could work with them much more effectively than many others can. He was patient, and yet impatient. And he always did his homework. He would dig and dig. . . . He was just one of those kind of salt-of-the-earth people to whom you literally trust your life."[77]

But WD came to the presidency of ANCA at a time the organization was experiencing internal division and financial stress. His predecessor, Bill House, was a Kansas rancher and an officer in the American Hereford Association and the Kansas Livestock Association. He was suspicious of the packing industry and opposed to WD's efforts to develop an industry-wide meat grading system that would establish new criteria for choice grades, replacing the old standards with a yield grading system that rewarded producers of carcasses with less fat, less marbling, and the smaller cuts demanded by chain stores.[78] WD had been developing his plan as chairman of ANCA's meat grading committee since 1956, but House was convinced the industry would suffer if cattlemen began raising and fattening "cheap Mexican cattle" in preference to the established breeds that he represented.[79]

The matter came to a head in 1968 at the Oklahoma City national convention. WD had persuaded the resolutions committee to bring his revised grading system to a vote, but House stood in the way. "I offended Farr," he recalled, "by following ANCA's by-laws and sent the matter to the floor for a vote. They thought they had it set up to pass, but we beat them by four votes."

House was also troubled by WD's interest in having full-time representation for ANCA in Washington, D.C. At the time, Charles W. (Bill) McMillan was in charge of ANCA's Denver office, but he was spending increasing amounts of time representing the association in the nation's capital. WD wanted McMillan to set up a permanent office in Washington, but House objected. He represented quite a few ANCA members who preferred a low profile for the association and who feared McMillan might easily succumb to "Potomac Fever" and become as worthless as "wadding in a shotgun."[80] House was even more suspicious because McMillan had been an employee of Swift and Company for four years before coming to Denver in 1959 to work for ANCA. Swift was importing South American beef, and House suspected McMillan would favor existing import laws at the expense of domestic cattle producers. He saw McMillan as a "Trojan Horse."[81]

Dissension around McMillan surfaced at the Honolulu convention in 1969. John Guthrie, president of ANCA from 1966 to 1967, urged delegates to dump House because of his inability to get along with McMillan. The executive board requested House's resignation. But when the matter came to the floor, Albert K. Mitchell, House's long-time mentor and a highly respected ANCA member, defended him. Because Mitchell was so respected as an owner of registered Herefords, the challenge to House's presidency died without further action. In the wake of this unpleasantness, however, ANCA vice president J. B. Smith resigned, and WD was tapped to replace him. Mitchell helped persuade WD to accept the position. He would be the first cattle feeder to serve as ANCA president, and WD knew House would ignore him. "We just didn't come up alike," House reflected. "We didn't have the same friends. I was around him for six years and best I can remember I never had a conversation with him."[82] WD had the same perspective: "I had to think about that [the vice presidency] quite a bit," he recalled, "but I agreed to do it, and I spent a tough year with [House] as his vice president. Then I took over in 1970."[83]

WD came into the presidency with optimism, but the cattle industry was in a steep decline, headed for the worst years since the Great Depression.[84] "You don't want to think things are all bad," he counseled. "They just change. You have to make it the best you can at the time, and then it's going to be up to the next generation. I am an optimist. I have always been, always will be. You know, life wasn't supposed to be easy. . . . You have to be patient."[85]

But you also had to face reality. Aside from internal divisions within ANCA, the organization was operating in the red. WD hired George Spencer to take over management of the Denver office when McMillan went to Washington as a full-time lobbyist. Experienced as a teacher of agriculture in Utah, Spencer had succeeded in landing a job with Swift and Company, where one of his assignments was to attend conventions and introduce cattlemen who had taken the "Swift Trip." After one such meeting, WD wrote a letter to Swift president Bob Renecker, extolling Spencer's fine character. He told Renecker to be proud of Spencer and to send him out into the world as a totally capable Swift representative. "Such a letter was typical of WD," Spencer noted. "It was complimentary, gracious, and kind, and it endeared me to WD Farr from the beginning."[86]

But the financial challenges Spencer faced in Denver were unexpected. In the process of overseeing incoming receipts and outstanding debt, he concluded ANCA was bankrupt. Because ANCA did not have significant assets or collateral, Denver banks refused to loan them money. WD convened the executive board to seek a solution. Among the board's members was an heir to the King Ranch, Belton K. "BK" Johnson, who was chairman of ANCA's finance committee and part owner of the National Bank of Commerce in San Antonio. If the board could persuade some well-heeled members of ANCA to produce a financial statement and sign a note in the amount of $5,000 each, the San Antonio bank would provide the funds necessary in the form of a line of credit to ANCA.

WD took the lead in making calls. "The members had such confidence in him," said Spencer, "they were willing to make a commitment. No one refused him." Although the ranchers probably expected to lose the money they had pledged, under Spencer's management, membership and dues were expanded, and by the end of the year all obligations to the San Antonio bank had been retired. "ANCA," Spencer noted, "was once again on a footing where we could begin to grow."[87]

As ANCA president, WD represented a $20 billion industry, by far the largest segment of American agriculture. Although consumers were lobbying in Washington for more foreign imports so beef prices would drop, WD argued that 40 percent of imported beef went into the restaurant trade, resulting in relatively little impact on fast food or chain store prices.[88] American producers could keep up with demand, he insisted, and the price of beef they raised was where it should be if cattlemen were going to be able to remain in business. According to WD, beef prices had risen only 12 percent in the previous decade compared with 23 percent in other industries.[89]

Assaults on the cattle industry were sometimes aggressive and based on emotion. As president, WD recognized he would be under attack from many quarters. Environmentalists claimed beef animals destroyed public lands, polluted water sources, and left unacceptable reminders of their bovine digestive process in areas otherwise considered pristine for hikers and campers. Feedlots were branded anti-social because of the smell of fermented feed and fecal matter that permeated nearby communities. Prominent public officials called for changes in import quotas that would eliminate all small producers. The only way to respond to such charges was to encourage ongoing research and up-to-date information that countered the multifarious unfavorable commentaries about the cattle industry.

WD looked beyond the controversies to a future that would benefit both the cattle industry and the American public. He expanded the payroll

WD Farr (*fifth from right*) and American National Cattlemen's Association directors with President Nixon (*fourth from right*), 1970, discussing price controls. Courtesy of the Farr family.

WD Farr (*second from right*) with Secretary of Agriculture Cliff Hardin (*center*) promoting beef, 1971. Courtesy of the National Cattlemen's Foundation.

of ANCA to fifty people, opened a permanent office in Washington so McMillan could become the association's first full-time lobbyist, and oversaw the transfer of ANCA records to computers. He continued to emphasize yield and quality grading, setting up a special study group with Dr. Zerle L. Carpenter of Texas A&M. Through ANCA's foreign trade committee, he encouraged research into a beef export program, planting the seed for what would later become the successful U.S. Meat Export Federation. He worked to bring affiliate organizations into ANCA and encouraged Spencer to work with the law firm Holland and Hart in Denver to develop ANCA's first political action committee. He established a foundation to support education and research, promoted trade shows at annual conventions, broadened ANCA's visibility internationally and in the corporate world, and introduced the Newcomen Society to the association at the Diamond Jubilee Denver convention in 1972.[90]

He also participated in establishing a general information network that came to be known as Cattle-Fax.[91] Conceived in 1968 during the ANCA presidency of John Guthrie, Cattle-Fax was a response to inflation, consumer beef boycotts, and the social unrest brought about by the Vietnam

War. According to McMillan, a "crisis meeting" in Denver generated a commitment by ANCA's market development committee to become more aggressive. "Cattlemen," he said, "felt they had become *price takers* and they wanted to become *price makers*."[92]

Cattle-Fax was organized as a corporation separate from ANCA but under the same leadership. Although legally constituted under the 1922 Capra–Volstead Act, Cattle-Fax presented some concern to ANCA board members because of potential liability associated with making market forecasts that might result in losses to members.[93] "Initially, it was a convoluted relationship," Topper Thorpe recalled. "We got most of our direction from the market development committee, but whatever thoughts they had went to the executive board of ANCA before they could be adopted."[94]

In fact, Cattle-Fax got off to a slow start. When WD became president, he made clear his dissatisfaction. "While he was always encouraging and supportive," Thorpe remembered, "he was also very plain and blunt about the fact that some of the stuff we were doing wasn't accomplishing what he thought, and others thought, we needed to accomplish. . . . I could tell that [WD] was very well informed and astute, but he was also critical of the things we were doing. I was new at this business myself, so I was probably naive, but it didn't take me long to find out that his real interest, and real concern, was not only Cattle-Fax, but the entire beef industry."[95]

As a result of WD's encouragement, along with a revision of the operating structure, Cattle-Fax was remodeled with revised computer programs and a wider network of data that was independent of USDA statistics. "We did use the USDA findings," Thorpe said, "but we became better scavengers, using every bit of information we could find that would be helpful in providing our members with a marketing advantage."[96]

Better marketing by cattlemen was a fundamental, lifelong goal for WD. In his vision of a better future for the cattle industry, producers and feeders would have to enhance their ability to promote what they sent to market, and they would be more effective if they were able to consolidate their interests to generate an advantage through industry-wide unity.

WD's biggest challenge to realizing a unified industry came from the National Livestock Feeder Association (NLFA). Officially created in 1960, the NLFA had been formed after World War II under another name to represent Corn Belt farmers and feeders who had some interest in government programs of price and acreage controls on grain. They saw themselves as "small, humble farmers" whose interests diverged from the "big, arrogant ranchers" of the public-land states, so they had no interest in belonging to ANCA.[97] Under the leadership of Don Magdanz, the NLFA grew to 10,000 members by 1970, thus representing a significant number of producers whose influence could increase the effectiveness of ANCA if a merger could be achieved.

In 1972, WD and George Spencer set out for Omaha to meet with the NLFA's Oscar Bredthauer, with the objective of reaching an informal merger agreement. On the way, Spencer recalled, "we decided to visit Lincoln first," so WD could visit Memorial Stadium, home of the Nebraska Cornhuskers. "We went right to the fifty yard line where WD was in awe of the surroundings. There were no people present at that time, but it was like a movie setting. You could just hear the roar of the crowd."[98]

Inspired by their visit to one of college football's most impressive shrines, the two men drove to Omaha, where they met Bredthauer and took him out to dinner. As Spencer recalled, they had a wonderful meal, but when the time came for WD to broach the idea of a merger, Bredthauer made it clear the evening was over. NLFA leaders, especially Magdanz, the organization's executive vice president, had great pride in their membership. They were unwilling to lose their identity among ranchers who had been so opposed to government subsidies. However, the 1972 trip set the stage for a merger a few years later. Because WD urged Spencer to maintain contact with the NLFA, and because Magdanz continued to hold WD in high respect, the two organizations were able to accomplish an agreement. The NLFA and ANCA became the National Cattlemen's Association in 1977. It was testimony to WD's leadership philosophy, his dedication to policies that would result in a better future for the industry, and his ability to cajole and guide others toward the ends in which he believed.

"He was such a gentle giant," Spencer concluded. "He had close friends in high offices in both business and government, and, in fact, throughout the world. It was only natural that people were drawn to him out of respect for the kind of man he was, the knowledge he had, and the approach he took to life."[99] He was successful, recalled Bill McMillan, because he was credible. In addition to his quiet touch, he was a "great innovator," always framing issues in the broadest context, willing and able to discuss his thoughts with others.[100] He led because he never asked anyone to do anything he would not do himself. Virginia cattleman Burton Eller, Jr, described WD as follows:

> He was a hundred and twenty-five percent engaged in anything he undertook, and you knew that if he stood up to support something, he was in it to the end, and he wouldn't leave you holding the bag. . . . He had a vision that enabled him to see and predict what would happen in the future, almost like a prophet, predicting how things would have to develop if the beef industry were to have a chance to be competitive and profitable in the future. . . . He refused to turn battles into personal conflicts, because he was sensitive to the views of others and could understand where they were coming from.[101]

Because of his courtesy, consideration of others, and his gentle persuasion, he was able to heal wounds and move people over to his way of thinking. He had no interest in taking credit for what he accomplished but always tried to get the best from others. In this sense, the chair of the National Cattlemen's Foundation Bob Josserand stated, "WD was the consummate facilitator. He was one of the most intelligent people I have ever met, but he was also a man who was humble, and he made a difference in the lives of other people."[102]

The ANCA presidency had proved demanding, but WD's ability to mute criticism and address entrenched biases with optimism, information, and solid plans for a better future strengthened the association for the presidents who followed him. After he left the office, WD came to be seen as an advocate of a business that had been weakened by internal discord and external critiques. Although he would have rejected the appellation, some saw him as a "true liberal" in the classic sense of one whose opinions are subject to constant modification on the basis of new, diligently sought information.[103] Others marveled at the map inside his head "that unfolds as he speaks," spreading out as the conversation moves "from water management to agriculture to the growth of northern Colorado."[104]

On the occasion WD being selected "Commercial Feeder of the Year" in 1969, *Feedlot Magazine* summed up his talent for leadership by noting that no matter how contentious the subject, he remained a gentleman. He was honest to a fault, willing to share his ideas with anyone, instrumental in bringing polarized groups together, available for discussions with anyone, willing to experiment, concerned about the impact of his decisions on other businesses and the community, and a first-rate teacher of young people.[105] With such talent and such a strong interest in life-long learning, WD in his early sixties could attribute many of his qualities to his father and grandfather, who set an example for him.[106]

Unfortunately, Harry passed away in 1965 after breaking his collarbone in a fall. The loss was hard on WD. Harry had a profound impact on him, setting standards for success in business and opening doors for WD through his membership in many organizations. At his death, Harry was still president of Farr Farms and Farr Company. He was one of the incorporating directors of Greeley National Bank, a director of the First National Bank of Denver, director of Home Light and Power Company, the first president of the Colorado–Nebraska Lamb Feeders Association, and president of the National Livestock and Meat Board. He was also a director of the Denver Union Stockyards and the Great Western Sugar Beet Company. In many ways, Harry had shown WD how to work with people, how to get the best out of them, and how to defuse controversy. As with most other facets of his life, WD proved to be a superb student under an extraordinary teacher.

Perhaps the one area of WD's expertise that emerged from within, not from Harry, was his fascination with the policies and agricultural practices of other countries. Beginning in the 1960s with travels to Europe, WD came to realize that the United States could learn a great deal by opening itself to the ideas and opportunities available in the rest of the world. Along with using his experiences in water development and beef raising, WD honed his vision of a better future with the knowledge he absorbed as a result of these international connections.

CHAPTER 6

Challenges

The gem cannot be polished without friction, nor man perfected without trials.
— Chinese proverb

By the early 1970s, WD had established himself as a hard-working, imaginative, and forward-looking community builder. As Malcolm Gladwell noted in *The Tipping Point*, successful leaders are "connectors," people who have a "special gift for bringing the world together."[1] These connectors, Gladwell wrote, are important not just for the number of people they know, but for the kinds of people they know. They are "people whom all of us can reach in only a few steps, because for one reason or another, they manage to occupy many different worlds and subcultures and niches."[2]

WD's connections were extraordinary. As of 1970 he was an officer, director, or board member in more than a dozen local, regional, and national organizations: ANCA, the Colorado Cattle Feeders Association, the Foundation of American Agriculture, the USDA's Cattle Advisory Committee, the Agricultural Committee of the U.S. Chamber of Commerce, the National Livestock Tax Commission, the Colorado Cattlemen's Association, the Greeley National Bank, the Greeley Water and Sewer Board, the Greeley Centennial Commission, Home Light and Power Company, Mountain States Telephone Company, the U.S. National Bank of Denver, the NCWCD, and the NCWCD Municipal Subdistrict charged with the challenge of building the Windy Gap Project. In addition, he was deeply committed to the Boy Scouts of America, Rotary, YMCA, the Congregational Church, the T-Bone Club, and the Independence Stampede, Greeley's annual rodeo.

But it was not just the numerous memberships that set WD apart. His personality, decisiveness, and the way he incorporated people into his life encouraged others to seek his counsel or his participation on governing boards. What attracted people to WD was his unique *Weltanschauung,* or worldview.[3] Connectors, Gladwell declared, "don't see the same world that the rest of us see. They see possibility, and while most of us are busily choosing whom we would like to know, and rejecting the people who don't look right, or who live out near the airport, or whom we haven't seen in sixty-five years, [connectors] like them all."[4] To make a difference, Gladwell concluded, connectors have to believe that change is possible, "that people can radically transform their behavior or beliefs in the face of the right kind of impetus," and those who can effect such change have an underlying attitude of hopefulness.[5] They manage challenges effectively!

By the 1970s, WD had begun to earn public recognition for his accomplishments. Like his mentor Charles Hansen, who oversaw the complex C-BT project when he was well into his sixth decade, WD at age 60 was energetic and interested in world affairs. Because of his growing reputation as a leader who helped others find constructive solutions to problems, he began to receive a number of awards that continued even after his death in 2007. These accolades started in the 1960s with the Greeley community's acknowledgment of his service in various local organizations. This recognition soon extended beyond Greeley. In 1969, the American Meat Institute honored WD with its top award. "I speak for the entire industry," said the institute's chairman Edward Jones, "when I say that no one in the cattle feeding business is more of a pioneer, more of a student of effective feeding programs, more of an innovator, or more copied far and wide, than Bill Farr."[6] In 1971, CSU awarded WD its coveted Livestock Industry Award, and the following year the *Record Stockman* recognized WD as Livestock Man of the Year. This award, stated editor Ken Archer, "is given to one who is first of all successful in the livestock industry and . . . who shares his talents for the good of the industry."[7]

Those who worked with WD already appreciated his willingness to share what he knew. He had an uncommon capacity to pursue and absorb knowledge, and he was never satiated. His advice was frequently sought and freely given, and because he grew up in a prosperous home with successful and hard-working parents and grandparents, he had a sense of entitlement about achievement that emerged in the form of guileless optimism. As Colorado Supreme Court justice Greg Hobbs said in 1999, when WD was designated Citizen of the West by the National Western Stock Show, WD might just as well stand for "Will Do." Indeed, WD hardly ever viewed worthy projects as impossible, no matter how difficult or radical they seemed, because his childhood and early adult years were filled with reminders that success was "a function of persistence and doggedness," as Gladwell would phrase it. His triumphs were also related to a powerful set of family circumstances and opportunities, a pattern of achieving rewards through effort and a "good dose of ingenuity and drive."[8]

WD spent little time worrying about the possibility of failure. He believed he would be successful as long as he could learn from others. He could always improve his own business and the organizations for which he held some governing responsibility, provided he was able to obtain knowledge from experts in the many fields in which he was involved. As dedicated as he was to the Greeley community, WD knew he had to reach out nationally and internationally to better comprehend the broad challenges of agriculture and livestock feeding. When he was invited by Professor Marion Eugene Ensminger to present a lecture on his imaginative approach to cattle feeding at Washington State University in the 1960s, WD initiated a thirty-year relationship with "Dr. E." that intensified his interest in other countries and added significantly to his global perspective.

Ensminger was the kind of person with whom WD liked to associate. He was an academic, a scientist, a hard worker, and a gentleman. He had been invited to Washington State University in 1941 to build up the animal science department. Over time, he and the department achieved recognition for establishing a highly rated doctoral program, for publications Ensminger authored on agriculture and animal science, and for the International Stockmen's Schools, which convened annually at the Pullman campus for a period of twenty years.[9] At one of these gatherings, Ensminger invited a Colorado rancher named Dan Thornton to give the banquet address. Thornton, who was well connected in the cattle business, received a standing ovation from an appreciative audience.[10] As Colorado governor from 1951 to 1955, Thornton was familiar with the Farrs' sheep and cattle operations, and it was probably his suggestion to Ensminger that resulted in the invitation WD received to speak at Washington State.

Ensminger and WD soon formed a synergistic bond. WD was fascinated by the agricultural technology schools Ensminger was establishing all over the world, and Dr. E. valued WD's business acumen and his unique capacity for innovation. Successful people, Ensminger believed, were not conformists. "It takes courage to innovate," he noted, but successful people often find themselves "pilgrims and strangers" amidst jealous competitors.[11] Believing that the nations most in need of scientific and technological information had been isolated by communism, Ensminger focused his energies on China, Russia, Cuba, and the Ukraine, notwithstanding the criticism he received from government officials and friends who thought his behavior unpatriotic.

President Nixon's visit to China in 1972 launched a diplomatic process that eventually established ties with the United States. As part of that advancement, Ensminger was invited to establish an agriculture–technology school in Peking (Beijing) under the auspices of the agricultural program faculty at Peking University. Several Chinese faculty members had received degrees under Ensminger at Washington State. They decided to take advantage of the thaw in relations to bring agricultural technicians to China, hoping they might learn how to increase food production for a population that was heading rapidly toward one billion.

The school was successful, and within a year Ensminger was invited to return with representatives from various areas of American agriculture and livestock production. Because he had been widely recognized for cattle feeding and his leadership of ANCA, WD was invited to join the group and to bring Judy with him. Although they were aware that living conditions would be difficult, the Farrs looked forward to the challenge. In 1974 the twenty-fifth anniversary of Mao Tse-Tung's victory over Chiang Kai-Shek's nationalist forces took place. Few westerners had been allowed in the country since 1949. Mao was still leader of the communist party and head of the People's Republic of China. Although some groups in the 1970s were beginning to challenge the long-standing Cold War polarizations between China and the United States, anti-communism continued to be a powerful litmus test for loyalty in America. Some advised the Farrs not to go, but as WD later recalled, the trip yielded information, opportunities, and perspectives he had never imagined, and it proved to be, without a doubt, "the greatest single learning experience I had ever had."[12]

The China trip, however, was neither his first foreign travel nor his first contact with agriculturalists in other countries. By 1974 WD had already concluded that the American beef industry would face increasingly stiff competition from countries with lower production costs. But there would also be opportunities for American beef producers, and in order to compete in the global market successfully, he would have to understand cattle operations in other parts of the world.

In 1967, WD and Judy joined a *Western Livestock Journal* European beef industry tour. At their first stop in Paris, WD attended a symposium on cattle raising, where he was asked to speak about ways to expand beef production on the continent. Aware of the marginal lands available to livestock raisers in Europe, he offered little hope for an increase in the size of European herds, but he came away from the Paris meeting "tremendously impressed" by the African representatives. The tour continued on to the *estancias* of Seville, where the Farrs learned that lunch (*la comida*) was both a social and business event lasting three to four hours. After visiting Spain, the group traveled to the Po River Valley in Italy, then to Denmark, England, Scotland, and Ireland before returning home. The trip enhanced WD's sense of the global market and enriched his thinking about how American beef producers might take advantage of export opportunities.[13]

Recalling their positive impressions of the African representatives, WD and Judy joined another *Western Livestock Journal* trip the following year, embarking with fifty others for a visit to South Africa and surrounding areas. They toured farms near Johannesburg for three weeks then spent ten days in Kenya and Uganda. WD came away impressed by the intelligence of local officials. He became convinced that developing countries should be left alone to develop themselves as much as possible.[14]

In 1970 he took ANCA's executive committee to Australia and New Zealand so they could develop a more balanced response to American beef producers' demand to restrict the importation of beef from down under. The widespread view among cattlemen was that Australian and New Zealand imports were depressing prices of American beef. WD spent three weeks in both countries learning how cattle were raised and slaughtered, getting to know the people, and establishing good relationships. He learned that Australia and New Zealand were shipping cuts of lean beef to the United States because of a limited capacity for refrigeration in their own countries. If American producers would buy this meat and mix it with fattier cuts, WD reasoned, they could sell a constant and guaranteed mix of hamburger to the fast food stores. Viewed from this perspective, Australian and New Zealand imports appeared to be less threatening.[15]

But expanding American beef exports would require additional attention. "On the return flight," WD recalled, "we decided that we had to do something to popularize U.S. beef so we could [better] sell it." On their way to Australia, the group had stopped in Japan. There they saw the results of WD's efforts to bring the Japanese secretary of agriculture to the USDA in Washington, D.C., where he was shown the prize steer from the National Western Stock Show. Sufficiently impressed by the animal he saw and the industry it represented, the secretary was able to introduce a modest program that allowed Japanese purchases of beef from the United States. "So, we had some friends in Japan," WD concluded, and "we decided we needed to start selling [more] meat overseas."[16] Not long thereafter, ANCA established a foreign trade committee. It expanded to include other commodity groups and began to function formally and energetically in 1976 as the U.S. Meat Export Federation (USMEF). WD's imprint was all over this successful organization.[17] When the 1974 China trip came up, he could see that along with the opportunity to gain knowledge, he would have a chance to assess the possibility of marketing American beef to the most populated country in the world.

The China trip began with an introductory meeting at the Holiday Inn in San Francisco. Ensminger pulled no punches in briefing the group: they would have to be punctual at all times, courteous to a fault, and attentive to Chinese restrictions. He would tolerate no excessive alcohol use, and he warned against drinking the water and eating the vegetables.

The next day the group flew to Hong Kong. From there it was a short train ride to the Chinese border. "Here were the Chinese Red troops," WD remembered, "with their bayonets and everything else that met us as we got off the train. We walked down the train platform for about two or three blocks with soldiers lining the way. You began to wonder if you were in the right place."[18]

After taking several hours to check passports, Chinese officials returned with a young man who spoke English. His name was Zhu Baochen, and he would become a friend of the Farr family for many years. Zhu explained that

WD and Judy Farr at the Great Wall of China, 1974. Courtesy of the Farr family.

everyone would have to indicate the exact amount of money they were bringing into the country. Receipts would be required for anything purchased, and no Chinese money could be removed from the country when they departed. If any of these rules were violated, the penalty was death.

Having gotten everyone's attention, the Chinese soldiers escorted the group back onto the train. Over the next three weeks, WD and Judy visited Peking, Shanghai, and Hangchow, but most of their time was spent in the rural areas. They lived in primitive conditions at communes of 60,000 to 80,000 workers, sleeping on cots with a blanket or two, using communal latrines, and eating out of bowls whatever food their hosts provided. Frequently, they did not know what they were being fed.

But the hardships were minimal when measured against the learning experience. WD was astounded by the industriousness of the Chinese people. He was astonished by what they had accomplished with their hands, with limited mechanization and with an organizational structure that suggested a burgeoning sense of democracy within the totalitarianism of communism. He marveled at "funny looking" sows that gave birth to twenty piglets, wheat fields that had numbered rows so kernels from each stalk could be identified and evaluated by weight to determine productivity, and the mass production of cloth that provided everyone with identical apparel. He learned from Zhu that no one had starved in China for fourteen years, that none of the peasants lived in caves anymore, that most had their own accommodations with electricity, and that men and women were retired from field work at age fifty-five so they could take care of the children. "The Chinese," WD concluded "are tremendously fine, intelligent people." It was just a matter of time before they would be the second strongest economy in the world, selling manufactured goods to the United States.[19]

This was the message he and Judy conveyed to friends and neighbors when they returned home. WD took 900 slides and used them when he gave talks, conveying a great admiration for the Chinese people. He told audiences that although China was a communist nation, it had become "one of the great producing countries of the world,"[20] with an educational system that required everyone to spend some time each day at manual labor. He had no doubt about China's future, and he warned listeners, not so subtly, that Americans, who were already tending toward smugness and laziness, might take a lesson from these hardworking people.

WD and Judy did not receive a warm welcome home in 1974. Some people thought they had been sold a bill of goods, and of those who heard WD speak, a few were repelled by his message. "My old minister from the Congregational Church," WD lamented, "told me we had gone soft on communism."[21] But if he was disappointed or surprised by such a response, WD had no intention of retreating from his interest in communist China, Russia, and other countries. The trip had been a watershed experience for him, because he esteemed a Chinese work ethic that was similar to his own, because the Chinese were detail-oriented and innovative like him, and because the Chinese search for knowledge from the outside world, he believed, would propel the nation forward into world markets that would ultimately impact the American beef industry.

In 1977 and 1983, WD received follow-up China invitations from Ensminger. On both trips, he revisited the places they had been in 1974 and noted immense progress. Mao died in 1976, and by 1977, with Deng Xiaoping back in power, China's Cultural Revolution had begun to change course.

In December 1978, President Jimmy Carter made a joint announcement with Deng that both countries were working to normalize relations. In stark contrast to Ronald Reagan's condemnation of this announcement, WD, also a steadfast Republican, described it as "the greatest peace move in the world today," a great step forward, and something he had predicted four years earlier.[22] In short order, Deng began to redirect China's energies toward modernization of agriculture, industry, national defense, science, and technology. During the twelve years he was in power, he also brought China into the world of international trade. This was exactly what WD had foreseen.

China appeared to be the nation of the future. WD traveled to Tibet and Mongolia, stayed in yurts used by yak herdsmen, and learned about the ancient Silk Road. He pondered the courage of medieval traders who went on three-year missions to deliver their silks and spices to Western Europe, and when he visited Chinese oil fields near the Russian border, he continued to be humbled by China's historic awareness of international markets. At one point he questioned the value of immense blocks of paraffin that had been removed from the oil. In response, one of the Chinese engineers asked if WD was aware that most of the world's population functioned without electricity. "They have to have candles," said the manager, "and we can sell more paraffin than we can produce." It was "simple things like that," WD recalled, "you don't ever forget. And it helps explain my great belief in China and all of the Pacific."[23]

The Russians were a different story. WD traveled across the Soviet Union as part of a People to People tour in 1982. He traversed nine time zones and saw everything the Russians would show him, from Moscow to the Black Sea. He was disappointed in their farms, their inability to understand irrigation, and the way they left broken-down machinery in the fields for want of qualified mechanics.[24] But mostly he was critical of the Russian brand of communism and how it favored the privileged and educated. He believed communism would fail in the Soviet Union because ordinary people were denied membership in the party. There was no incentive to work hard, as in China, because the upwardly mobile were chosen from the elite while the vast majority of Russians struggled without hope.

These trips and a half-dozen others WD took to Europe and South America provided education, perspective, and ideas. He paid his own way and expected the benefits of such travel to be realized through an improved comprehension of the world's problems. A visit to Colombia introduced him to the danger of disappearing rain forests. In Peru, he became aware of global climate change and El Niño and La Niña's impact on fisheries. In Argentina he sampled "the true beef flavor" of grass-fed beef,[25] and in Brasilia, Brazil, he learned about city planning and the consequences of not preparing adequately for explosive urban growth. All of these experiences comingled in the sponge that was WD's mind. He loved the challenges and the adventures of travel, and because he was such a great listener, he stored enormous quantities of data in his head and used it for perspective when discussing future trends and developments. He was not clairvoyant and not especially cosmopolitan. However, WD was globally enlightened, and in his later years, he fully expected Denver and its new international airport (completed in 1995) to become the hub of trade with Pacific Rim countries.

Always looking to the future with the goal of adapting his own business to an expanding world economy, WD began designing an improved feedlot a few years before his first trip to China. In contrast to the old one, which was feeding approximately 10,000 Farr-owned animals yearly, the new lot would custom-feed other people's cattle. Charges would be based on actual costs and a percentage of overhead that would secure a profit. WD was already known for having studied feeding operations in other countries,[26] but when construction of the new feedlot began in 1972, his principal concerns were environmental protection and a facility that would keep animals as healthy as possible. He wanted to build a commercial operation that would incorporate the science and technology that had been unavailable forty years earlier. "When I started feeding cattle," he confessed, "we didn't know a damn thing. Education and knowledge are keys to the future."[27] And also the keys to success!

The new feedlot was situated six miles east and downwind of Greeley on 240 acres. Its concept reflected WD's experience as a member of President Nixon's Water Pollution Committee. One hundred and forty-four pens, each with a capacity for 250 head of cattle, were constructed with feeding efficiency, animal health, and environmental safety in mind.[28] An underground drainage system, designed by agricultural engineer Tom Norton, made possible the removal of liquid wastes even during winter

WD at the new Farr feedlot east of Greeley, Colorado, ca. mid-1970s. Courtesy of the Farr family.

months when temperatures dropped below freezing.[29] Large manholes caught runoff water from the feeding pens, while the alleys in between were v-shaped to direct water to the underground system. Fresh water from two wells served the cattle population and also satisfied the Farrs' commitment to reduce blowing dust by sprinkling the ground and road-ways with specially designed water trucks. Storm sewers drained the liquid wastes into large holding ponds, and a sixty-foot-wide greenbelt surrounded the site along the north and west county road boundaries. Solid wastes were collected in stockpiles, awaiting removal to nearby fields as fertilizer; the liquid material was available for irrigation from the settling ponds. Large, concrete-lined pits were built to hold 100,000 tons of silage and 50,000 tons of ground high-moisture corn. The large pits ensured a constant food supply for a cattle population estimated at 35,000 to 40,000. WD banked on farmers' willingness to plant and harvest an additional 20,000 acres of corn. Because the company (Farr Feeders, Inc.) could guarantee the purchase of locally grown high-moisture corn, even at a discounted price, he assumed farmers would cooperate.[30] They did, because they had confidence in him and believed he would always cut them the best deal.

The computerized mixing facility was a technological marvel. A feed mill, operated by computers and a punch-card system that provided mixing orders, was capable of blending a ton of feed every minute. A thermalizer was installed to steam roll corn for greater digestibility, heating the kernels until they were almost ready to pop, then rolling the corn so each kernel was about the size of a quarter. Seventy-five percent of a normal ration was corn and silage, but the computerized mixer also added grain, vitamins, minerals, dried beet pulp pellets, dehydrated alfalfa pellets, brewers malt pellets, molasses, and animal tallow as determined by nutritionists.[31]

Special consideration was given to the health of the animals. Upon arrival in the feedlot, they were vaccinated for red nose, leptospirosis, and black leg. They were injected with vitamins A, D, and E; implanted with a growth stimulant;[32] branded; and dipped in pesticides to kill host insects. Animal health inspectors visited the pens daily to look for sick animals. In general, WD opposed the use of horses. "On horseback," he contended, "the man can't hear the cattle because of the noise of the horse. He's not able to see something wrong with the animal as well as when he's on foot." While some people claimed that men on foot would disturb the cattle too much, WD believed that after a few days, the animals would get used to them.[33] If sick animals were encountered, they were taken to one of four on-site clinics, where they were treated by a veterinarian and either cured or disposed of as a bad risk.

The $4 million facility was completed in the spring of 1974. It was a first-class feedlot, and its construction was supervised in every detail by WD himself. His frequent revisions in design required engineers to mark plans with the day and time of changes so they could be certain they were working with the most current documents.[34] After construction was finished, WD paid little attention to operations. Sons WR and Dick operated Farr Feeders. Because it was a state-of-the-art facility, because the weather was generally mild and dry, and because the Swift packing plant was nearby, the new feedlot was expected to do well. WD never worried about making money. He was a perfectionist in building things, even if the quality he aimed for required borrowing money to meet high standards. Any job well done, he believed, would make money.[35]

To make sure everything worked smoothly, Farr Farms ran some of its own cattle through the system. Electronic controls monitored all the operations so that if any part of the system malfunctioned or exceeded temperature limits, the entire mill would shut down. By October of 1974, when WD and Judy were involved in their first trip to China, the feedlot began to receive cattle for custom feeding. Unfortunately, the successful completion of this state-of-the-art facility coincided with a destabilized economy, but WD appealed to cattle producers to give the new feedlot a try. "With the *current conditions* in the cattle industry," he noted, "the [new] facility can offer a specialized service, providing the rancher or investor with a complete package, from receiving to marketing, all with the most efficient methods of production."[36] Those conditions, having steadily worsened since 1972, were being described by many in the business as an outright "cattle wreck."

One did not have to look far to find the cause of economic instability. Food prices for consumers began to climb late in 1971. Against the advice of economists, President Nixon imposed temporary wage and price controls, but the upward pressure on retail prices continued throughout 1972. Retail meat prices increased 50 percent between 1968 and 1972.[37] Consumer advocacy groups were becoming increasingly active in many states, causing Nixon to consider price freezes.

WD found himself on the horns of a dilemma. Already a member of Nixon's Cost of Living Council, he was named to the president's Food Industry Advisory Committee in February 1973. On March 23, while enjoying a morning shower, he received a phone call from the White House. His presence in Washington was expected that afternoon, and plane tickets were waiting for him at the Denver airport. When he arrived in Washington, he and other committee members met with Secretary of the Treasury George Schultz. They were told that Nixon had decided to freeze wholesale and retail red meat prices for seven months. The following day, Nixon made his decision public.[38]

WD was philosophically opposed to price controls because he believed they interrupted the cattle market's natural cycles and caused exacerbated swings in supply and demand. But he was loyal to the Nixon administration, and while Weld County farmers vented anger at the president's announcement, WD expressed support. "I think he [Nixon] made the right decision," WD said, explaining his position by pointing to the rising costs consumers faced for red meat. "I think I would have done the same thing."[39]

But events during the rest of 1973 made things even worse for the cattle industry. A severe drought in Russia followed by grain shortages meant that the Soviet Union was on the world market paying premium prices for wheat and causing feed grain prices in the United States to rise by 65 percent.[40] Inflation precipitated soaring consumer prices plus a 10 percent increase in interest rates, and when the United States announced its support for Israel in the three-week Yom Kippur War against Syria and Egypt, Arab members of the Organization of the Petroleum Exporting Countries (OPEC) declared an embargo on oil to the United States. As energy costs skyrocketed, farm costs rose further. By 1974 it was clear that the damage to cattle feeders would not be repaired quickly. "It will take a while to recover from the losses we have sustained in this market so far," lamented WR.[41] He estimated that up to 20 percent of cattle feeders might have to fold their tents before the market turned around. In addition to blaming energy costs, inflation, high interest rates, and swollen grain prices, he noted that cattlemen had failed to "promote the sale of beef at the customer level as much as [they] should have."[42]

The unexpected energy of consumer activism hit cattle producers broadside. The consumer price index, along with all retail foods, showed an alarming increase of 30 percent between 1967 and 1973, but the retail meat index was 20 percent higher than that. Boycotts began in Denver, where protestors railed against retail store green stamps, games, and gimmicks, and when they realized the chain stores actually netted very little from meat sales, they went after the middle men: feeders, packers, and wholesalers. "Inflation and escalating food prices were their concerns, but beef was their target. They still considered beef the 'King of Meats,' and they thought they were being ripped off by *cattlemen who drive Cadillacs*."[43]

The net effect of the so-called cattle wreck and consumer boycotts was an increase in the cattle population that reached a historic peak of 132 million in 1976.[44] Consumer prices improved for a few months, but for cattle feeders in general, losses of $100 to $200 dollars per animal, along with bankruptcies and mergers, indicated that these were watershed years for the cattle industry. WD commented on this transition in a 1982 speech to the National Livestock Grading and Marketing Association,[45] but he had become convinced many years earlier that the cattle business could be successful only if it reorganized to produce the kind of product consumers demanded at a reasonable price.

For most of the 1970s, WD remained optimistic the beef industry could survive if it would learn to speak with one voice and take lessons from the poultry and pork industries regarding the use of science and genetics to produce premium carcasses. Cattle, he believed, would have to be bred and sold on a performance basis like hybrid seed corn. Three- or four-breed crosses, based on statistical proof of high-yielding carcasses, would increase the quality and yield of slaughtered animals, reducing the fatty wastes that increased the price of meat to consumers. Unfortunately, he noted, "the beef industry works on averages. The poor, inefficient animals in every herd drag down the good animals. I do not believe any industry can exist on averages for a long period of time."[46] Far more productive, he argued, was a system within which cattlemen would receive a premium if they produced superior animals. Although the American people were angry about high food prices, they clearly preferred beef over pork and chicken, at least through 1975. The annual per capita consumption of beef had reached roughly 100 pounds by then, and WD thought that figure had the potential to rise to 130 pounds.[47] Furthermore, from what he had been hearing at conferences, the appetite of fast food restaurants for beef appeared limitless. "As I analyze our industry in 1979," he said, "I am absolutely confident that the cattle industry is in the early stages of the most radical change we have ever known." The cow-calf operators had reason to be sanguine about their future, he said, "because this demand is permanent. I believe the fast food outlets are here to stay."[48]

Unfortunately, the cattle industry as a whole failed to meet his expectations. Some organizational progress was made in 1977 when ANCA and the NLFA merged to form the National Cattlemen's Association (NCA). But in WD's view, the producers and feeders still remained stubbornly unresponsive to consumer demands. They continued to produce overly fat cattle. New meat grading standards advocated by WD as chairman of the National Cattlemen's Association's meat grading committee were ignored, and the association's membership failed to approve a self-imposed tax, or check-off, that would have assessed a $1 charge per head to tell the beef story to the public.[49] Meanwhile, the American Agricultural Movement organized a "tractorcade" on Washington to protest low prices, and a Senate committee generated a study that, among other things, urged Americans to eat more poultry and fish.[50] Economic data for the decade clearly showed that beef's dominance in the meat industry had ended. From 1975 on, beef's share of consumer meat purchases steadily lost out to poultry, while pork production and sales continued to be relatively steady.[51]

By 1980 WD had become less sanguine about the cattle industry's future. The Farrs were operating two feedlots, two grassland ranches (LF Ranch and 70 Ranch), and seven farms on which they raised potatoes, sugar beets, alfalfa, pinto beans, corn, oats, and onions. A fertilizer company and a potato company rounded out their enterprises. Inflation at 12.5 percent and interest rates at 21.5 percent challenged every business across the country, but the cost of money hit agriculture especially hard: "$15 billion in inventory loss and $5 billion in operating loss."[52] In scarcely three years, cattlemen lost $20 billion.

In contrast to the optimism he had promulgated in the late 1970s, WD now realized that the economic pressures on farming and cattle feeding demanded decisive action. He had taken on considerable debt to build the new feedlot and to renovate the 70 Ranch. Under the debilitating economic pressures of the early 1980s, the repayment of borrowed money became onerous. Writing his good friend Andy Russell in the fall of 1982, he bemoaned the difficulties of the past two years and noted in addition that Farr Farms and Farr Feeders were in trouble, "because we acquired too much debt, and it has been very hard to service the debt."[53] A year later he told Russell that the situation continued to be a "drain on our financial resources," and by 1984 both ranches had to be put up for sale to raise cash.[54]

For a man who loved ranches and ranching, this was a difficult decision, but it was indicative of the way he approached most challenges. He studied his options, determined which was best, made a decision, and never looked back.[55] Even so, the ranches were more than just businesses. The LF Ranch represented WD's innovative foray into the cattle business in the 1930s, and the 70 Ranch was the fulfillment of his dream to own river-bottom land where hunting, water, and development combined with the joys of owning historic property.[56] Both ranches were used to run steers for the old feedlot, but they were also family destinations for work and hunting recreation.

Even though WD rarely looked back with regret, the ranch sales were traumatic. He had always been a prudent businessman whose conservative principles, inherited from father and grandfather, required a thorough evaluation of risk when borrowing money. Having to liquidate properties, their equity eroded to retire unforeseen debt, placed WD in unfamiliar territory. Believing his choices were limited, he said it was time to recognize that the Farrs were essentially cattle feeders, not ranchers, committed to producing fat, marketable animals. "Actually," he noted, "we're in the hotel business. We sell room and board for livestock, and we try to make five bucks for every head we put up."[57] Without the responsibility of the ranches, WD reasoned, he would have more time to spend on the Greeley Water Board, the NCWCD, and the Colorado Water Resources and Power Development Authority. He was seventy-four and determined to look forward.

But he was putting a good face on what was clearly a painful and emotional experience. When the LF Ranch sold in 1986, WD noted, "It was not easy to sell. It [took] a lifetime to build . . . [but] we had to do it; there comes a time for everything."[58] Since his grandfather Billy Farr had begun his sheep feeding operation in the late nineteenth century, the Farr family had built a large empire in Weld County. Its complete dissolution in less than four years, including the two ranches, seven irrigated farms, and the new feedlot, took place in a businesslike manner without any attempt on WD's part to place blame on anyone or on any circumstances. WD said he was just recognizing his age and adjusting accordingly. "It's time to get your house in order and get things in order when you're as old as I am," he said. "Circumstances and age and conditions change. . . . The world doesn't stand still."[59] Looking back on those years, son WR noted that when the feedlot finally sold in 1988, his father did not appear upset. "It was the end of a chapter," he said, "and we got the price for it. If you need to sell, you just have to get on with it. [Feeding] was a tough business, but I never saw him display depression or sadness. He just gradually separated from the cattle and got into water."[60]

But WD guarded his emotions very carefully, even with his family. When problems arose, he preferred to ask rhetorically, "What do we do now?"

rather than finding fault or dwelling on what might have been. He found nothing constructive in censuring people, preferring instead to make the most out of situations that would have caused others to seek retribution. It was a leadership trait that revealed his forbearance and compassion for others. As his good friend Nick Kosmicki noted, WD was a product of the Great Depression. People who survived those difficult times learned to deal with life's injustices. Although he was a perfectionist when it came to machinery and systems operations, he understood the imperfection inherent in humans with whom he interacted. Those who knew him well praised WD's total absence of pettiness and recrimination. He was grounded in the practicality of the world, inspired by change and challenges, and able to deal with adversity as a natural condition of life. These were the qualities of leadership that drew people to him. Instead of lamenting unfortunate developments, or yearning for different outcomes, he made the most of every circumstance, respected the feelings of other people, and refrained from turning disappointments into personal conflicts. In WD's own words,

> We have had lots of financial hard times that [came] and [went]. But I don't have any advice for anybody on that. It . . . depends on the people's temperament and how much they want to make out of [the hard times]. It's like other things. If you accept life the way it is, and if you want . . . to make progress, or change the bad circumstances . . . you just have to make up your mind to do it. . . . It isn't easy, but I have seen so many people let something destroy them when it wasn't necessary. It would have been much better if they had just taken a firmer look and gone on.[61]

And that is what WD decided to do in the early 1980s. He realized that farming and cattle feeding would continue to fall on hard times. His sons were not interested in ranching. He deeply felt the loss of what three generations of Farrs had established over almost 100 years. To his Italian friend Bruno Borhy he pulled no punches: "When you have built up a business all your life, it is difficult to gradually sell it away piece by piece. It certainly is not what I had planned or hoped for."[62]

But WD had also become concerned about recent changes in agriculture, and he was willing to shift his energy to endeavors that could produce more positive outcomes with greater impact on the future. The discussions, negotiations, and compromises that went into water-related planning gradually replaced much of the time and commitment he had given previously to farming and cattle feeding. Water work gave him great pleasure. It allowed him to use his leadership skills as a connector to bring together diverse groups of people for the purpose of bringing about more efficient use of a scarce resource. The region's rapid population growth would place demands on water, requiring cooperation among leaders of farming, industry, and urban centers.

The focus on water also allowed WD to exercise his commitment to good management. He believed that much of the state's concern about water scarcity could be alleviated by concentrating on waste and inefficient water distribution. Appointed as director and first chairman of the Colorado Water Resources and Power Development Authority (CWRPDA), he found himself well positioned to influence the way Colorado's water projects were studied and funded, but he was not prepared for the disparate voices that would oppose him in ensuing debates.

The CWRPDA was Colorado's response to President Jimmy Carter's hit list and President Ronald Reagan's decision to prevent the federal government from building new water projects. Colorado developed the CWRPDA to replace the role of the then-dormant federal government. Its purpose, according to Senator Fred Anderson, was to develop water storage for Colorado.[63] The group was composed of nine members who represented each of Colorado's major stream systems, plus the city and county of Denver. Organized by statute in 1981, the authority held its first meeting in January 1982. With demands on existing water sources expected to escalate with energy development—coal, oil shale, oil, natural gas— and with some observers concerned that the CWCB was not acting fast enough, the state legislature created the authority and made available $30 million from the CWCB's construction fund for the CWRPDA to use as it saw fit.[64]

In his role as the CWRPDA's first chairman, WD presided over an operational shift from building water storage to acting as banker for the many entities in the state needing financial help with water projects. The authority accomplished this function by developing a funding program that allowed them to loan money at low interest rates under the "moral authority" of the state of Colorado. Under its constitution, Colorado could not take on debt or borrow money, but WD drew on his extensive banking experience to shape a plan that leveraged EPA money appropriated to the state for loans rather than for grants to specific projects where there had been previous accusations of graft.[65] Using these funds, plus interest earned from the $30 million as seed money, the authority was able to issue bonds under the state of Colorado's name "like it was an official bond of the state," WD recalled. "We could borrow money and enlarge it almost to anything we needed, [and] we loaned at one percent to two percent interest. The last year I was on the board, we got the mechanics of it set up."[66]

This creative financing allowed for more efficient management and funding of the state's water needs. The CWRPDA became a banker, in contrast to the construction entity originally conceived by the state legislature. But to maximize its financial capability, the authority would also need a professional staff. WD persuaded Ival Goslin to come out of retirement to act as executive director. Goslin had overseen the Upper Colorado River Compact for Colorado, Wyoming, New Mexico, and Utah, and he had spent a lot of time in Washington. He understood the politics of water at the state and national level, and he was highly respected.[67] Daniel Law was hired as the authority's engineer. Because WD understood the peculiar needs of each river basin in the state, he was pleased to observe Law's attention to financial details, crediting him with the authority's record of issuing funds without a single loan default.[68] And WD was also influential in bringing in John U. Carlson as the authority's attorney. "He was, without question," WD said, "the best water attorney in the state. . . . He was the dean of all the water attorneys. I learned a lot from him."[69]

With adequate funding and a professional staff on board, the CWRPDA began studying water projects submitted by the state's eight river basins. Even before he was appointed to the board, WD was convinced that each basin should be operated by a set of rules unique to its own history and circumstances. He disapproved of the state engineer acting as czar for the entire state, preferring a system in which each river basin would be managed by an authority made up of representatives from its own ditch companies, conservancy districts, water users, river commissioners, cities, and rural domestic water servers. To maximize the benefit of assistance from the authority, all water systems in each drainage basin would have to be correlated in one overall plan, and these plans had to be flexible.[70]

Some projects were caught up in politics or proved impractical. But each river basin had its chance to present requests to the authority. In one year, for example, the Animas–La Plata Project received the entire $30 million state appropriation. The money had been authorized by Congress in 1968 but had become a victim of political discord, environmental regulations, and President Jimmy Carter's 1976 hit list, which reduced USBR funding for Colorado Water Storage Projects. Animas–La Plata was Ival Goslin's favorite, however, and was one of the most practical projects Colorado congressman Wayne Aspinall had proposed as a quid pro quo for his endorsement of the Central Arizona Project. The authority recognized the importance of providing water to the Ute Mountain, Southern Ute, and Navajo tribes, but even with $30 million, Animas–La Plata was not expected to be completed before 2012.

Loans were available for other projects, such as Stagecoach Reservoir on the Yampa River, which was successfully planned and overseen by John Fetcher of Steamboat Springs. WD was a keen supporter of Fetcher's well-planned storage project, but he was also a strong proponent of financing general river basin studies across the state. Consistent with WD's approach to understanding complex problems, these data collection inquiries helped the authority to grasp the needs and interrelationships of the state's major rivers. WD was always interested in the big picture.

In the South Platte River drainage, the authority soon confronted the multiplicity of interests that would confound easy consensus. The Coffin Top Dam proposal on the St. Vrain River met objections from citizens who learned that geological studies suggested the possibility of structural failure. Likewise, popular opposition arose against the NCWCD's plan to build a dam and reservoir midway up the Cache la Poudre River. The authority found that in addition to popular resistance to the dam, testing of the site revealed the possibility of structural failure. The next study involved the NCWCD's scheme to dam the Cache la Poudre River where it emerges from the canyon. Because the South Platte basin lost a lot of water to Nebraska every year, WD supported studies of the project, convinced that it would better manage water for the expected population increase and inevitable drought in the Fort Collins–Greeley corridor. His membership on the NCWCD board required that he excuse himself from CWRPDA votes that allocated funds for these studies, but he was fully engaged in the ensuing debates. Because he was recognized as an outstanding agriculturalist, his credibility was unmatched when he spoke to farmers who opposed any project that would limit their access to the Poudre River. "It was a tough sell," WD remembered. "By God they wanted to go up and build their reservoirs where they wanted to, and they didn't like the idea that they could never build another reservoir themselves."[71]

A greater challenge for WD came from Poudre River residents and more recent arrivals to the community, who saw a dam on their river as a violation of a covenant with nature. They wanted the river preserved in its natural state, ideally freeing it from any future development. If reservoirs were needed in the area, they argued, these could be dredged and filled by the farmers on their own lands.

The CWRPDA funded a study in 1985, but the disharmony between adversaries for and against Poudre River storage continued unabated. Senator Hank Brown tried to get the interested parties together. He remembered the situation as follows:

> I got all the farm groups and environmental groups to sit down. They wouldn't even talk to each other, and when they did, they would get mad as hell. We negotiated for three years, I think. It was just hell to get them to come and talk to each other, but we finally worked out a rough compromise. . . . When we got to Congress, the Sierra Club changed its mind and withdrew their support. . . . But we sat down [again] with all the groups and worked out another compromise, although [none of them] were too sure they wanted to do it.[72]

Anguished about the possibility of another failure, Brown went to WD to explain what had been going on. "What can I do?" WD asked. Brown replied that he felt there was something good in the compromise for everyone: a tentative agreement that seventy-five of the Poudre River's eighty-three miles would be designated "wild" or "recreational," and the lower eight miles of the river would be protected for possible future development. "Within a couple of weeks," Brown recalled, "WD had everybody on board. It was just a miracle. When they knew it was okay with WD, everybody fell in line and we got it passed. . . . People had so much confidence in him that if he would sign off on something, it would make the difference."[73]

It all boiled down to trust. At the time, WD was in his mid-seventies. He had earned the respect due a man of his age and experience. But as Brown perceptively explained, the deference he received had more to do with WD's many years in the cattle business:

> The cattle business is where you develop a reputation, and people either trust you or they don't. The reason it's so important is that if you don't have a reputation that people can take you at your word, it's very tough to do [anything]. It's not that people sue you; they can't win law-suits, but people just don't do business with you. WD had the finest reputation of anybody in the state. Everybody knew his word was good, that he would go the extra mile to [effect] a square deal.[74]

This trust carried over when WD advanced ideas that challenged the way water users guarded their rights under Colorado water law. Instead of demanding water delivery regardless of actual need, he argued, water rights owners should be persuaded to accept water from a centralized authority in their basin only when crops required moisture. The central authority he envisaged would have power to deliver water on the basis of need and would be able to select the source of that water based on computerized data of the region's available water supplies. Traditional water rights would still be recognized, but a savings of 20 percent would result if water were to be allocated on a so-called volumetric basis.[75]

Volumetric water distribution was a management concept WD wanted to apply broadly to the state's limited water resources. Diversion by second-feet (cfs), he contended, was just plain wasteful. It resulted in farmers taking water from the river their crops did not need, solely to prevent junior water rights users from getting it. Furthermore, he argued, it would be much better for Colorado to proactively manage its own water at the local level rather than to have either the state or the federal government step in.[76] Grass roots management was always best where water was concerned.

The idea was probably not saleable in the mid-1980s, WD admitted, "but it will come. And we'll have two great blocks of water—the City of Denver and Northern [NCWCD]. They'll run the Front Range . . . they'll run it with tremendous efficiency, and they'll be able to switch water back and forth between the two systems."[77] Down the road, he predicted, twenty-five years from now, the Poudre and Big Thompson rivers would be managed more on a volumetric basis. "It won't change the law; we will leave the old priorities. We will protect people, but we will give people [only] what they need. There is no use giving them any more. It is a waste to run twenty feet of water down the ditch if they are going to use only ten of it. If they need twenty, we will see they have it. That is the way it should be run."[78]

WD also entered actively into the debate about whether or not directors appointed to water conservancy boards should have the power to spend taxpayer money. Even though the 1937 Conservancy District Act specifically stated that courts should appoint directors, the culture of northern Colorado had changed significantly in fifty years. More urban and environmentally focused inhabitants of the Front Range were hostile to the business-as-usual approach they saw coming from water leaders. They accused the NCWCD and other water districts of taxation without representation and rallied a diverse coalition of thirteen organizations under the heading Taxpayers for Responsible Water Projects (TFRWP).[79]

WD recognized the challenge to sitting boards. He was not opposed philosophically to the existence of elected officials, but in the case of water boards, he maintained, continuity was essential because of the extensive time required to complete most projects. "Taxation without representation," he asserted, was "a fallacious charge, because the assessment capability of the conservancy district is limited by the state legislature and can be adjusted by this elected body at any time." What he feared about elected boards was the possibility of having ill-informed directors with selfish interests who wanted to use the conservancy district as a soap box for their own ideas.[80]

But he also recognized the validity of TFRWP's criticism. Conservancy districts had been too smug in assuming they knew what was best for the citizenry. They failed to explain themselves sufficiently to the public, and they were paying the consequences. WD believed the state legislature should be urged to provide judges with criteria for appointing board members, and courts should be given the specific charge of removing directors who were not doing their job. As with most challenges he faced, WD recognized the constant need for improvement. But in the case of the state's conservancy districts and the Greeley Water Board, where he already counted thirty years of experience, he was convinced that the appointment process would keep directors out of roller-coaster politics, enabling them to act responsibly as the independent bodies they were intended to be under the 1937 law.[81]

WD was not an ideologue. He had strong convictions, but they were based on practicality and what was required to improve northern Colorado's water supply. He was able to be flexible when necessary and willing to abandon certain beliefs, or commitments, if by changing course the community's water security could be assured into the future.

The city of Thornton's experience and the demise of the Two Forks project in the mid-1980s serve to illustrate this adaptability. Denver, the metropolis adjacent to Thornton, had been filing conditional water decrees in South Park and on the West Slope since experiencing exponential population growth after World War II.[82] The Two Forks Dam and Reservoir on the South Platte River was envisioned as a means of providing water for Denver and its growing suburbs. One of Denver's rights on the Blue River resulted in delivery of water to the city through the Roberts Tunnel into the South Platte River; however, Denver's consistently pugnacious approach to transmountain water diversion had alienated the West Slope, because the city never seemed interested in providing compensation in any form for water permanently removed to the Front Range. Denver's planning was also frustrated by the 1974 Poundstone Amendment, which forced the city to gain voter approval prior to annexation of land in the suburbs. Consequently, Denver and its suburbs lacked unity. When Governor Richard Lamm created the Metropolitan Water Roundtable in October 1981 to discuss how best to provide additional water and storage for the Denver metropolitan area, dissident groups on both sides of the Continental Divide voiced objections to the Two Forks Dam and Reservoir.

The Denver Water Board was the only entity with sufficient authority and financial clout to sponsor Two Forks, and no other project was seriously under consideration. The city had filed on the Two Forks reservoir site in 1902, and the U.S. Forest Service had granted a right-of-way in 1931. Even though the project would flood thirty-one miles of the South Platte River Valley, it was an ideal location for a dam and reservoir that were expected to deliver almost 100,000 acre-feet of water annually from the Colorado River plus more than a million acre-feet of storage at a cost of $370 million.[83]

For the Denver suburbs, Two Forks seemed at first to be a good way to secure their own water future. In a loosely drawn contract, Denver agreed to provide 80 percent of Two Forks water to the suburbs, where the principal growth was occurring. But agreements began to break down when the cost of Two Forks was made known and its environmental impact— including potentially adverse impacts on recreation, wildlife, and downstream users of the South Platte River—was revealed. When some of the suburbs began to withdraw their support from the project, the city of Thornton followed suit. It had a claim to the largest portion of water the suburbs were due to receive, but Mayor Margaret "Maggie" Carpenter feared the impact of the new Denver International Airport and a new highway on Thornton's escalating growth. She was afraid that the delay imposed by environmental objections would cause the price of Two Forks water to become prohibitive. In 1986, the city began clandestine moves to the north, with its eye on the farms of Weld and Larimer counties and on the direct-flow rights provided to these farms by Water Supply and Storage Company (WSSC). If Two Forks water was going to cost $10,000 per acre-foot, as Carpenter feared, and farmers would sell for $4,000 per acre-foot, Thornton would benefit by abandoning the Denver Water Board and seeking its own solution to the north.

WD was appalled by Thornton's raid on agricultural lands and the base water supply in northern Colorado, but he doubted much could be done to reverse the encroachment. "I don't like to see water go from northern Colorado agricultural lands to what is basically the city of Denver," he lamented, "but I don't see how it can be stopped."[84] He had urged Governor Roy Romer to approve Two Forks, believing that Colorado could only become a great state if there was a "dependable water supply for the Front Range and some entity, such as the Colorado Water Authority, [to] be the one entity that controls storage, has the ability to exchange water, has the financial strength to sell bonds, and [has] the foresight to develop the system as Colorado grows."[85] Two Forks fit with WD's view of good management practices in regard to water resources, and he saw that project as the best solution to keep Denver and the suburbs from drying up productive farmland.

But Thornton was doing exactly that. By the summer of 1986, Thornton's purchase of seventy farms and 40 percent of WSSC stock became public. Ultimately, the city would purchase over 100 farms and slightly more than 51 percent of WSSC stock. Thornton also purchased over 1,000 acre-feet of the Greeley–Loveland System, leading some critics to conclude they had been attacked by a municipal entity that had invaded their inner sanctum with impunity.[86]

In this overheated emotional climate, WD, as chairman of the Greeley Water and Sewage Board, was faced with the task of explaining to the elected Greeley City Council that a deal with Thornton could actually work to the benefit of Greeley residents. At a public meeting of the two boards in 1986, he urged acceptance of a proposal whereby Greeley would give up ownership of five mountain lakes,[87] high upstream on the Poudre River, in exchange for Thornton's recently purchased 1,305 acre-feet of Greeley–Loveland water on the Big Thompson River, plus $5.2 million in cash.

"This is purely an economic decision, not an emotional one," WD explained. Greeley could keep the high mountain lakes the city had purchased in the 1940s, when doubts prevailed about the C-BT ever being completed, or it could trade those lakes to Thornton to secure additional shares of water from the Greeley–Loveland system and receive enough cash to buy additional C-BT or Greeley–Loveland water. Although Greeley residents might see the lakes as a future source of the purest water and as a connection to its past, repairs to these reservoirs would cost the city up to $4 million, which would result in a 20 percent increase in water rates.[88]

"It was a hell of a deal for Greeley," WD recalled, "and something that Greeley should have done." But his logic and impeccable presentation of the facts could not overcome the emotions of the moment. Led by a local preacher, seventy-five citizens came to the meeting to protest Greeley's possible loss of "pure mountain water." They had "tears in their eyes," WD remembered, because of the potential loss of "this Christian, high-mountain storage way up there, right where the snow fell, and they couldn't get it through their heads that the only way that water could be used was through exchange."[89] The city council heard their plea and responded by voting 4–3 against the Thornton proposal. It was the only argument the Greeley Water Board had with the city council during WD's tenure as chairman, and within a year the vote was overturned. But this experience, along with the hard-fought battle over the Poudre River's "wild and scenic" designation, underscored the challenge of trying to increase water storage at a time when environmental concerns were beginning to trump the arguments expressed by proponents of long-range planning.

WD felt the frustration keenly. Rooted in the values of the Old West, he was disturbed by the region's emerging culture of opposition to water projects. Newly arrived residents voiced antagonism toward what they perceived as water grabs by water buffaloes,[90] and they made themselves heard repeatedly in different forums. Some believed that water security should be achieved by improved methods of conservation. Others were just anti-government, anti-establishment, or anti-development. Their hostility was difficult for WD to accept, but as noted by so many of his friends and colleagues, he remained a gentleman, determined to work persistently to achieve the goals in which he believed.

When the Sierra Club Legal Defense Fund filed a complaint in federal district court stating that the USDA and U.S. Department of the Interior had failed to claim federal reserved water rights for the twenty-four wilderness areas in Colorado, WD sensed the possibility of a considerable restriction on northern Colorado's water supply.[91] The 1964 Wilderness Act required the federal government to administer these areas in such a way that the public's recreational enjoyment would never be impaired by a diminution of water for the benefit of private interests. To this end, the Sierra Club was asking for a federal water right in the national forests that would protect and pre-date most of the projects that diverted and stored water for beneficial use on the Front Range.

The Sierra Club's goal was laudable, but Front Range communities dependent on transmountain water diversion were alarmed. Consistent with his general misgivings about government intervention in the management of water, WD opposed the Sierra Club's suit and joined with others on the NCWCD board of directors to support allocation of funds required to oppose the federal reserved rights claim in court. After initial victories for those who favored the Sierra Club's claim, a court of appeals ruled in 1990 against the Sierra Club, and the district court was given instructions to dismiss the complaint.[92]

Although the decision provided considerable relief from a potential
threat to the NCWCD and other entities diverting water from national
forests, the goal of bringing Denver and the Colorado River Water Conservancy District (River District) to the table to effect an agreement that would
allow completion of the Windy Gap project proved even more challenging
to WD. Known as the Four Party Agreement of 1986, the consensus WD
obtained among representatives of four stakeholders representing East
and West slopes stands alone as an example of his ability to achieve agreement when all parties had practically given up hope.

Since 1981, the NCWCD and the NCWCD Municipal Subdistrict (MSD)
had been trying to figure out how they could substitute a commitment to
build a compensatory reservoir for the River District with a cash settlement.
The Azure Reservoir site on the Colorado River, preferred by the River
District, appeared increasingly problematic because of environmental
restrictions and the high cost of rerouting Union Pacific rail lines through
Gore Canyon. River District attorney John Carlson counseled his client
not to let the NCWCD–MSD off the hook, but River District board members
were increasingly interested in owning and operating their own reservoir.
Because he was so well-connected and attuned to how organizations worked,
WD sensed a window of opportunity that might be used to everyone's
benefit, including Denver's, at a time when the city was struggling to keep
the Two Forks project on track.[93]

When attorneys representing the NCWCD–MSD and the River District
tried to work out a compromise in regard to the mitigating reservoir,
negotiations became contentious. In his role as chairman of the MSD and
a director of the NCWCD, WD began making telephone calls to individual
River District board members. He believed a deal could be brokered, and
he put his integrity on the line to suggest a process that required considerable trust. At a National Water Resources Association meeting in San Diego
in 1985, he obtained agreement from both boards to meet at a later date
without benefit of counsel on either side. It was an unprecedented move,
but it represented WD's conviction that both sides wanted a deal that
could be worked out if common sense and good faith were allowed to
replace acrimony and litigious behavior.

The essence of the Four Party Agreement, officially signed in December
1986, was crafted at a meeting in Kremmling, Colorado, near the site of what
would be the Wolford Mountain Reservoir on Muddy Creek. Grand County,

which was represented on the River District board, preferred the Muddy Creek site over the Azure site because of its accessibility and recreational possibilities. But the real achievement in bringing about an agreement between the East and West slopes occurred when the Denver Water Board (DWB) expressed an interest in providing funds to assist in construction of the reservoir if they could, in return, use a greater volume of water from Dillon Reservoir via the Roberts Tunnel.[94] The DWB also hoped to curtail West Slope criticism of Two Forks. The lack of unanimous support for Two Forks in Colorado's Washington delegation, and the fact that the decade of the 1980s was the wettest in history, combined to undermine Denver's case that Two Forks was desired and needed statewide.

It was WD's keen sense of opportunity and his passion for working with people that accomplished the Four Party Agreement between the NCWCD, River District, MSD, and DWB. He was ready when the challenge presented itself, and he had the connections with Denver and the West Slope to pull it off. As onetime CSU president Albert Yates remarked, WD's leadership was manifest in the fact that all adversaries claimed him as one of their own. In addition, Yates noted, he had an "absolute commitment to scholarship," not in the university sense, in which publishing prevents perishing, but in the sense that he communicated a special respect for both the data and the people involved in negotiations, and he was able to verbalize this respect as he worked toward common goals and successful conclusions. "We use the term 'Renaissance Man' somewhat loosely when we speak of talented leaders," Yates said, "but WD had the depth and breadth of knowledge that earned him respect from all sides of a controversy, and he did that by reflecting a mediating ability that created trust. The foundation of that trust was integrity, and WD at his core was a man of integrity. There are only a few leaders whom we can truly designate standard bearers."[95]

True to his reputation and amicable demeanor, WD complimented everyone involved for their good work in achieving the Four Party Agreement. At the 1995 dedication he said, "The Wolford Mountain Project is to Windy Gap what Green Mountain Reservoir was to the C-BT" almost sixty years earlier.[96] In other words, it was a milestone in successful negotiation. Although he had not participated directly in the 1930s negotiations between East Slope and West Slope that made C-BT construction possible, WD had learned much from that history. When it was his turn to bring adversaries together for an equally critical deliberation, he acted like a statesman. Entering his ninth decade, he had earned the public's respect. He was honored in many circles, and he was seen as a leader who consistently promoted the public good.

CHAPTER 7

Statesmanship

*In spite of illness, in spite of even the arch enemy sorrow, one can remain
alive long past the usual date of disintegration if one is unafraid of change,
insatiable in intellectual curiosity, interested in big things, and happy in
small ways.*

—Edith Wharton, *A Backward Glance*

Achieving the Four Party Agreement muted any disappointment WD
experienced from the sale of the Farr farms and feedlots. His zest for life
and the realization he probably knew more about cattle, agriculture, banking,
and water than most people in positions of responsibility sustained him.
He was not arrogant, but he exuded confidence. During his last two decades,
he enjoyed the role of senior statesman, frequently sharing his vision of
the future with those who sought his advice. Approaching his eightieth
birthday, WD's leadership talents were sought by groups needing direction,
and his support was often requested by those aspiring to political office.
He saw himself as an amalgam of consultant and historian. "I still know
more about [certain things] than anybody else," he said, "and I can help
out here and there. . . . I can always point out what might be a better way
than somebody [who] is thinking short-term. Or, I can give the reason why
something is the way it is."[1] Far from viewing himself as an oracle, WD
viewed the world pragmatically: he could assist people who were fearful
of change, and he could provide guidance to those willing to listen.

William Haw from National Farms, Inc., of Kansas City was one of many
who heeded his advice. National Farms had purchased the Farr feedlot
east of Greeley, and WD suggested that if they would also purchase the yet

unsold 70 Ranch, it could provide National Farms with a perfect conduit for feeder cattle destined for the feedlot. Haw agreed, and the sale was consummated. Only a few months later, however, the Bass Brothers, owners of National Farms, authorized establishment of the largest farrow-to-finish hog farm in the world on the 70 Ranch. The $50 million operation was designed to hold 16,800 sows, which were expected to produce 6,000 finished hogs weekly.

Even though the proposed site of the hog farm was downwind and fifteen miles east, some Greeley citizens feared the impact of strong odors and the potential for pollution of groundwater supplies. Scores of petitions were circulated against the project, and a lawsuit was filed in state district court initiated by Adolph Coors and Philip Anschutz, both of whom owned adjacent lands they used for hunting and entertainment. Anschutz's Eagle Nest Ranch bordered the 70 Ranch on the east, where prevailing winds could transport unpleasant odors, so he led the challenge in court against National Farms' right to build a hog farm without a special state permit. Finding no violation of existing laws, the district court judge ruled against him. Construction began in 1990, with plans for completion of the facility in two years.[2]

WD now found himself in the position of defending an industry that had been increasingly competitive with cattle. For years he had preached to the cattle industry that they needed to consolidate, improve breeds, and form alliances to better compete with poultry and pork. Now, separated from his own farming and cattle feeding operations, he accepted the role of consultant to National Farms. "I know about the [70] Ranch," he wrote his good friend Bruno Borhy in Italy, "and [I know] how to build things, so I am their ramrod."[3] Because he had always been essentially a business-man who believed agricultural enterprises had to consolidate to survive rising labor, machinery, and grain prices, WD viewed the hog farm as a good example of concentrated agricultural production, serving the best interests of the food-buying public.

"You have to understand," John Farr commented, "Dad saw Weld County as an agricultural zone and having a pig farm made sense to him. . . . In my view, he saw the big picture, and that was food production."[4] In fact, WD openly promoted the National Farms operation. He assisted in conver-sations with county commissioners, hosted tour busses for the public, and explained his conclusions in a carefully reasoned essay in the *Greeley Tribune* without ever attacking Anschutz or his cohorts directly. He wrote,

> Opponents of the swine operation are asking that National Hog Farms be made to use a secondary wastewater treatment system similar to the City of Greeley's First Avenue Plant. On the surface, this sounds like a sound solution, but the facts are different. Wastewater plants discharge directly into the river with a permit from the state to do so. The discharge must meet stream standards of nitrates content. Municipalities legally dump nitrates into the water. To ask National Hog farms to do likewise is not a solution, it simply adds to an already troubling nitrate problem. . . . The only way to rid water of nitrates is through oxygenation and plant uptake. National Hog Farms incorporates both of these methods into its water treatment system [two steel tanks, each with a capacity of 1.2 million gallons]. First the effluent is oxygenated, then it is pumped through center pivot sprinklers, using very light applications over 2,000 acres of grass. . . . These light applications allow both the native and planted grasses to use all the nitrogen as a necessary nutrient source. . . . No water returns to the river.[5]

But WD's support for National Hog Farms, based on science and his vision of what was best for the community, provoked criticism. The culture of northern Colorado had changed. Denver International Airport south of Greeley and east of Denver was scheduled for completion in 1993. Population had begun to drift south from Greeley toward the airport, and some experts, including WD, saw northern Colorado as the perfect locus for a burgeoning agricultural trade that would connect Denver with Pacific Rim countries.[6] Public hostility in Greeley regarding potentially increased animal odors and contamination of groundwater fanned the spark of animosity into a roaring fire. Organizations such as Protect Our Water and the Platte River Environmental Conservation Organization—allegedly financed by Anschutz—held rallies and demanded laws to restrict hog farms. As recalled by *Greeley Tribune* reporter Bill Jackson, "WD was the first one to stand up at meetings and say, 'This [hog farm] is good for Colorado. It's good for Kersey and good for Weld County. And this is a top-notch operation.' He never wavered, never changed that attitude."

Jackson said that when Anschutz's men argued that the hog farm was

> stinking up the area out there, WD responded, "Hey, let's go out
> there. Let's take a drive and I'll show you." And we did. You could get
> up close to one of those tanks holding all that effluent [from the hogs]
> and you couldn't smell a thing until you got right up underneath.
> [Anschutz and Coors] had their little playground out there, and by
> God, they were going to do everything they could to protect that. . . .
> The saying around here was that [the controversy] between National
> Farms and the forces of Anschutz and Coors was nothing more than a
> pissing contest between billionaires.[7]

In fact, hog farm opponents had both money and influence. After opponents spent two years trying to get the state legislature to pass laws restricting hog farm operations, in 1998 the Colorado Legislative Assembly was able to agree on Amendment 14, a ballot initiative that was submitted to the public and approved. The amendment contained new rules and regulations requiring commercial hog facilities to obtain special permits, and it gave local governments enhanced authority to control odors and waste disposal. As a result, National Hog Farms faced unacceptable expenditures that forced the company to shut its doors in 2000. Having already spent millions on legal fees, Bill Haw decided to terminate the operation rather than continue to fight local regulations. The Colorado Department of Public Health and Environment saw this as a victory, as did the Anschutz camp, but the jobs lost to Weld County and the opportunity for local farmers to sell feed had disappeared. Haw claimed bitterly that the hog farm had never received a validated odor complaint and that CSU scientists had rated his operation "the best in the state."[8] But the public's perception of animal-related pollution, the political clout of monied interests, and poor management on Haw's part combined to run the hogs out of town.[9]

WD maintained considerable respect for the Bass Brothers and was pleased when National Farms hired Dick Farr's son, RD, to work at the feedlot.[10] WD never criticized the hog operation, but as with other aspects of change in agriculture with which he was very familiar, the social and economic forces that combined to eliminate the hog farm signaled another shift in the landscape that required adaptation. WD knew it was time to accept what had happened and move on. He had done what he thought was right to preserve an important economic engine for Weld County, and he had formed his opinions after studying the scientific data. He lost the battle but not because of skewed data or personal bias. Haw failed to manage the facility as promised, resulting in environmental damage to the area. WD had provided selfless leadership based on a factual understanding of a complex problem. If any criticism should attach to his advocacy, it would have to focus on his tendency to trust other people too much.

A few months before his eightieth birthday in 1990, and shortly after his thoughtful essay supporting National Farms was printed in the *Greeley Tribune*, WD joined son John on a fishing trip to Argentina. Responsibilities at home had decreased considerably, and it was time to unwind and go fishing with his oldest son.

The two men flew to Buenos Aires then boarded a flight to Esquel, a small town in the northwest corner of the Province of Chubut in Argentine Patagonia. Esquel is set in a colorful amphitheater, surrounded by extinct volcanoes. For more than half a century, the town has been connected to the outside world by a narrow gauge railroad known locally as *La Trochita*, the Old Patagonian Express,[11] which was part of an Argentine rail system designed to connect rural areas to the capital. Esquel is a paradise for fisherman, hikers, and skiers. It was also an ideal site for father and son to share the sport they both enjoyed in an atmosphere that inspired long talks during secluded sessions on the river, angling for trout.[12]

The trout proved elusive at first, but John and WD were enchanted by the rivers and an environment conducive to long talks. After five days in and around Esquel, the men headed for San Carlos de Bariloche, where WD had spent a memorable time with Judy on a livestock tour. He was saddened to see the resort hotel boarded up, a victim of Argentina's ongoing problems with inflation and general economic instability, and he remarked on the unfortunate tendency of people to be shortsighted in planning for the future.

From Bariloche, they drove north 155 miles to Junín. First fall colors had begun to paint the landscape as they descended into the Chime-huín Valley, where six streams pour down from the Andes to create ideal conditions for fly fishermen. Brown and rainbow trout were so plentiful that John and WD managed to catch and release over a hundred fish in one day, some weighing upwards of three pounds. It was a spectacular experience, accented by a float trip and another day of phenomenal fishing. WD commented that he had not slept in a tent since hunting with

Andy Russell almost fifty years earlier in Canada. He was also reminded of the rustic life he had so enjoyed during two summers of working cattle as a teenager north of Hayden, Colorado, in the 1920s. He and John talked at length about family, the indigenous peoples of Argentina, the lack of irrigation in farming communities, the traditional Argentine barbecued meal called *asado*, and the crystal clear waters of the valley. WD was optimistic about the future. He saw a bright time ahead, but the joy of meeting new people and experiencing the Patagonian culture was somewhat diminished by the catastrophic circumstances of the collapsed Argentine economy.

Since World War II, Argentina had been through almost a dozen cycles of hyperinflation and reform. None of the reforms had been able to keep inflation under control for more than a few years. The central bank never seemed to have a solution, except to crank up the presses and print more money. As inflation increased, productivity declined. The public's attitude was a combination of a desperate wish to eliminate inflation along with a deep-seated cynicism about the prospects for effective anti-inflationary policies. For the most part, the monetary system was defunct. Local banks were unwilling to make loans, and savings accounts were virtually eliminated. Commerce was practically at a standstill.

WD recalled how important a strong banking system had been in the development of northern Colorado. Communities suffer when currency is unstable and when local banks lack confidence and capital to make appropriate loans. Ever since 1894, when his grandfather (Billy) had been invited to join the board of the Union Bank of Greeley, the Farrs had been at the center of Weld County banking. Harry Farr was a director of Greeley National Bank and the First National Bank of Denver, and he was on the board of the Federal Reserve Bank in Kansas City. WD followed in lockstep, serving as director of the Greeley National Bank for forty-one years and the U.S. National Bank in Denver for twenty years. "Through the bank," WD commented, "you could help your town grow."[13] But sometimes the demands on small banks far exceeded their ability to satisfy local needs even in a stable economy.

Comparing his own experiences to Argentina's plight, WD shared with John his pleasure over WR Farr's recent appointment to a position in a Colorado bank that was part of Affiliated Bankshares of Colorado (ABC).

This good news, that another Farr had made a move into banking,[14] inspired WD to recount his own role in the formation of ABC some years earlier. He still believed in 1990, as he had in the 1960s, that the strength of local communities would continue to be inextricably connected to the power, independence, and security of local banks. But the problem for small banks in Colorado had been that until the mid-1960s, they were prevented from forming conglomerates. They all had correspondent relationships with bigger banks in Denver, but Colorado was a "unit banking state," which meant that mergers and branch banking were illegal. The only way small banks could match the capital and loan capability of larger banks was to join together under holding company laws recently approved by the Federal Reserve System.

ABC came together under these laws. After witnessing firsthand the debacle of Argentina's failed banking system and how the financial disintegration was punishing the Argentine people, WD recalled the formation of ABC and why it had succeeded. John reminded him of a hunting trip they had taken in Wyoming in 1969, when the weather had been unexpectedly mild. Instead of hunting, they had rested on a log and talked. WD wanted to inform John about a novel concept to which he had been privy because of his position as chairman of the board of the Greeley National Bank. Several officers from the First National Bank of Boulder had come to Greeley National to explore the possibility of forming a holding company. WD and the Greeley bank executives were interested. They outlined a plan whereby banks in several communities would come together, exchange old stock for new, and form a holding company in which each bank would maintain its independence but would become part of a larger entity, thus making possible larger loans, shared expertise, and related business activities.

It was an exciting concept, but it was brand new. When WD shared the details with John during the course of that Wyoming hunt, he swore his son to secrecy. Shortly thereafter, banks in Boulder, Greeley, Loveland, and Colorado Springs embraced the plan. Denver already had its own holding companies, and some of the outlying community banks had considered joining them. But loss of identity and the fear of being dictated to by larger, more powerful institutions discouraged smaller banks from making a deal with the "big boys."[15]

ABC became a reality with thirteen banks in the spring of 1970.[16] Board members represented each member bank. After appropriate deliberations, they selected WD as their first chairman, a position he held for thirteen years. Although WD never sang his own praises, especially when reminiscing with his family, others have noted that WD was voted chairman because of his exemplary financial talents, his unselfish community orientation, his foresight, and his well-known integrity. "I have often said," remarked Leo Hill, ABC's first chief executive officer, "that if you're going to pick out somebody to be associated with, [WD] Farr would be the person. He was so genuine, honest, and so bright, and he was anxious to do things that would be helpful. . . . He and Judy both were just the nicest people you could possibly be associated with." In addition, Hill recalled, WD exuded the finest qualities of leadership: "He had the ability to put a consensus together, to cover the facts, cover the alternatives . . . very unselfishly, making it very easy for people to come to conclusions. He was magnificent in a quiet way at board meetings. He didn't dominate or dictate in any way; he led. He would tell you honestly how he felt about things, but he wasn't one to force people. He really led them here, and we all loved him."[17]

In a little over a year, the holding company was able to declare a 17.5 percent dividend.[18] Twenty-nine banks ultimately joined ABC, and the communities they represented were able to deal with the growth pressures and business expansion of the 1970s and 1980s without having to spend too much time in Denver, Omaha, Chicago, or New York requesting loans. "There was never anything but complete support for [WD]," Hill recalled. "[ABC] made it possible for us all to serve our communities in a more aggressive way. We knew where things were going. The people who really needed significant support, we could provide it to them very easily."[19] Right up until Banc One purchased ABC in 1993,[20] the working arrangement among member banks was outstanding, providing borrowers and lenders the kind of financial security and cooperation necessary for consumer confidence.

The inflation and absence of such growth conditions in Argentina stood out by contrast. They provided a context for WD's recollection of ABC's success, but they did not dampen the pleasures of a warm father–son adventure on the trout streams of Patagonia. The Argentine experience simply sharpened WD's awareness of the power of banks to drive the economic engine of any growth-oriented community. He and John continued their conversations as they flew home. WD remained sanguine about the U.S. economy, the increasing globalization of the world, and Colorado's role as exporter of agricultural commodities. His optimism was unflagging. For John, the trip stimulated a desire to return annually. "Argentina became for me what the Dean River was for Dad," he recalled. "The relationship with the people and the fishing were all similar. We both shared each other's realm. That was a special bond."[21]

That bond would grow even stronger when they landed in Denver. Judy was not well. For several years she had shown signs of memory loss and confusion, the telltale indicators of Alzheimer's disease. John's wife, Leslie, stayed with Judy while John and WD were in Argentina. The two women toured Taos, Santa Fe, and Breckenridge, and Judy felt secure, "always cooperative and charming," Leslie recalled, "as though she was trying very hard to be my perfect guest. I was thankfully appreciative. Even while fighting Alzheimer's, she still had her dignity and her pride."[22]

Judy had much to be proud of. Her life as wife, mother, community builder, athlete, philanthropist, educator, and family executive was exemplary. "She was enchanting," Greeley banker Larry Scott remembered, "and could have been the 'grande dame' of Greeley. Everyone cared about her."[23] She spearheaded the 1966 initiative that brought into existence the University of Northern Colorado Foundation.[24] As first president and chair of the board of directors, she led that organization for ten years (1966–1977) through demanding times. The university was attempting to develop an outreach program in other parts of the nation and world without sufficient comprehension of the potential for jealousies within the university and the financial resources required to succeed. "We all could have fallen apart," Scott noted, "but Judy kept us at the task, kept us working with it." Her relaxed leadership style, what Scott referred to as "casual consensus," was Judy's way of making everyone feel comfortable, "encouraging everyone to visit and talk, sort of like being in her front room, not really at a board meeting, until everyone had talked themselves out. Then she would call for a vote, and lo and behold, we would all generally agree on what we might have disapproved half an hour before. She did it so casually and easily, we didn't know what was happening. It was fun to watch."[25]

Judy and WD were a strong team. She championed his endeavors and cultivated close personal relationships. She knew how to bring people together and get them to cooperate.[26] She treated everyone individually and earned their respect. From behind the scenes, she provided assistance to groups and organizations, focusing especially on education and those less fortunate in the community who required intervention. She led the parent–teachers' council four times in twenty years, chaired a committee to study foreign language in elementary schools, and promoted efforts to bring national recognition to the University of Northern Colorado (UNC). "When we had the grand opening of the James A. Michener Library," UNC vice president for public affairs Gilbert Hause recalled that "Michener was reluctant to attend and make a speech," but Judy made contact with Michener's wife, Mari, who was charmed by Judy and prevailed on her husband to participate.[27]

With the influx of Hispanic workers into the Greeley area, Judy became involved in the Weld Information and Referral Services (WIRS). Established by the First Congregational Church, WIRS soon became a community organization to which Judy gave much of her time as a volunteer and as president of the board for three years in the early 1980s. WIRS's main function was to connect people in need with appropriate aid agencies, and as Weld County agriculture and meat packing expanded, the work of WIRS became increasingly valuable.

Judy was smart and sensitive to the community's needs. Her attraction to Republican politics matured as WD's interests and influence advanced around the country. She was a delegate to the Republican National Convention, a precinct chairwoman, president of the Weld County Republican Women, and a guest at the Nixon White House soon after WD stepped down as president of the National Cattlemen's Association. "She got to be a pretty good Republican," WD said. "In fact, they wanted her to run for the [state] senate, [but] that part of politics she didn't like."[28]

What Judy did enjoy were the many trips to foreign countries with WD; the gardening and orchids she gifted to people; the opportunity to host large family gatherings for home-cooked meals; fishing trips to Encampment,

which she referred to as "my town";[29] her Philanthropic Educational Organization (PEO) sisters;[30] the Social Science Club of Greeley, where she
presented numerous talks; and Denver Broncos football games. Judy was
an athlete herself, but she especially savored the Sunday outings to Denver
with WD and other family members for home games. They had season
tickets under a balcony, where they were protected from rain and sun. It
was a great place to see and be seen, as Larry Scott remembered, and
every time the home team scored, WD and Judy would wrap up in a hug
and kiss. "It wasn't just a cheerleader hug or a Hollywood hug," Scott remembered. "It was a hug hug, six points worth of hug, and it was wonderful.
I'm sure they were unaware that I was observing with a big smile. They
related to each other so well."[31]

Judy also loved to hunt. She realized early on that hunting and fishing
were enormously important to her husband. "If I wanted to be part of this
family," she told her friend Tate Todd, "I had to learn to hunt and fish
and camp."[32] But the experience was something she anticipated more
keenly with each passing year. When duck or pheasant season opened,
she was known to take WR out of school so they could enjoy the camara-
derie and success of being among the first to shoot game birds. She also
kept a shotgun in the car when she traveled through the prairies east of
Greeley. On one occasion, while returning from a PEO meeting in Sterling
with her mother-in-law in the car, Judy stopped along the road and, while
dressed in her best go-to-meeting clothes and high heels, shot a couple
of pheasants and continued the drive back to Greeley with dinner in hand.
To some extent she was a tomboy, Sharon Farr recalled. "She was really
athletic, but she was feminine. . . . The last thing a woman would want to
be when she grew up in those days was a jock. You wanted to be a feminine lady, but she had the athletic ability [and] loved the outdoors and
gardening. She wasn't into sewing, weaving, painting or those sorts of
things. She was into outdoor stuff."[33]

That interest meant a lot to WD. For many years Judy accompanied
him on elk hunts to Budge's White River Resort in the Flat Tops Wilder-
ness Area, north of the Colorado River. Having made his first hunt from
Budge's in 1934, WD returned on many occasions with Judy and the boys.
In 1984, after a five-year interlude, he again made reservations, inviting
WR and John to join them. It was a bad year for hunting, WD recalled.

WD and Judy Farr, ca 1980. Courtesy of the Farr family.

"We had about a foot of snow up there and it was cold. Judy was seventy-two years old, and she was still up there riding horseback in the snow. She didn't try to hunt, but she liked it so well that she went just to be with us and to have the thrill. . . . What she loved most was to be on top of the mountain and see first light."[34]

Perhaps WD was describing the spirituality he and Judy shared. They were solid members of the First Congregational Church in Greeley and frequent donors. Because they traveled a great deal, Sunday attendance was irregular, but Al Slighter, the church's senior minister from 1975 to 1992, described the Farrs as loyal, faithful in worship, and generous to the church. "Their spirituality was very much the golden rule," Slighter said. WD often described himself as a fatalist, Slighter added, but "I don't think he meant predestination, [the idea] that everything in life is pre-determined. It's more like the fatalism of servicemen who believe that if the bullet has [their] name on it, it's their time to go." More to the point, WD and Judy focused on what they could do to make their community and the world a better place, treating everyone with equal respect and dignity. "The people who worked for the Farrs knew that," Slighter noted. "Regardless of their status or power, all were treated equally. . . . The family went through some tough times," but Judy and WD refused to lament the discouragements, preferring to move ahead with the cards they were dealt, making things better, and improving life for themselves and others. "They didn't spend a lot of time talking about [those] things, whining, or having any sense of self-pity." They just accepted the way life was and set their minds to improving the things over which they had some control. That philosophy, along with their love of the outdoors, was, in effect, their most profound spiritual belief.[35]

Judy complemented her spiritual side with a quick wit and an impish sense of humor. As a young lady, she insisted on being called "Bill," and when she wrote home in the early years of her marriage, she signed her letters that way. "I never knew her by any other name," recalled her younger sister. "She wouldn't answer unless we called her Bill. She was going to be Bill, and that was that."[36] She just had a twinkle in her eye and she enjoyed being unpredictable. When asked why she stopped at four children, she replied, "Because every fifth child born in the world is Chinese." When Halloween came around, she once dressed herself and her boys like bums and went around the neighborhood asking for money. At a PEO meeting in her home, she gave everyone in attendance little seed packages that were supposed to be flowers. To everyone's surprise, the seeds produced carrots and radishes. She loved to play practical jokes on people, and she was a good sport when she was the object of a joke. On a trip to the Colorado River, a guide told her how the fish had developed the ability to swim backward to keep sand out of their eyes. When she recounted this bit of information to the rest of the family, they broke up in laughter. Of course, it became a family joke.[37]

But Judy's vivacious approach to life only added to the admiration people felt for her. Her reputation as an outstanding contributor to the community was first recognized in 1970, when the Farrs were honored as Greeley's "Centennial Family" during the celebration of the community's first one hundred years. In 1977 Judy received the Bill Hartman award for significant service to UNC. In 1983, she was chosen for the Greeley Sertoma Club's Service to Mankind Award in recognition of her involvement in community activities. And in December 1988, at the winter graduation ceremonies, UNC president Bob Dickerson awarded Judy and WD honorary doctorates: to Judy, a doctorate in humane letters; to WD, a doctorate in laws. It was the first time in the ninety-nine-year history of the university that honorary doctorates were awarded to a husband and wife. The honor was a measure of the community's respect for the Farrs. It acclaimed their role as disinterested promoters of the public good and leaders who worked for the benefit of others without narrow partisanship. In other words, *statesmanship*!

The university bestowed the degrees at a time Judy was beginning to experience the early signs of Alzheimer's disease. WD did not immediately recognize the seriousness of her condition, but over the next four or five years it became obvious she needed full-time medical care. For WD, the gradual loss of his partner, best friend, hunting and fishing buddy, and family advocate was overwhelming. Her life had been intertwined in his for almost sixty years. But practical and realistic as always, WD dealt with the circumstances as they developed, and he tried to maintain routines and habits he thought Judy would appreciate. Her doctor prescribed a lot of medications, and WD would count them out for her every day. "He would talk to her like a stern uncle," Judy's sister remembered, "and she took the pills even though she didn't want to. He was just so good to her. She had shrunk a lot when I was visiting, and when WD came downstairs and knelt in front of Judy so she could tie his tie, that was a tear jerker."[38]

Meanwhile, WD was dealing with his own health issues. Not long after his return from Argentina in 1990, he was driving home from Denver when he suddenly experienced a clouding of eyesight in the center of his vision. He could see laterally if he turned his head, but frontal sight had disappeared. It took him thirty minutes to go the remaining ten miles, and he never drove again. The diagnosis was macular degeneration. For a man who was such a student and who read everything he could get his hands on, this diagnosis was a blow. But it was not a defeat. Machines were available for enlarging print. WD bought three of them, one for his office on the sixth floor of the First National Bank building, where he had located after the feedlot was sold, and two others for his homes in Greeley and Encampment, Wyoming. He read headlines, a few articles in newspapers, and occasionally a book. During an interview in 2003, he said he had read *The Silver Fox of the Rockies*, the biography of another Greeley water pioneer, Delph Carpenter. "It's hard for me," he confessed. "Took me a month. It's just slow going."[39]

But WD refused to be deterred by physical adversity. He hired a driver, went to his office every day, continued his work on the Greeley Water Board and the NCWCD, and lent his stature as one of Greeley's leading citizens to a campaign that opposed moving the county's administrative offices to north Greeley. The Concerned Citizens for Weld County's Future committee chose WD as president. In newspaper editorials and speeches, the committee contested a four-to-one vote by Weld County commissioners to move the offices away from downtown over a period of fifteen years.

The fur that flew back and forth from June through October 1991 brought out jealousies and past grievances, accusations of heavy handedness by landowners in downtown Greeley, and suggestions that the county commissioners and their supporters had distorted the facts and overturned the democratic process. There were even suggestions of racism from Hispanic groups who believed the Concerned Citizens Committee was trying to keep county offices from relocating in an area that was good enough for Mexican families but not worthy of government administration.[40]

It was a shouting match on both sides, and it seemed to bring out the worst in everyone. When a vote was taken, almost 60 percent of the eligible electorate decided the commissioners should be allowed to go forward with their plan. The Concerned Citizens group was defeated. "It's too bad people made that decision," WD said. "They will live to regret it. When Weld moves its offices, you're going to destroy the image of a real class community."[41]

WD received his share of censure. Ken Monfort's widow, Myra, accused him of using a negative approach, launching personal attacks, and ignoring the facts. Roy Moser, a former county commissioner, demanded an apology from WD for "stooping to ignominious criticism of our elected officials, when all they have done is to proceed to serve as they were elected to do."[42]

In fact, WD's position was consistent with his long-standing belief that business had to be vibrant at the core of any community. He had lived long enough to appreciate the impact to the downtown area when the I-25 corridor was constructed west of Greeley and when the Greeley mall siphoned off additional businesses to the south. Removing the major center of county business to the north of the city seemed to him to invite further evisceration of the downtown area. But the poor organization of Concerned Citizens, coupled with the public's feeling that the old guard was just trying to protect its downtown property investment, combined to produce a defeat at the polls.

WD was disappointed, but he had no reason to doubt the principles in which he believed. Eight months earlier the Denver Chamber of Commerce had recognized his business acumen by inducting him as the first living member of the Colorado Business Hall of Fame. Noting the importance of "strength of character and steadfast integrity," the chamber named the late Spencer Penrose (Cripple Creek mining baron), Benjamin H. Eaton (Colorado governor), John Evans (Colorado governor), and Jesse Shwayder (founder of Samsonite) as fellow members of the 1991 class of inductees. Four years later, WD was inducted into the Colorado Agricultural Hall of Fame because of his significant contributions to agriculture in the state and nation. His statesmanship continued to be acknowledged, even as his active role in agriculture, banking, and water development had begun to decline. But his youthful spirit was indomitable. At age eighty-five, with his physical abilities somewhat compromised by macular degeneration, WD invited sons John and WR to join him for an expedition to the Dean River in British Columbia to fish for big, hard-fighting steelhead trout. It was the summer of 1995.

The Dean River is the shrine of steelheading. It is home to chinook and coho salmon, as well as the sea-run rainbow trout (steelheads) that can weigh over twenty pounds and are considered "tackle busters" when hooked on a fly rod. WD first experienced the Lower Dean River when he flew there with Robby Stewart in his floatplane before any accommodations were available. After pulling up to a sandbar on the river, they fished long enough, and with enough success, to recognize that the Lower Dean could be a major attraction to sportsmen. With his partner, Dick Blewett, Stewart returned the following year to build a tent camp on the river. Over the years, the Lower Dean River Lodge came into being, along with cabins raised up on large timbers so flood waters would pass below the main structures during spring runoff.

For anyone with a love of the outdoors and a passion for fishing, the Lower Dean River is paradise. Located in a wilderness setting with the bay of the Dean Channel not far to the west, the fishing camp is surrounded by mountains of the British Coastal Range, most with year-round snow and some reaching an altitude of over 8,000 feet. The natural beauty of the valley, combined with potentially great fishing, made the Dean River a coveted destination for WD and his family for many years.

About 5:30 on a July morning in 1995, WD stepped from his cabin on the way to the bath house. Because of impaired vision, he failed to properly calculate the distance from the raised cabin floor to the ground. WR, who was rooming with him, heard a thud. WD had missed a step and had fallen back against the large timbers supporting the cabin, shattering his shoulder blade, cracking several ribs, and breaking his right hip where he hit the ground. WR shouted for John. With additional assistance from Rob Stewart (the founder's son) and Dr. Robert Rothwell, also a guest at the lodge, the men placed WD on a recently acquired back board. They took him to the main lodge, where WD expressed sorrow at having started the day badly, urged everyone to go fishing, and admonished John to get his pants on.[43]

Stewart called for a medivac helicopter. It arrived mid-morning, landed on the only clearing available at the river's edge, and whisked WD off to

WD Farr fishing on the Dean River, British Columbia, Canada. Courtesy of the Farr family.

Bella Coola for X rays. A doctor determined the extent of WD's injuries and made arrangements for him to be flown to Vancouver General Hospital. A team of doctors was ordered to perform surgery, but because WD's condition was not critical, he had to wait his turn while more seriously injured patients were treated. Surgery finally commenced at nine o'clock Friday evening, thirty-nine hours after the accident occurred.

The long wait was difficult for everyone, but the Canadian doctors repaired the damage expertly; total hospital charges were $300. John stayed with his father in Vancouver, while WR flew back to Greeley to make arrangements for WD's return. He contacted Kenny Monfort in regard to possible flight arrangements. Kenny referred WR to son Charlie, who was in partnership with Jerry McMorris as co-owner of the Colorado Rockies. They agreed to fly the Rockies' plane to Vancouver with Sharon Farr, WR's wife, on board. With less than one-half inch to spare, hospital staff loaded WD on a backboard into the small jet aircraft, along with John and Sharon, for the flight home. "He was alert on the entire trip," John recalled. "I described the rugged country we flew over and what Encampment looked like from forty thousand feet. He was fascinated to hear my description of the cabins, the valley below, and everything I could see from that elevation. Twenty minutes after passing Encampment, we were preparing to land at Crozier Field in Greeley."[44]

The return flight in the Rockies' jet was expensive—$12,000—but as a favor to the Farr family, the cost was half the usual charge. WR did not even consider a flight on commercial airlines because of WD's condition, and he turned down a no-cost offer to fly his father back in a twin-engine propeller aircraft. The time involved would have caused his father considerable discomfort. WD arrived at the North Colorado Medical Center ready to begin two weeks of rehabilitation. He amazed the doctors with his resiliency, his desire to get healed, and his gratitude for the quality of care he received. In a letter to Dr. Judith Vaughn, head of the rehabilitation department, WD expressed his thanks and included a check for $100 for "some equipment your aids [may] need in the exercise area or something like the plants that the patients helped water and trim."[45]

His outspoken appreciation extended beyond the hospital. He wrote thank you letters to each person who sent a card or flowers or called him in the hospital; he thanked Dr. Rothwell for his timely advice right after the accident and expressed his appreciation to Charlie Monfort for arranging the flight to and from Vancouver. He had a lot of time to think during his stay in the hospital and the month of rehabilitation that followed, but what he said to his sons probably reflects his deepest emotions:

> I have often told you I am a fatalist [because] I believe some things are meant to happen at certain times. . . . That Thursday, Friday, and Saturday were three tough days for all of us. Thank God you were both there, or it would have been more difficult. . . . Between the two of you, everything turned out extremely well. . . . I am certain this unfortunate accident has drawn the three of us closer together than ever before. We all supported each other. . . . Thank you both for all you did to get me out of a bad situation.[46]

He probably knew he would never return again to the Dean River, but it was hard to give up the hope. "I don't know what to say about 1996," he wrote Rob Stewart. "When I can't step off a step without half killing myself, maybe the good Lord is saying, 'You need to slow down.' For the time being, I would like to hold the reservation. I am not convinced that I want to give up a yearly event that has meant so much for so many years."[47] By the middle of September, he was spending afternoons in his office and getting around with the aid of a four-legged cane, but he admitted that he hurt.

Four months later his self-evaluation was slightly modified. He was still having trouble getting back a good walking stride. The five-eighths-inch lift he wore in his right shoe was a reminder that the injured right leg was shorter and would continue to create some instability. He had had his share of great trips to the Dean River, he wrote Dick Blewett. It was time to recognize that he would not be coming again.[48] The decision was difficult. He had begun fishing the Dean River with Judy and remembered that year as "the greatest thrill I ever had."[49] Judy was a real fisherwoman. There were times she outfished WD, Rob Stewart recalled, "because women pay more attention to the guide, and because fish have an unusual sense of smell."[50]

It was sad for WD to admit to himself that the Dean River era was over, but his enthusiasm for life remained undiminished. In addition, the recognition he was receiving as elder statesman continued to grow. Still healing from his accident, he spoke at the dedication of Wolford Mountain Reservoir as the East Slope representative for the agreement that brought formal recognition to the Windy Gap project. WD had been the primary driver behind Windy Gap, and he had persevered as its leader through years of frustration. Acknowledging that the East Slope–West Slope bargaining had been filled with controversy, confrontation, and litigation, WD gave credit to West Slope negotiators in general and to Chris Jouflas, the Colorado River Water Conservation District's board president, in particular. Jouflas had sat on the other side of the table from WD when they had hammered out the Windy Gap Settlement Agreement ten years earlier. Giving credit to others, as was his nature, WD applauded Jouflas's "efforts and fine negotiating skill" as the key to a complex settlement that would ultimately benefit both sides of the Continental Divide.[51]

WD's words characterized the breadth of vision and planning he had demonstrated during forty years of leadership on the board of the NCWCD.

He had served longer than any other director in NCWCD history, and he had worked with every manager and legal counsel since his appointment in 1955. But it was time to resign. "It has been a wonderful experience," WD reflected, "and a great satisfaction to have participated in all these developments and to see northern Colorado change from a dry, water-short area into the rapidly developing northern Front Range of today."[52] The future, he concluded, would require attention to additional water storage, maintenance of aging structures, modernization of facilities, and recognition of endangered species, minimum streamflows, and non-point sources of pollution.

Few directors had WD's talent to look so intelligibly into the future. In recognition of his unique history and his ability to grasp the essence of broad-ranging problems, the judges who appoint NCWCD directors named WD director emeritus, marking the fourth time in district history such an honor was bestowed on a director.[53] Bob Barkley, who had been recognized previously for his distinguished record as manager of Northern, complimented WD and noted somewhat teasingly that WD's emeritus status eclipsed Barkley's honorary degree from CSU.[54]

Both the Northern and Greeley water boards honored WD at a public reception in the Union Colony Civic Center in Greeley. Two hundred people gathered to honor him and to applaud with gratitude his foresight in providing northern Colorado with an adequate water supply. Representative Wayne Allard, a Colorado congressman, entered a statement in the *Congressional Record* calling attention to the "lifetime commitment WD Farr has made to ensuring that the Front Range has an adequate supply of water year after year."[55]

It was a heady moment for WD. He was speechless, accepting the accolades with great humility. He believed he still had a role to play in helping those tasked with protecting and developing the water supply. When NCWCD monthly board meetings resumed, he was in attendance, observant, soft-spoken, gentle, and incisive. Boulder County director Ruth Wright recalled the following about WD:

[He] had a mind that was really remarkable, and he had historical perspective. He could recall names, places, and dates, and this was useful to us on the board. We really miss that, and I miss him, because I thought he was extremely valuable. He was a treasure, sitting there at the board meetings. Invariably, something would come up at almost every meeting when we would turn to him and ask what happened. . . . And he would remember everything. . . . He was very focused in answer to questions, and he was a resource.[56]

He was also the single person most familiar with all phases of C-BT history, development, and operations. He had helped persuade reluctant farmers to place a lien on their land in the 1930s. He had guided the city of Greeley toward purchase of a large block of shares of C-BT water long before the water was available. And he had been the leader of the Windy Gap project since the 1970s. If Charles Hansen was the "Father of the Big T," WD was its oldest son, amply filling his late "father's" shoes.

No one recognized WD's importance to the C-BT more than NCWCD's general managers Larry Simpson and Eric Wilkinson. *Greeley Tribune* editor Charles Hansen's name had already been used to identify a canal that brought C-BT water into Horsetooth Reservoir, and three other facilities in the C-BT system had been named for other important dignitaries.[57] Many felt that the Farr family deserved recognition, and when a window opened during final discussions of the 1993 Colorado Wilderness Act,[58] Senator Hank Brown was able to add a statement in the legislation authorizing the Granby Pumping Plant to be renamed the Farr Pumping Plant.

Completed in 1951, this plant has long been considered the heart of the C-BT system. Its role is to pump water from Lake Granby, the C-BT's principal collection system, into the Granby Pump Canal, where it flows by gravity into Shadow Mountain Lake. It then flows into Grand Lake, through the Alva B. Adams Tunnel under the Continental Divide, and down to the East Slope reservoirs, where it is distributed to farms and cities. The sixteen-story pump plant building, two-thirds of which is under water, houses three 6,000-horsepower motors that pump water 186 feet so it can flow eastward to its destination on the Front Range. Literally and metaphorically, it is the beating heart of the C-BT system.

This pump plant now bears the Farr family name. John M. Sayre, WD's friend and accomplished NCWCD attorney, perceptively noted in a letter to WD that "even though your father and grandfather had a lot to do with northern Colorado, the principal reason for renaming the pumping plant

Dedication of Farr Pump Plant, 1994. Courtesy of the Northern Colorado Water Conservancy District.

was because of your many years of devoted service to the District and Municipal Subdistrict. You have made a terrific contribution to both districts, and it is only because of your farsightedness, efforts, and wisdom that many of the policies and procedures which the districts now have are in place."[59]

In his mid-eighties, WD received frequent acknowledgment of a life that had been dedicated in large part to the amelioration of water supplies for rapidly growing communities near Front Range farms in Boulder, Larimer, and Weld counties. These counties were among the most productive in the nation. He accepted the pump plant honor with modesty and admitted to Senator Hank Brown that it was "the proudest day of my life. The Farr Pump Plant," he said, "is a personal part of my life and [a part] of my efforts to make northern Colorado a better place."[60] He also received the Headgate Award from the Four States Irrigation Council (Nebraska, Wyoming, Kansas, and Colorado) in recognition of his outstanding contributions in irrigation and agriculture and his efforts to encourage water resource development. Around this time when WD's legacy in water matters

Daniel Tyler and WD Farr at Farr Pump Plant dedication, 1994. Author's collection.

was being celebrated, the cattle industry turned to him in difficult times because of his well-recognized leadership over a period of six decades.

By the summer of 1995, and after three years of meetings, officers of the NCA and the Beef Industry Council of the National Livestock Meat Board (Meat Board) voted to join forces and hoped to include the U.S.

Meat Export Federation (USMEF) and the Cattlemen's Beef Board in a new unified organization. Although the USMEF and Cattlemen's Beef Board eventually opted out of the partnership, the two largest beef organizations were on their way to becoming a single entity, if the merger was ratified by a membership vote at the upcoming NCA convention. WD had protested for many years that cattlemen manifested the unfortunate tendency to create new organizations for every new problem. The result was that the industry was fragmented, bickering, and ineffective. He decried the multiplying advantages of poultry and pork producers as the beef industry became more vulnerable. He wrote letters to key figures, urging cooperation and consolidation among all segments of production, feeding, slaughter, and marketing.[61] The NCA leadership hoped their membership would approve the merger they had agreed on, but everyone knew before the San Antonio convention in 1996 that the spirit of independence, so visceral to cattlemen, could result in a defeat of the proposed consolidation.

Some feared takeover by the so-called Gucci loafer crowd, whom they suspected of being in control of the Meat Board. Others feared a raid on check-off funds by "cowboys who wanted to control it all."[62] For his part, WD was solidly behind the merger proposal, capitalizing on his statesman's role and occasionally incurring criticism. Although he was not on any of the boards involved in crafting the merger plan, WD was engaged behind the scenes. He encouraged industry leaders to move forward and generated letters to half a dozen livestock journals, urging their support and criticizing those who had expressed an editorial bias against the plan.[63]

The vote was scheduled for the NCA's membership and business meeting at the San Antonio convention on January 30, 1996. A considerable floor debate ensued prior to the vote. Some of the criticism was led by the California delegation, which argued that all members of NCA, whether or not they were in attendance, should be allowed to vote. "Paul Hitch of Oklahoma [finally] stepped to the mic and declared, '*The world is run by people who show up.*'"[64] Members in attendance agreed. They voted 744 to 133 to terminate the old NCA and replace it with the National Cattlemen's Beef Association (NCBA), whose expressed focus would be on "pasture-to-plate"[65] control of the beef industry.

WD was in attendance. As recalled by Greeley friend Bob Tointon, WD arrived during the middle of a large luncheon in a room that was crowded and noisy. Tointon described what followed:

I was sitting near the back end of the room. . . . I happened to look around, and there was WD standing at the doorway. This was after he had lost most of his eyesight. . . . I got up and went over to him. He had gotten from the airplane to the convention center on his own, but naturally it was confusing to him. There weren't many seats left, but I helped him to a table where there was one seat. I asked him who he was with, and he replied, "I came on my own. It's a direct flight here, not too bad."[66]

Rather remarkable, in fact, for a man just short of his eighty-sixth birthday, with severe macular degeneration, a bad leg, and a wife in the final stage of Alzheimer's. But he had anticipated success with the merger vote, and he wanted to be part of the consolidation he had advocated for many years. When he returned to Greeley, he sent letters of congratulation to those who made it happen. To his old friend Burton Eller he wrote, "We won by a healthy margin. Now we have to prove our points." Although it had been an exceptionally tough year for the cattle business, he added, "You can always accomplish more when the economics are bad. . . . We now have a beef association, not a cattle association. It will take a lot of education and patience. I wish I could be here twenty years from now to see how the beef industry finally develops."[67]

As often happened, WD's instincts proved accurate. The standing ovation and cheering that followed the convention vote were soon replaced by suspicion and acrimony. Criticism emerged regarding the name of the new organization, who the policymakers would be, the role of affiliate organizations, and new meat grading standards. WD was frustrated, but he knew that change always brought some pain. The beef industry's sour mood was exacerbated by financial losses to cow-calf operators, depressed markets for feeders, and corn prices predicted to escalate 75 percent. If these circumstances were not enough to cause general rumblings, the entire beef industry found itself on the defensive when Mad Cow Disease broke out in the United Kingdom. In the United States, accusations of "cow cannibalism" were directed at feeders by anti-beef activists who charged that "ruminant-derived proteins" were being fed to cattle. When Oprah Winfrey opened one of her television shows with a discussion about "cow cannibalism" in April 1996, Texas cattlemen responded by filing a lawsuit, claiming she had violated food disparagement laws and had caused the beef market to enter a downward spiral.[68]

Public suspicion regarding the safety of beef continued during the next two years. Texas cattleman Paul Engler, no stranger to confrontation, organized the legal battle against Oprah. WD urged him on. "I admire you for filing the suit," he wrote. "More importantly for the industry, if you win, it will stop a lot of misguided people from unnecessary attacks on our industry. . . . Keep after it. People like you can do more to change viewpoints than any officer of the organization, college professors, packers, or politicians."[69]

But WD was surprised by the extent of the nation's concern about food safety, and he was disappointed in the outcome of the litigation. A five-week trial in Amarillo ended in a decision for Oprah "with prejudice."[70] The twelve-member jury concluded the primary issue was free speech; Oprah's First Amendment rights trumped the Texas food disparagement laws. The NCBA expressed disappointment, but analysts recognized that those same laws were still on the books of many states, and in the months ahead, the NCBA persuaded Oprah to clear up unanswered questions and set the record straight on a follow-up show.[71]

Meanwhile, WD was asked to serve on the editorial board for a book (*Building the Beef Industry*) that would celebrate 100 years of the cattle industry. The year 1998 marked the 100-year anniversary of the National Livestock Association, the first successful organization representing cattlemen in the United States. Among other plans to celebrate the moment, a Centennial Task Force voted to publish a history of the cattle industry that would be available for the 1998 Denver convention of the NCBA. The National Cattlemen's Foundation (NCF), an organization WD established when he was president of the NCBA's predecessor, accepted this responsibility.

WD's imprint can be seen all over the book, but the summer of 1996 proved a tough time to be raising funds for such a publication. The cattle industry was staggering from bad market conditions. Even though he openly admitted his inability to do anything "to straighten out the mess," WD expressed a commitment to what he thought could be a useful promotional piece for an industry dealing with increasingly negative press.[72] Drawing on his long and amicable friendship with the Monforts, WD asked if the family might be interested in underwriting the publication. Kenny Monfort did not hesitate. At a meeting of the governing board and trustees of the NCF in January 1997, WD reported that Kenny Monfort would sponsor the entire book project with a gift of $400,000.[73]

As a member of the editorial board, WD was asked to review manuscript drafts. He believed the marketing plan was thorough, but he felt obligated to rewrite the segment on the Monforts, noting the importance of the family's pioneering work in cattle feeding, its development of a single-species packing plant, and its production of boxed meat for the retail market. He also noted how the Monforts had survived brutal competition with Swift, Armour, Cudahy, and Wilson and how Kenny Monfort's persistence ultimately led to his presidency of the American Meat Institute.[74]

WD also faulted author Charles Ball for taking a narrow approach that focused too much on cattle producers and feeders. It was necessary, he argued, to give adequate credit to all the associated industries: the food chains, fast food businesses, pharmaceutical companies, packers, hide plants, and the feed companies. In view of the recent merger of several beef organizations into the NCBA, and the problems anticipated by the loss of individual group identities, WD asserted the need to recognize everyone who had a hand in the raising and marketing of beef. He also emphasized the importance of a final chapter that would hold out "hope for a better, more stable industry in the future."[75] His suggestions that the book reflect "the bigger picture, the longer view," while avoiding the "narrow viewpoints," marked the final draft with WD's brand.[76] Seeing issues broadly, being inclusive, giving credit to others, showing optimism— these were hallmarks of WD's life, and they influenced the final version of *Building the Beef Industry*.

Project director Susan Borg well understood the value of WD's counsel. At the request of several people, and in recognition of his standing among cattlemen, Borg asked WD to write an epilogue titled "The Next Hundred Years." He accepted the assignment but was delayed by escalating concerns for Judy and his excruciatingly painful decision to place her in the state's only Alzheimer's institution in Brush, Colorado. His friend and secretary, Susi Seawald, recalled that WD never really forgave himself for making this decision. But he had no choice. The disease had advanced to the point where Judy needed twenty-four-hour care. Although he was depressed and guilt-ridden about his wife's situation, WD managed to write the epilogue with an expression of optimism, hope, and a restatement of many of the ideas he had articulated during sixty years of association with the cattle business. Sadly, Judy passed away six months later in February 1997.

WD was deeply affected by Judy's death. According to Susi Seawald, the morning after Judy's death, WD came into the office and said, "'Our Judy is gone,' then he just kept on working that whole day. . . . He grieved for Judy, cried in his office, but he wanted to be strong for the kids. He told me wonderful things about Judy, showed me pictures of the two of them hunting and snowmobiling. . . . They were such a close couple. . . . Judy was his one love. . . . He was broken-hearted, but he trudged on."[77]

The blow to his personal life never fully dissipated, but he found the will to refocus energy on *Building the Beef Industry*. If the cattle industry was to survive, he wrote in the epilogue, "it must adapt to new consumer demands and adopt scientific knowledge . . . to create a better product. . . . The industry's real challenge is to produce a constant product of high quality. . . . Today, with fewer than half of fed cattle grading Choice, we are not producing the kind of product that the consumer wants. . . . Beef must be the same quality twelve months out of the year." The industry would have to focus on strengthening alliances, spending money on research and development, and investigating the global markets. "During the next decade, those who are not willing to be optimistic and forward thinking will be lost in the dust of what promises to be the greatest century the world has ever seen."[78]

It was vintage WD. Although he worried that he might be "preaching to the choir," his admonitions surfaced from a visceral level. "I feel strongly," he told Susan Borg, "that [what I have written] is the only real option the industry has."[79]

Borg accepted the draft epilogue and made few changes. She also called on WD to use his influence in persuading James Michener to write a foreword.[80] For a time it appeared he was having success, but Michener was ill. A month after WD completed his epilogue, the author of *Centennial, Texas, Hawaii, Alaska, Mexico, Chesapeake,* and many other engaging books was dead. Hugh Sidey, *Time* magazine's expert on the American presidency, whose roots were in rural Iowa, accepted the invitation to write the foreword. He was considered a fine writer who understood farming and livestock raising. His call to cattlemen to unite, to accept and master change, and to understand the modern marketplace echoed themes WD had also stressed. Sidey's foreword served as an appropriate bookend for WD's epilogue.

Building the Beef Industry emerged from the printer in the fall of 1997. WD sent fifty copies to friends and family members. The editorial board included him in a plan to run a special train of vintage parlor cars from Greeley to Denver at the beginning of the 1998 NCBA convention. The idea was conceived as a marketing tool to celebrate the centennial, help sell books, provide credence to the NCBA, and create a media event. Participants would terminate their journey at the Brown Palace Hotel, where they would sign books. It would have been a happy occasion, a fitting conclusion to all the work the book represented, but the volunteer funds expected to pay for the event never materialized.

WD moved on as he always did. Other honors awaited. The Greeley Water and Sewer Board designated him chairman emeritus, recognizing his thirty-nine years of service to Greeley. A two-page ordinance cited his "illustrious service to his community, state, and nation" and praised his vision in local and regional water planning for six decades. Asked why he retired, WD replied, "I'm getting old. They asked me to stay on the board because I know more about water (than other board members), [but] we need to be training some new people." Respected for his historical memory as well as his ability to ask how decisions made today would affect Greeley's future, WD was viewed as "the grand old man. . . . a true statesman, a gentleman, and a person with great vision of the future," noted Dick Boettcher, who was elected to replace WD as head of the Greeley Water and Sewer Board. Because of that vision, Boettcher added, "we've never been forced to play the expensive game of catch-up."[81] With thanks for his outstanding service, WD was presented with a bronze statue of the Greeley Stampede's representation of western protagonists—cowboy and bronco—entitled "When Champions Meet." It was an appropriate gift, because it spoke to the long ride WD had endured on the water board, and it was symbolic of his "cowboy-up" outlook. It was also fitting because WD had served on the Greeley Rodeo Committee from 1938 to 1952, was its chairman for two years, and was selected grand marshal in 1985.

Further recognition followed in 1997. The El Pomar Foundation in Colorado Springs awarded WD the Russell Tutt Excellence in Leadership

Award. A $15,000 check came to him with the stipulation he donate $10,000 to charity. WD gave it all away. At the National Western Livestock banquet, he received the Jerry Litton Award for achievement in agriculture. The United Way named him "Humanitarian of the Year" because of his "incredible commitment to people, whether [by] small acts of neighborly kindness or in big projects that improve the life of the entire community."[82] For his business acumen, northern Colorado business organizations honored him with the inaugural Bravo Entrepreneur Lifetime Achievement Award.[83]

As the twentieth century drew to a close, WD received another prestigious honor that caught him by surprise. The National Western Stock Show designated him the 1999 Citizen of the West at its ninety-third meeting in Denver. This award is the stock show's highest honor. It is given annually to individuals who embody the spirit and determination of the western pioneer and who are committed to sustaining the West's agricultural heritage and principles.

The January banquet, held in the Westin Hotel, was a fundraising occasion for the National Western Scholarship Fund, which provides grants to students studying agriculture and preparing to practice medicine in rural areas. Seven hundred friends and family members gathered to witness the presentation of the branding iron award to WD. With rain gauges as party favors and Michael Martin Murphey singing a medley of songs, including "Cool Water," master of ceremonies Hank Brown and Colorado Supreme Court justice Gregory J. Hobbs saluted WD for his many accomplishments. Poetically, Hobbs captured the essence of WD's legacy: "You've always been coming from the future," he noted. "That's what makes you a Citizen of the West. Thinking about the future optimistically is what the western experience has always been about. . . . Your initials mean, 'We'll do,' for you have said there's no one else to do the job as well as each of us will do together. . . . Take to heart this iron, symbol of the mark we bear of you. You have sealed in our hearts and minds the initials, WD."[84]

"Dad said very few words," John Farr recalled. "He was speaking very little then and was always quiet. He thanked everyone who honored him and with whom he had worked over the years, and he urged people to continue working together for the future and the new century."[85]

No one doubted WD's gratitude or the intense feelings that were stimulated by the recognition of his peers, friends, and family members. Charles P. Schroeder, chief executive officer of the NCBA, underscored the evening's accolades with a letter written soon after the dinner, praising the role WD played in history: "Your reputation for innovation, integrity, and statesmanship still resounds, and the standard you set for leadership is still the mark to which others aspire. . . . Surely, we need that continued reminder in the cattle industry."[86]

It was a fine compliment, but while WD was appreciative of all the kind words, "it was *just* as meaningful to him that the results of the Denver event would provide scholarships to further the careers of talented kids, who would keep the torch lit for American agriculture."[87] That's who WD was: thoughtful, grateful, forward-looking, and self-effacing—a statesman.

CHAPTER 8

Leadership

If your actions inspire others to dream more, learn more, do more and become more, you are a leader.

—John Quincy Adams

Good leaders must first be good people.

—Albert C. Yates, CSU

WD celebrated his ninetieth birthday on May 26 and May 27, 2000. Because of his many friends and acquaintances, the invitations were spread over a two-day period. Landscaper Gerald Nelson spruced up the garden WD loved so much, working for two weeks to encourage early spring blooms. At ninety, WD was no longer gardening, but he was passionate about each plant, flower, shrub, and tree as it emerged from dormancy. Though his strength and endurance had declined significantly, he was alert, inquisitive, and as mentally vibrant as ever. "Dad is still looking toward the future," WR Farr mused. "He lives the way he thinks."[1]

Most often, he thought about Greeley's economic future and about the decisions requiring action in the present to ensure greater opportunities and a better life for the community down the road. He wrote letters to the newspaper, urging the city to annex land west of Greeley to the north–south interstate, I-25. This area, between the Cache la Poudre and South Platte rivers, would have businesses and subdivisions within five years. He also foresaw commercial and light-industrial operations along the east–west corridor of Highway 34. Those companies would use little water, he advised, and their contribution to the municipal tax base would be significant.

WD in his garden on his ninetieth birthday. Courtesy of the Farr family.

The Greeley/Weld Chamber of Commerce concurred with WD's annexation plan, and Mayor Jerry Wones supported "the spirit" of it. But some were afraid that neighboring towns also had expansion plans, and they feared that WD's vision was "sure to stir up controversy" in those municipalities.[2] They dragged their feet and expressed misgivings.

WD was undeterred by the criticism. As he had done in the past when he believed strongly about something, he presented his case to Greeley's decision makers:

> This city council and city administrative staff have the great opportunity to plan and build a fine city in the next thirty years if this large area of land can be annexed and planned now. Think of the millions of dollars that can be saved in the planning and location of parks, storm sewers, arterial roads, fire station locations, and proper sizing of sewer and water mains. . . . Greeley has the water and the infrastructure to plan and build a great city.[3]

He understood the need to work out intergovernmental agreements with other stakeholders and applauded those efforts that had taken place to date. But he also believed Greeley should be the principal annexing body. Over the course of his life WD had been the architect of many plans to bring water to the area, and those water projects required intense negotiations between the different cities and counties. He believed that once the land was annexed, "an army of developers would come to the city with ideas." He had spoken to the Water and Sewer Board, the city's finance director, and the Greeley/Weld Economic Development Action Partnership. Even if it proved necessary to borrow money for a few years, "the City of Greeley," WD concluded, "is in wonderful shape to take on this new challenge. . . . I hope that I have described a vision for the future that you will move forward on."[4]

But the city council's leadership was more conservative. The city manager was afraid Greeley could not provide services that far out, so the aggressive action WD hoped for did not materialize. Greeley lost some choice land to more determined neighbors.[5] Undeterred, WD continued to urge officials to think broadly about water supplies and to envision their community thirty years hence. He had seen the city grow from 5,000 to 75,000 people, and he knew the demographic trend would continue, especially with the success of Denver International Airport, completed in 1994. "Mr. Farr was never stuck in one spot," Eric Wilkinson recalled. "He was flexible way into his nineties and delighted in the challenge of change."[6]

WD connected his vision of a growing and prosperous community to the availability of water supplies. He recognized two potential water projects Greeley should endorse. The first was an expansion of Seaman Reservoir on the North Fork of the Cache la Poudre River. Because of the lengthy planning and permitting required for any water project, he knew it would take twenty years before the 20,000 to 30,000 acre-feet of new water would be available. Arrangements should commence immediately. The second project would involve a pump on the Cache la Poudre River near its junction with the South Platte River. Approximately 80,000 acre-feet of non-potable water could be delivered to Galeton Reservoir twenty miles northeast of Greeley, where it would be stored for agricultural use. The irrigation ditches in that area could then exchange their potable water for this non-potable water, thus making available new sources of purer water for domestic uses. "This project," WD conjectured, "is probably twenty-five years away before it will be needed if Greeley continues to grow. And if the dry-land areas [expect to receive] water, it will have to come from these new sources. . . . If the city of Greeley wants to maintain the position of being a leader and having water available for the future, [it] must be in a position to sign up for significant quantities of these two new water projects. This is the last water that can be developed. Water will be finite after that."[7]

Even at ninety, the future was still on his mind. He continually ruminated about it, always compiling, always assimilating data, Eric Wilkinson recalled.

And it was a dynamic kind of thing, too. It wasn't just the facts. It was the cause and effect, the human relationships. . . . To me his whole target, long distance, far down the road was [to ask], "Where are we going as a community, a ditch company, a city, a region, a water district, whatever? Where are [we] going, and what's best for the constituents of that group?" He was constantly weighing those things. I think his visionary gift really helped him with that.[8]

For WD the future always seemed brighter, filled with the promise of enhanced benefits for Americans—at least until September 11, 2001. He had spoken frequently of the twenty-first century being the greatest ever for the world, and he yearned with a passion to live another fifty years to see it unfold. He was an optimist, but even though he would regain his positive attitude, the events of that day shook him to the core. John Farr recalled the events:

Dad and I were in Casper [Wyoming] at the Super 8 Motel, where we always stayed when we fished up there. I had walked up to get breakfast and the TV had the weather channel on. We were all watching the weather, since the place was full of travelers and fishermen. A lady came into the room and almost screamed, "Why weren't we watching the news? A plane has just hit the Twin Towers." My first thought was [of] a small plane, and so what? No one moved to change the channel, and this lady *really* yelled and [the station] was flipped to the live coverage. I went to get Dad, and he had turned on the news . . . we sat rather dumbfounded and watched for over an hour. . . . We had planned on going to Rock Creek to fish, about ninety minutes north of Casper. We discussed the situation, and Dad said we might as well go fishing, since this event was still unraveling, and the news folks knew little of what was really going on. . . . We needed to do something, and Dad thought that fishing with our friend Paul Kiser was the best way to spend the day.[9]

Close to Kaycee, Wyoming, Rock Creek was a spectacular fishing area, surrounded by the ranching country WD loved so well. The narrow valley was green and lush, fishing conditions were perfect, and a blue sky overhead made the setting ideal. WD fished a bit, but the impact of what he had seen in the morning distracted him from what had been a lifelong pleasure. "I just couldn't fish," he recalled. "I knew the world would never be the same."[10] Returning to Casper in the evening, conversation in the car with John was about the impact of the attack on America's future. "How could the nation's security have been so lax?" WD wondered. "The attackers knew where to hit the buildings so they would collapse, and this information came from engineering schools."[11] He was dejected. "The next morning we drove home," John remembered. "We were all upset [and] glad to live in the western U.S. We wondered what the ripple effect would be."[12]

WD probably wondered more than most people. His active mind regularly sought explanations of puzzling circumstances and ways to work with the unexpected misfortunes of life. Susi Seawald, executive secretary of the Colorado Sugarbeet Growers Association and WD's amanuensis, friend, and confidant, remarked that "WD believed there was a reason for everything and that there was no great plan for mankind. You made your way or not. He believed that if you wanted to accomplish something, you would have to work for it. With such reasoning, he described himself as a fatalist, [but] he believed things could be turned around by effort."[13]

That frame of mind was one of WD's hallmarks. It was nurtured by the cyclical fortunes of agriculture and the disappointments of his own life, which had been turned around by effort. Consequently, WD was able to ponder changes in American policy triggered by the tragedy of 9/11. He never totally got past the horror of seeing the United States under attack, but he gradually returned to the global nature of national events and expressed hope that the president would soon become more flexible in his dealings with the world. He lamented the declining image of the United States and remained convinced that the nation's leaders should become more malleable in international affairs.[14]

Perhaps WD was looking for qualities in the nation's leaders that so many people saw in him: integrity, trust, generosity, and compassion. He seemed to have an ability to view the future positively, recognizing at the same time that constructive change was inevitably limited by the depth of people's resolution to learn from the past. Five months after 9/11, the NCBA recognized these qualities in WD with the first-ever Swan Leadership Award. Developed by the NCBA in cooperation with the Idaho Cattle Association, the award was named after Bill and George Swan, whose dedication to the beef industry stretched over several generations. WD was honored on February 9, 2002, at a ceremony during the Cattle Industry Convention and Trade Show in Denver. Considered a pioneer in cattle feeding, the patriarch of an internationally recognized business, and a champion of technology in the cattle industry, WD was lauded for a lifetime of accomplishments. NCBA president Lynn Cornwell called attention to WD's "incredible life of leadership. . . . He has never said no to a request for his guidance, and the cattle industry, and all of agriculture [has] been a huge beneficiary of this dedication. We are very appreciative of his wisdom and foresight and the endless generosity he has shown with his time and energy. . . . The entire Farr family [has] always been known for [its] innovations, keen business sense, and vision," Cornwell said. "More importantly, they helped the industry move from one era to the next."[15]

Greeley mayor Jerry Wones agreed: "It's amazing to talk to a guy who's ninety years old and have him be able to think so clearly and envision what's going to happen fifty years from now. . . . People in leadership positions could take a real lesson from him—sort of like Cal Ripken in baseball."[16]

Clearly, WD's leadership talents began with this discerning ability to look ahead, to anticipate the tasks required in the present so a brighter future would be assured. It was an attribute of his character that helped him place the horrors of 9/11 in perspective, and it also defined him as an unusually effective leader.

Vision, as Steven Sample has written, is one of the key strengths of good leadership, but "creative imagination," which relates to the ability to think freely, "may in the end be every bit as important as vision."[17] Anyone who pretends to lead, Sample wrote, must be able to hear, consider, and appropriate the fresh ideas of one's associates and colleagues. In other words, good leaders know how to listen. Furthermore, Sample noted, vision alone is worthless unless the leader can find the right words to articulate the vision. When this happens, effective leaders and followers are able to work toward the same goal.[18]

Because he was such a good listener, WD amassed encyclopedic amounts of information and ideas from everyone with whom he came into contact. He remembered what he heard, even into his ninth decade, and he was able to synthesize the verbal and written data into concepts, plans, and programs that others failed at first to visualize. By validating everyone's opinion and maintaining a steadfast focus on outcomes desired by the various stakeholders, he was able to overcome the territoriality and jealousies that prevented participants from working together. He could explain his ideas exceptionally well, and, in that sense, WD was also a teacher. As John Gardner has written, "every great leader is clearly teaching—and every great teacher is leading."[19] WD maintained a pragmatic and comprehensible approach to what could be accomplished. He was what some might call "a practical dreamer,"[20] spending enormous amounts of time contemplating changes that would bring about efficiency, financial benefits, and societal improvements. At the same time he was aware that "life is not easy and that nothing is ever finally safe"—not even your own country.[21]

WD had not only great vision, but also the will and the courage to see visions fulfilled. He was patient and flexible, and because he was also highly respected and trusted for the knowledge and confidence he brought to the table, he was able to achieve successes over time periods that tended to frustrate most would-be leaders. As Warren Bennis has observed, real leaders persist, because they are unwilling to accept anything less than the best in themselves, their followers, and their organization. Like poets and children, they can look at things in new and creative ways. They question everything, trust their instincts, and never stray from moral and intellectual honesty. "Good leaders," Bennis concluded, "are generalists, capable of seeing the interconnectedness of science, esthetics, and ethics."[22]

WD was a generalist. The many insights he verbalized and defended—as an active farmer, cattleman, water guru, banker, and community builder—frequently took into account the reality and interconnectedness of a global society. He came to embrace free-market and supply-and-demand principles for agriculture and livestock because he believed that more business would come to American producers if every nation specialized in what it did best. The United States, for example, had a vibrant cattle industry, but it was competing with cheaper meats—especially poultry and pork—and would have to concentrate itself into fewer and larger enterprises if its leaders expected to survive global competition. Cattlemen and the NCBA would need to rely more on genetic research, with the objective of producing consistently flavorful and tender meat, and they would need refrigerated storage buildings in order to market beef when retail and export demands were strongest.[23]

But even though he was loyal to the cattle industry and to the people who had worked so hard to succeed in it, his later years were dominated by a conviction that the future for beef in America had peaked. The fate of cow-calf ranching, WD sadly acknowledged, was probably in jeopardy, except for very large grassland ranches or as a way of life for people who just enjoyed the outdoors, the rugged life, and the independence associated with ranching.[24] Consolidation of production, feeding, and slaughter of cattle might restore competition. But even with vertical integration of all the industry's elements, WD had to concede that the cattle business seemed to be going downhill, "so I wouldn't spend time with it," he concluded. "It's almost an impossible situation. I would either stay with irrigated farming that I think has tremendous potential, or I would go into smaller banking like my son [has]."[25] Even though he felt great pride in the one family member (RD Farr) who seemed to have the right instincts about cattle raising and feeding, he was pessimistic about the industry as a whole.

Big banks seemed to be addressing the needs of cattlemen and farmers who borrowed large sums of money, but WD felt they had lost touch with average people. There was a future, he supposed, for those interested in small banks and in technology. "When I started as a director," he recalled, "we did everything by hand. All the bookkeeping was with a pen you dipped in a bottle of ink and then wrote it down." When it was time for an audit or examination, "I used to have to go into the vault and we had to count the money out, every single penny and account for it with the examiners. So with computers nowadays, it's just a matter of a day and you can do so many things. . . . If I had the education, I'd certainly be trying to get into that field where you can use that kind of information."[26]

He also recognized the value of technology in matters of water acquisition, storage, and distribution. WD was proud to have convinced so many people of the need to think ahead for their organizations (NCWCD, Windy Gap, Greeley–Loveland Ditch Company, Greeley Water Board, and others), and he knew that computers would play a powerful role in tracking the ownership and delivery of water. Considering all the changes that had occurred in his life—the end of the lamb industry, decline in cattle feeding, consolidation of banks, and the immense population growth along the Front Range—what meant most to WD in his waning years were the successes associated with bringing permanent water to the semi-arid Front Range. His thoughts about the future still involved the need for additional storage, and he knew from experience that water projects took a long time to build. Even in his later years, he repeatedly urged officials to prepare for future droughts and to manage water supplies with the anticipation of exponential population growth.

The controversial Northern Integrated Supply Project (NISP), with its plan to build an off-channel reservoir northwest of Fort Collins, was an extension of WD's efforts to make better use of the Cache la Poudre River. Planned and supported by the NCWCD, NISP was going through the intense process of public commentary, environmental impact statements, and permitting at the time of WD's death in 2007.[27] In an earlier configuration, that project had been presented and discussed while WD was still on the NCWCD board. He was a champion of the concept. In some ways NISP was the final stage of efforts he began in the 1950s to assure enough water storage for the inevitable growth and future droughts expected in northern Colorado. He knew what he was talking about, principally because of the Dust Bowl and economic depression he lived through in the 1930s with his father. Today, while many powerful individuals are absorbed in seeing NISP completed, WD's shadow looms large. "You can say what you want about all these other people who are involved," commented *Greeley Tribune* reporter Bill Jackson, "but [that] project is still WD Farr. . . . It was WD who said that we needed more storage on the Poudre River, be that Grey Rock [Dam] on the river or [Glade Reservoir] off the river." NISP, therefore, is a legacy of WD's long-lived foresight in providing water to a semi-desert region.[28]

WD foresaw the need to develop a system of integrated management for the entire South Platte River and its tributaries. He felt that water would be more efficiently distributed and utilized if Denver and the NCWCD shared management of the entire system. He believed that surface water and groundwater should be integrated, and that district boundaries should be expanded. Some members of the NCWCD board disagreed and argued against him, but WD's tolerance, patience, insatiable curiosity, and enthusiasm won him respect, if not concurrence, from most board members taking part in these discussions. Director Nancy Gray, a former Fort Collins mayor, was somewhat troubled that WD seemed to be treated with such reverence. But when she recognized that he was always the best prepared board member and had the best grasp of the future, she conceded that he commanded attention justifiably when he spoke.[29] That ability to listen, avoid judgmental comments, and master sometimes complex data prior to deliberation earned WD respect even from critics.

He also attracted a sympathetic audience when he revealed his thoughts about the growing importance of Colorado in international trade. Whether or not he changed any minds, his musings about the twenty-first century reflected many hours of deliberation. The greatest growth in the world, he asserted, "will be in the Pacific Rim. All of the new growth here [in Colorado] will develop as the Pacific develops. . . . The future is in the Pacific. There will be a fantastic amount of trading to do with them. . . . If we could only get a plan for the next thirty years and do it, we could be a better country. We are too politically minded. We need longer range plans."[30] Denver International Airport, he believed, was positioned to export and import goods to and from the area. Los Angeles and San Francisco, in WD's view, were already at capacity. With the great tradition of manufacturing in the United States and with Colorado's capability of producing corn, grains, vegetables, and dairy products, Denver stood to become a major trading hub in the twenty-first century.

"It seems to me we are going to have a global society," WD surmised. In his judgment, globalization would distribute wealth more evenly in the United States. "Over time, we won't have the . . . high-priced salaries and extreme wealth we see today. . . . I think we will level more and be a more uniform society . . . [because we will have to compete.] Other countries can do some things better than we can, and we are going to have to trade with them."[31] In America of today, WD contended, young people are spoiled, labor unions demand too much, and management and business leaders are overpaid. Just as Russia and China faced social upheaval in the twentieth century, here in the United States, he warned, we need to face the uneven distribution of wealth in order to remain competitive and to avoid violent social revolution.[32]

Respected because of his visionary deliberations, WD's personal traits inspired further confidence. He was a gentleman with few affectations. He was always respectful, taking time to listen to people of any age, from any walk of life, and he never ridiculed or made fun of others' ideas. He could have a conversation with anyone, and he accepted others on their own terms. Unknowingly, people were guided by him. Two of his closest collaborators in the NCA articulated this characteristic. "[People] often believed they had come forth with an idea WD planted," Bob Jousserand recalled, "because he did so in a very gentle fashion."[33] Agreeing in principle, Topper Thorpe noted that "WD led with gentle persuasion. He shared his thoughts and ideas with yours, and had an ability to pull things together in a way that came across as being very sincere, very genuine, reflecting a concern on his part about your thoughts, your feelings, while sharing his own."[34]

WD never tired of refining his ideas. He was forever searching the world and its people for the best information he could find. He was tireless in this pursuit and was more intellectually active than many who had undergraduate and graduate degrees. He took an interest in the Newcomen Society, an organization that promoted, researched, and honored success in the free enterprise system.[35] WD brought the national meeting to Greeley in 1970 and then introduced it to the NCA convention in Denver, where cowboys in pearl-button shirts and boots were asked to acknowledge the British origins of the society. "We didn't do it as well as the Newcomen people might have liked us to," George Spencer remembered, "but the dinner went over well." The Queen of England was honored by a gentleman "who was getting along in years with a little palsy, so when he raised his glass, he showered the platform guests with his wine as he was making the toast."[36]

Even if the occasion had its minor flaws, it represented WD's indefatigable curiosity about life, customs, ideas, and events. This inquisitiveness was a WD trademark; he brought people to his office and to his home even after he had become bedridden. Some sought his blessing when they contemplated running for political office. Others came just to hear his stories, because WD was a consummate storyteller—not in the sense that he sought out and described American creation myths but, rather, as a senior statesman and motivator who could recount an extraordinary number of experiences and weave them together in a single tapestry that made sense. The diverse events of his life were generally accessible in his mind. They could be discussed easily, sometimes in a stream of consciousness but more often as a gentle discourse to explain a strategy or a concept he had been examining. He did talk a lot when questioned, but he spoke softly, smiled, and engaged his listeners directly. At meetings, however, he usually remained quiet until everyone had spoken. He never wrote anything down, but he heard everything that was said, weighed the value of every remark, and offered his own thoughts with respect for all the views that preceded his.

Most people were eager to listen to him. WD had the ability to place his experiences in historical context, recounting an assortment of details. "All the facets of his life and activities," recalled Greeley Museum's Peggy Ford, "were microcosmic punctuation points within the larger macrocosm. He understood the composition of things around him, and he made others see and feel it. . . . The information, power, and persuasiveness of his views and logic raised both individual and community awareness about the efficacy of many issues and projects." But even more to the point, WD found a way to bring his listeners into the stories he told. "He wanted people to be on the same page about important issues, and he valued open discussion," Ford observed.[37] At times his historical recall was inconsistent with the facts, but he was an observant student of the past, both recent and distant, and he knew how to connect the broad sweep of previous eras and events to the sometimes frightening changes of the present and future. Because he could do this with tranquility, optimism, integrity, and humility, he led almost by default.

Integrity and humility were powerful forces in WD. Albert C. Yates, president of CSU for thirteen years and a lifelong student of leadership, commented that to be the type of leader who can attract people on all sides of an issue, "you have to have complete integrity. You have to reflect a mediating ability that allows others to trust you, and you have to show a special respect for people. The foundation of good leadership is, in fact, integrity."[38] WD was impatient with people who were intellectually dishonest, but individuals who dealt with him knew he was "rock solid, straightforward, and wasn't trying to catch you on anything."[39] He would never ask someone to do something he would not do, and he was "humble enough to get things done, sometimes by delegating. He knew how to get people to work for a vision."[40] Because he was good at pouring oil on troubled waters, because he never took conflicts public, and because he was reliably respectful of others' views, even the people who disapproved of his ideas respected him.[41]

Compared with other leaders, WD probably falls into the "human relations" category described by Warren Bennis. In contrast to the classical scientific management theory, which describes successful leaders as those who believe in strengthening organizational structures because of an underlying conviction that humans are "regrettably unpredictable and unstable," human relations leaders focus more on emotions, ideas, and attitudes. In this context, Bennis argues, the leader is a facilitator, working "as an agent of change who helps smooth the pathway toward goal-achievement."[42]

When WD was in leadership positions, he proved himself to be an effective facilitator. But he was also much more than that. The passionate loyalty he elicited from the different groups with which he associated, and the true feelings of affection he inspired from colleagues, make it difficult to place WD's leadership in a particular scholarly niche. Bennis also examined a burgeoning group of so-called revisionists: those who attempt in different ways to see leadership as the "fulcrum on which the demands of the individual and the demands of the organization are balanced."[43] WD was certainly conscious of the structures within which he led, and he was also aware of the need to make connections with the humans who functioned therein. But as Bennis concluded, revisionists fail to understand fully the nature of change, and change was, without doubt, the one aspect of leadership with which WD was totally at ease. Perhaps the best summation of WD's leadership is that he inspired others through his mastery of information, his compassion for people, his willingness to listen attentively, and his ability to articulate visions that had solid and practical roots in the past and the future. He led with persistence, confidence, patience, and energy, and those who encountered his style marveled at the results.

During his later life, when he was no longer involved in boards and committees, WD deeply missed the feelings of usefulness and the challenges of problem solving he experienced while actively serving various organizations. But he was still able to savor good memories of past leadership

successes, and he remained determined to follow daily routines and continue living usefully. He hired drivers so he could get to a Greeley office
he rented in the First National Bank building. Harry Bauer, perhaps his
favorite, drove WD to meetings, appointments, shopping, family affairs,
and to Encampment, Wyoming. They became good friends, sometimes just
riding around in the car, observing the farms, fields, and water systems.
When they returned to the office, WD would always provide his assistant,
Susi Seawald, with a report on where they had been and what they had seen.

WD and Harry could talk about almost anything. They were a perfect
match for each other. Harry was a baseball fanatic and loved to talk
statistics. WD listened and attended a few games with Harry, but he still
enjoyed football more. When Harry complained of a sore hip, WD advised
him to see a doctor. Harry delayed the visit, partly because he feared he
might lose the job of driving WD after hip replacement surgery. When he
finally sought out a doctor, it was too late. He was diagnosed with inoper-
able cancer and died a few weeks later. WD was devastated. "I thought we
were going to lose Dad right there [spring of 2005]," John Farr remembered. "He really was down for a month, but he rallied as usual, and that
is when we began [around-the-clock] care for him."[44]

Susi Seawald was a source of encouragement to him. She divided her
time between WD and the Sugarbeet Association, typing twenty to thirty
letters a day from WD's drafts and dictation. Gradually, she became the
person on whom WD depended for paying bills, buying clothes, performing
household duties, and, most important, providing emotional support. For
WD, she was the daughter he never had, the one who brought him up short
when he was tempted to write an inappropriate letter, the liaison between
WD and his sons, and the person who sat with him when the infirmities of
age became frightening. WD preferred not to bother the boys when he
was sick or had an accident. He would call Harry or Susi, relying on both
of them as if they were his family. Susi was his anchor. When she had to
be away from the office at an association meeting, he would also make
plans to be elsewhere. He did not like being at the office without her.

When she was there, he divided his time between letter writing and
reading. Most of the letters were to thank people for what they did for
him. All his life he had written letters of appreciation, but in his final years
he had the time to thank people for everything, even Christmas cards.

When Susi brought him baked goods, he wanted to dictate a letter of thanks to her. She objected, with good reason, so WD suggested writing her husband. "But my husband didn't do the baking," she told WD, "so I never had to write a thank-you note to myself for my own baking. But I had to fight him on it. He was just in the habit of thanking people."[45]

He also enjoyed receiving mail. Once, when he was in the hospital and Judy was still at home, letters stopped arriving at the house. Susi looked into the matter and found that the U.S. Postal Service had stopped delivery to his 14th Avenue home. Upon further investigation, she discovered the reason: WD's little dog, Pepe, had managed to get her snout through the mail slot and had bitten the mail carrier. "I went to the Post Office," Susi said, "and picked up two hundred pieces of mail I had to sort through, including overdue bills. It was four months before the post office would resume mail delivery to the house." WD loved Pepe. He spent a princely sum to have CSU veterinarians repair her battered body after Pepe was almost killed in a canine brawl in Encampment. She died shortly thereafter of old age, and WD never replaced her.

He continued to receive letters regularly after Pepe's death and looked forward to reading his mail, newspaper articles, and an occasional book. The large Telesensory reading machine in his office magnified printed words, but its insertion tray required placing material backwards and then moving it in a direction opposite to normal page turning. It was slow going and confusing. Words were difficult to focus, the machine regularly broke down, and WD often fell asleep while attempting to put it all together. But even with macular degeneration, WD read all the time. The now-defunct *Rocky Mountain News* was always delivered to his home, and Susi made sure that new carriers were handsomely tipped to guarantee the paper was always delivered on his porch.

Susi also helped WD with scheduling. "We always filled in the calendar at least a year in advance with all his events." Business meetings, social occasions, and vacations were all booked. Rotary was always scheduled on Wednesdays, and as long as he was able, sometimes with a cane, or on the arm of a fellow Rotarian, he insisted on walking to Rotary luncheons a few blocks from his office.

Fishing trips were also planned. As he aged, those trips became more difficult, but he looked forward to them with passion. Because of arthritis, his hands had lost some strength, so he purchased a new rod with a "fighting butt." It had a rubber cap that he could shove into his stomach for stability and a custom-made cork handle that made gripping easier. The last few years he fished with a guide and his sons. They lashed him into the boat while they drifted down the North Platte River. He could cast well enough, but his sons and the guide worried that if they hit a rock, he might be thrown overboard. Sometimes he just enjoyed the warm sun and the rhythms of the river, occasionally falling asleep in his seat.

But the fighting butt proved its worth. On one of his last trips he hooked a ten-pound rainbow trout on a nymph. The fish had probably never been caught before. Instead of leaping from the water, as most trout that have been caught more than once do, this fish ran like a steelhead. WD worked for fifteen minutes to land that rainbow, eventually winning the battle. It was not the last fish he caught, but it was one of the biggest and most memorable.

Unable to hunt and fish as he had in the past, WD looked to his garden for serenity. It was his last real connection to nature's beauty. He had a keen aesthetic appreciation of the many flowers, shrubs, and trees planted by landscaper Gerald Nelson, and he wanted the garden to reflect a Tudor look to match his Tudor-style home. Although he had used chemicals in farming and in his garden, Nelson persuaded him to apply mulches and compost. The results were so spectacular that he authorized Nelson to rework all the flower beds. It was an expensive project, but the net effect was magnificent.

WD loved to try new varieties of plants and trees he had seen on trips to other parts of the country. He enjoyed having specimens unique to Greeley, and he encouraged people to tour his garden. His favorite tree was a Tri-Colored Beech. With variegated leaves, throwing off shades of green, pink, white, and purple, it made a statement on the north side of the house. When he died, the tree was moved to the cemetery near his grave site.[46]

Unfortunately, WD was not permitted to enter his garden once his legs began to fail. The risk of a fall was too great. In response, his neighbor Susan Wickham cut samples of emerging blooms and brought bouquets to WD while he languished in bed. She joined forces with Nelson's daughter to prepare a video of the blossoms that were emerging in May of 2007.

WD with North Platte River rainbow trout, 1995. Courtesy of the Farr family.

"He watched the video three times," Susan recalled, "and he cried. He was so moved and so thankful that he could experience his [garden], but there was also sadness that he couldn't get outside."[47] His appreciation of all things sensory, especially food and flowers, became sharper in his last years as his vision declined. He shared his love of British Columbia with Susan, and when she showed him pictures of a visit to Victoria's

Butchart Gardens,[48] "he cried with great joy, thinking of the past . . . about the beauty [of the area] and how exquisite the flowers were." On another occasion, when Susan and her husband brought him chocolates after a trip to New Orleans, he had to stop talking so he could fully appreciate the taste of such an exquisite sweet. "He would talk about the beauty of everything," Susan remembered. "When something moves you to the point of tears, it must represent a great part of who you are."[49]

Fortunately, WD was able to share this essential part of himself with son Randy. The youngest of WD's four boys, Randy was seventeen years younger than John, the oldest. Randy left Greeley to pursue his own interests. He was a gifted writer who took pleasure in sharing his love of gardening with WD. His descriptive letters about the flowers, vegetables, and plants he cultivated elicited a warm response from WD. "It pleases me that you get so much enjoyment from your garden," WD wrote, "plus some good eating."[50] Interspersed with the exchange of gardening information were thoughts about future fishing trips; Randy's shop in Grant's Pass, Oregon; computer work; and a book Randy was writing. It was good father–son communication, and it was enhanced by the many gifts of fruits, candies, special nuts, cakes, and occasional plants Randy sent his father.

WD's letters to Randy further demonstrated his love of beauty in nature. They also disclosed a gentleness that had characterized WD's leadership in business. Although he was admired for the tough negotiating skills required to produce accomplishments, WD's leadership was also attributable to a gentle and empathetic nature. No pleasure or honor validated this personal disposition more than the award he received from the National Cowboy and Western Heritage Museum in Oklahoma City. In 2007, four months before his death, he was inducted into the museum's Hall of Great Westerners.

In many ways this recognition was the climax of WD's life. "Mr. Farr's nomination came from the floor in our Western Heritage Awards Committee last year [2006]," recalled Charles P. "Chuck" Schroeder, executive director of the museum.[51] The pool of candidates in the formal nomination process was deemed inadequate. Schroeder and Linda Mitchell Davis, a previous inductee (2000), suggested WD as someone who met the personal and professional criteria for the Hall of Great Westerners. After museum staff assembled background information on WD, the nomination was presented to the awards committee, which approved it unanimously.

Randy and Melanie Farr with WD Farr (*center*), Trail Ridge Road, Continental Divide, 2003. Courtesy of the Farr family.

Inductees for this award are expected to have made exceptional contributions to the advancement of western heritage and traditions and to have promoted this heritage through their leadership and patronage of organizations dedicated to art, business, industry, the environment, education, humanitarian causes, government, or philanthropy. Their achievements must command national recognition and historical significance, and on a personal level, they are required to exemplify traditional western ideals of honesty, integrity, and self-sufficiency over their lifetime.[52]

Schroeder had observed WD for forty years, and he had known WD for twelve years. He made the nomination because of WD's uncommon vision, reflected in water development, livestock feeding, and other leadership positions he held in various cattle industry organizations. In press releases Schroeder called attention to WD's impact on changes in farming methods, his foresight in planning and completing water projects, and his ongoing inspiration as a leader in the West. "We are reminded daily," Schroeder wrote, "that the West is not just another piece of real estate, but a place that continues to intrigue and provoke big dreams for people around the world. In his mid nineties, Mr. Farr still epitomizes 'the Great Westerner' who is always looking forward, solving near-term challenges in order to achieve a grand ambition for people well beyond his own fences, and making the world a more interesting place [by] just being himself."[53]

The tribute to WD was warm and immensely satisfying. For months he did physical therapy to strengthen his legs in hopes he would be able to attend the ceremony. Family members discussed the possibility of hiring a private plane to take him to Oklahoma City, but in the end his body would not cooperate. He was disappointed but respected the family decision to leave him behind. During the last four months of his life, he was bedridden and under hospice care.

For his caregivers, there was only one option: celebrate the event at home while WD's family represented him in Oklahoma City. They dressed him in western attire, put his "Citizen of the West" hat on his head, and read out loud from *Persimmon Hill* magazine, the museum's flagship publication. They read about WD's achievements and why a plaque with his name would join such notable inductees as Dwight Eisenhower, Kit Carson, Levi Strauss, Sacajawea, Lewis and Clark, Sam Houston, Will Rogers, Charlie Russell, Frederic Remington, Abe Lincoln, John Muir, Teddy Roosevelt, Bose Ikard, and many others on the wall of the marble hallway leading to the historic galleries.[54] WD was grateful and emotional. He had been honored many times in his life, but the "Wrangler" sculpture award his sons brought back later from Oklahoma represented the highest praise that could be bestowed on any man or woman of the West.

WD died at home on August 13, 2007. He often said that the extraordinary events of his life were "just circumstances," but the celebration of his life at Greeley's Union Colony Civic Center belies that assertion. Instead, it exhibited the extent to which he had touched people's lives, both directly and with purpose. The hundreds of people in attendance knew they were witnessing the end of a remarkable life, one that had transformed the community, the region, and the West through innumerable acts of kindness and hard work, new ideas, projects built, and changes made to advance the lives of others. It was a life filled with such a rich assortment of activities and experiences that, as one writer commented, "not even Michener could describe WD and get it all."[55] If any doubt remained about the legacy he had created, it surely vanished when WD became the first person inducted into the Cattle Feeders Hall of Fame in August 2009. Recognized as an agricultural pioneer with extraordinary contributions to water, banking, cattle feeding, and government, WD was acknowledged posthumously as a distinguished western leader.[56] With comparable admiration, the U.S. Senate approved legislation (H.R. 4238) naming the WD Farr Post Office in West Greeley in August 2010. A few months later, the Meat Industry Hall of Fame inducted WD along with Ray Kroc, founder of McDonald's; Colonel Harland Sanders, founder of Kentucky Fried Chicken; and Dave Thomas, founder of Wendy's.

These posthumous awards would have pleased WD, but the measure he took of his own life was better expressed in cowboy lingo. In one of the folders that now constitute the Farr Papers in the Water Resources Archive at CSU, there is a card in WD's handwriting, most probably copied from remarks he heard during a cattlemen's convention he attended in Lubbock, Texas. The card has no date and no identification, but its message reflects the core of WD's thinking as he looked back over his life. "If I had her to do over," it said, "I'd let her go just like she went."[57]

There may not be a better epitaph for this cowboy in the boardroom.

Postscript

Everyone hopes to leave a legacy of some sort, and WD was no exception. While many people were profoundly influenced by their contact with WD, it was his grandson, Richard Daven (RD) Farr, who developed the talents of business management and people skills in the cattle industry that reflected the profound influence and devotion of his admiring grandfather.

The only son of WD's third child, Harry Richard Farr, RD first learned about cattle from his father, when the new Farr feedlot was constructed in Greeley in 1974.[1] Like his grandfather, RD always wanted to be a cowboy. He loved horses and cattle, disdained traditional school sports so he could work at the feedlot or the 70 Ranch in his free time, and studied at Oklahoma State University for a degree in agricultural economics. After college he accepted a job as cattle manager with National Farms, which had purchased the Farr feedlot while he was still in college. He was in charge of shipping, receiving, and general care of feedlot animals. He had a keen sense of animal behavior, what WD called "livestock sense," and he earned respect from his family and feedlot work crews because he tackled projects with enthusiasm and took pride in manual labor.

He also earned the admiration of Ed and Lee Bass, who were pleased when he agreed to manage their ranches in Kansas. The Bass brothers, owners of National Farms and ranch operations in Kansas, Oklahoma, and Texas, were leaders in cattle raising and feeding. They were known for urban revitalization projects in the United States, sustainable management of the tall-grass prairie, and service to their alma mater, Yale University. Lee Bass saw potential in RD and invited him to become director of agribusiness and livestock operations on several of his ranches. RD now manages

WD (*left*) and RD Farr on the Dean River, 1993. Courtesy of the Farr family.

the irrigated farms and ranches, buys and sells cattle, and controls the progress of up to 40,000 animals from weaning to feedlot. The responsibility is enormous. The talent RD manifests is both innate and a reflection of his grandfather's guidance.

"Unlike most cowboys," RD recalled, "my grandfather always looked ahead, not backwards. For him the next twenty years were going to be the most exciting, and I found that hard to believe given what he had been through in ninety years." WD cautioned him about change, not as something to rue, but as an inevitable cycle of life. "Whereas I grump and groan about all the changes that have happened to Greeley since I went to school there, my grandfather always relished new circumstances and opportunities, developing ideas and possibilities for a better future. From the time I was just a kid, he would ask me how the feedlot might be run better, what mistakes we were making, and what I thought about different procedures. I couldn't believe he was taking me seriously, but I learned that he truly sought out better ways of doing things from almost everyone he met."

WD enjoyed people and was gregarious. RD observed from him the importance of joining industry associations and dressing professionally in order to convey serious interest in the business at hand. From both grandparents he learned to pursue various tasks to completion, to associate himself with leaders of successful companies, and to keep an office in a bank or credit union where he would be surrounded by community decision makers.

Most of all, RD learned from his grandfather's example that true leadership is composed of both humility and hard work. WD shared his mistakes with RD, urged him to research all aspects of the cattle business, and advised him to pay attention to those individuals who were achievers. Without specifically directing his grandson, WD demonstrated by example that effective leadership included flexibility, patience, and a good sense of the potential of each person with whom he worked. RD soon comprehended that his grandfather's unlimited interest in the world around him—especially the changes brought about by technology, innovation, and globalization—could be emulated and put to good use. If WD had lived long enough to understand and make use of a Blackberry cellular phone, RD concluded, he would have been euphoric. The weather that fascinated him for so long would be available to him daily. Seeing its effect on water deliveries, crops, and livestock markets would prove once and for all the value of seeing opportunity in change.

THE FAMILY OF WD FARR: A GENEALOGICAL CHART

Dates refer to birth years

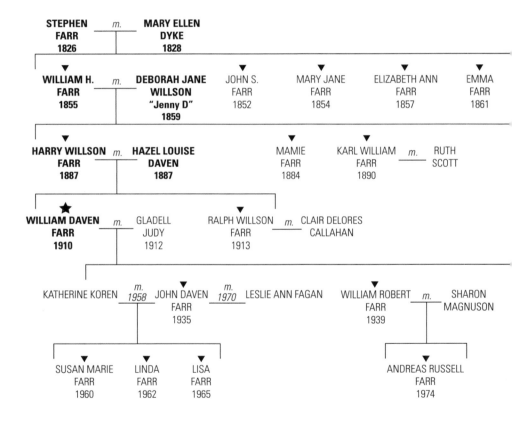

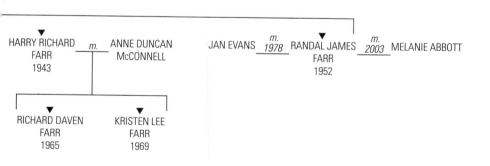

WALTER J.
FARR
1859

THOMAS E.   *m.*   MAY
FARR   O'LERY
1861

CHARLES AUGUSTUS   *m.*   MARY G.
FARR   DUNN
1862   1865

ANNA   *m.*   ROSSWELL
FARR   HUTCHINSON
c. 1869

LLOYD ALBERT   *m.*   LAURA ELIZABETH
FARR   CONGDON
1899

HARRY RICHARD   *m.*   ANNE DUNCAN
FARR   McCONNELL
1943

JAN EVANS   *m. 1978*   RANDAL JAMES   *m. 2003*   MELANIE ABBOTT
                        FARR
                        1952

RICHARD DAVEN
FARR
1965

KRISTEN LEE
FARR
1969

233

Notes

In researching this book, I interviewed dozens of people, including members of the Farr family, business associates of WD Farr, and experts in the cattle, farming, banking, and water resource communities. I selected those people who had a special area of expertise or a unique association with WD Farr. Most of these interviews—whether they took place in person or over the telephone—were taped and transcribed. I donated these tapes and transcriptions to the Water Resource Archives, Colorado State University, Fort Collins, Colorado.

INTRODUCTION

1. A history major with a degree from the University of Toronto's Trinity College, Gladwell first worked as a journalist for the *American Spectator* and *Insight on the News.* He then became the science and business writer for the *Washington Post* and has been a staff writer for the *New Yorker* since 1996. See Gladwell, *Tipping Point, Blink,* and *Outliers.*

2. Allison Sherry, "W.D. Farr: Greeley Man Pioneered Efforts to Improve Water Use," *Denver Post,* August 7, 2000.

3. David McCullough, "Leadership and the History You Don't Know" (Jack R. Anderson Distinguished Lecture, Miami University , Oxford, Ohio, Nov. 9, 2009).

CHAPTER 1

1. In the last thirty years of his life, Farr was referred to as WD, resulting from a time when he and son Bill (also known as WR) shared an office. Frequently, when people came to visit, they would ask to speak with "Senior" or "Junior." Neither liked the nicknames, so "WD" came about as a way to separate father and son. For consistency, I use WD throughout the book to avoid confusion with his grandfather Billy and his son Bill. It should be noted, however, that WD was also called Billy and Bill at various stages of his youth and career.

2. The Dorset History Centre contains marriage, baptism, and burial records for Beer Hackett and other Dorset County townships and civil parishes. See www.dorsetforyou.com/archives.

3. Stephen Farr of Beer Hackett, will dated 1858 and inventory and evaluation dated 1864, FFOOKS and Darlington Archive, Dorset County, file reference D/FFO/16/3, 1858–1864, www.dorsetcc.gov.uk/archives. Land ownership information is located at www.dorset-opc.com/BeerHacketFiles/BeerHacket.htm.

4. Mary Gladys Farr (Aunt Gladys) Reynolds, born in Greeley on July 9, 1893, was one of four daughters of Charles A. Farr. She wrote an undated letter to "Bill Farr" in which she stated that Stephen, age twenty-five, and Mary Ellen, age twenty-three, left England for America "soon after the ceremonies" because Stephen had been disinherited. Two half-sisters continued to live on the Farr estate in Dorset County and two brothers were killed in steeple chase activities. Between 1900 and 1905, Stephen's son, William H. Farr, visited the estate, where he found a "village of retainers" numbering 200 "who cared for the crops and the many other needs." Loose material, Papers of W.D. Farr, Water Resources Archive, Colorado State University, Fort Collins, Colo. (hereafter cited as Farr Papers, Water Resources Archive, CSU).

5. Eton College, a boarding school for boys, was founded in 1440 by King Henry VI. It is located in England near Windsor Castle. Eton is one of the original nine English public schools as defined by the Public Schools Act of 1868.

6. "Examining the Transatlantic Voyage."

7. Until 1867, Canada was a colony of the British Empire and subject to its laws. Colonials rarely challenged British ships in violation of imperial laws. After 1867, Canada became a self-governing dominion, a federation of provinces that maintained a loose relationship with the British monarchy.

8. 1901 Census of Canada, province of Ontario, East Elgin District, Malahide Sub. District, p. 11, shows John Farr, age 48, a farmer, married to Emily Leverton, with one child, Ethel Farr, age 18. Available at www.search.ancestrylibrary.com.

9. Kettle Creek, which descends through Ontario into Lake Erie at Port Stanley, divided the townships of Yarmouth and Southwold. According to the Ontario, Canada, Census of 1871, Samuel Farr, a possible relative, was born in Ireland about 1811. He was an Anglican farmer who had settled not far from Port Stanley in Southwold Township prior to 1864. The George R. Tremaine Map for Elgin County notes his land in Range 1, north of Union Road, Lot 14. Barbara Hoskins, St. Thomas, Ontario, Public Library, located this information for the author.

10. Ontario GenWeb, html. For general reference, see also Rayburn, *Place Names of Ontario*. The seven townships in Elgin County were as follows: Aldborough, Dunwich, Southwold, Yarmouth, Malahide, Bayham, and South Dorchester. Regarding Colonel Talbot, see Arnold Raymond Firby, "The Firby Family History," www.execulink.com/~firby/history.html.

11. Economic data for Elgin County between 1850 and 1880 can be found in Hall, *Economic Development in Elgin County*. See also Cumming, *Historical Atlas of Elgin County*, pp. v, vi, x.

12. Jean Bircham of Aylmer, Ontario, found Stephen Farr listed as a teamster in *Church at the Bend of the River*, a locally published history of the Port Stanley Anglican Church.

13. See Sims, *Sims' History of Elgin County*. See also Obituary of Mary Ellen Farr, *Aylmer (Ontario) Express*, July 30, 1903.

14. I am indebted to Jean Bircham of Aylmer, Ontario, for locating the tax rolls, censuses, and land registry records that describe Stephen Farr's status as tenant farmer. See Land Registry, Yarmouth Township, Elgin County, Concession 4, Lot 21, pp. 22–22L; Yarmouth Twp. Assessment/Collectors' Rolls, 1861–1878; Malahide Twp. Assessment/Collectors' Rolls, 1878–1890; Assessment Roll, Municipality of Malahide, 1890; and Elgin and Malahide counties, census records, 1861–1901, St. Thomas Public Library, St. Thomas, Ontario.

15. Unless otherwise noted, information on Billy Farr's travels from Ontario to Greeley, Colo., is based on several interviews of WD Farr by Greg Silkensen, 1997; by Sally Mier, 1999 and 2000; and by the author, 2006 and 2007.

16. Affidavit signed by WH Farr, n.d., Greeley Museum, Greeley, Colo. When asked to fill out a form for the Meeker Memorial Museum, Billy Farr wrote that he started for the Black Hills in 1877.

17. In 1877, Crazy Horse fought his last battle and was finally captured and murdered by a soldier in Nebraska. Sitting Bull led his Lakota band of Sioux into Canada to escape ongoing harassment by the soldiers of General Nelson Miles, and all of northeastern Colo. was opened for settlement when bands of Arapaho and Cheyenne Indians were defeated in1869 at the Battle of Summit Springs near present-day Sterling, Colo.

18. Greeley was the principal community of the Union Colony founded in 1870 under the guidance of Nathan Meeker, agricultural editor of the *New York Tribune*. Named after the paper's owner, Horace Greeley, the community was located in Weld County near the junction of the South Platte and Cache la Poudre rivers and on the route of the Denver Pacific Railroad between Cheyenne and Denver. Greeley farmers had begun to benefit from an expanded irrigation system that diverted water into Ditch No. 2 from the Cache la Poudre River to farms within a twenty-mile radius north of Greeley.

19. WD Farr, interview with the author, December 22, 2006; and with Sally Mier, December 21, 1999. WD proudly noted that his grandfather took the stage driver to the 1904 Paris Exposition as payment in full of his debt. "That's the kind of man he was," WD noted, "and that's how I, too, learned to take advantage of opportunities."

20. See Ford, "Greeley, Colorado: Agricultural Mecca of the West," sect. titled "City of Saints."

21. Boyd, *History*, 12–17. Meeker and his wife were followers of the French social reformer Francois Marie Charles Fourier, who believed that a superior society could be formed based on innovative social and economic policies. Horace Greeley embraced these ideas and financed several Fourier communities. What Meeker envisioned for the Union Colony was a homogeneous Fourier-style community of Anglo-Saxon Protestants who had money, high moral standards, a strong work ethic, conservative values, adherence to temperance principles, a belief in coopera- tion, and an understanding of agriculture. The founding of the Union Colony coincided with the last wave of utopian societies in the United States. Greeley was the third temperance colony, and anyone who manufactured or sold liquor would forfeit the deed to his property. See also A. F. Tyler, *Freedom's Ferment*. Tyler places the Union Colony in historical perspective with other utopian colonies of the nineteenth century.

22. Boyd, *History*, 69, 70.

23. Ibid, 159. Boyd explains: "the limited development attained in agricul- ture during the first seven years dwarfed the business of the town and impaired its growth as a whole."

24. Webb, *Great Plains*, 152. According to Webb, during the first half of the nineteenth century, and possibly until after the Civil War, "there existed in the public mind a Great American Desert situated to the east of the Rocky Mountains. . . . To them the region was actually a desert, wholly uninhabitable with the methods and the implements and instruments of pioneering which had been previously used east of the ninety-eighth meridian, and wholly undesirable. The occupation of the region was impossible without the complete alteration of methods of utilization."

25. As quoted in Ubbelohde, Benson, and Smith, *Colorado History*, 188.

26. Wentworth, *America's Sheep Trails*, 611.

27. Deborah Jane Willson was the daughter of Mordecai Willson and Rachel Van Syckle, who had married near Ancaster, Ontario, on November 16, 1830. The Willsons seem to have come from New Jersey, where Mordecai was born in 1808. Deborah Jane's brother, George Mordecai Willson, also came to Greeley with his wife, Mary J. Harding, in order to escape the "deadly consumption" from which George was suffering. He lived to the age of 91. See his obituary in the *Greeley (Colo.) Tribune*, August 5, 1941.

28. Under the preemption acts of 1841 and 1843, citizens were allowed to squat on eighty acres of the public domain, gaining title to the property by right of prior settlement and by cash payment once the land was surveyed. When Congress passed the Homestead Act in 1862, some squatters chose to seek ownership under the new law. Existing records do not make clear when Billy Farr first worked his land, but Wentworth refers to the "Jenny Farr Preemption" in *America's Sheep Trails*, p. 352, and anecdotal references handed down through the Farr family point to some activity in the area prior to 1884. In this year Billy applied for a quarter- section under the Homestead Act, and on July 12, 1889, a patent was issued to

him for the southeast quarter of section 18 in township 5, north of range 65, west of the 6th principal meridian. The Homestead Act required five years of improving the property before a patent could be issued.

29. Hartman, *Century of Remarkable Progress*, 11.

30. Ibid. The system in place today allows farmers to order water when they need it.

31. This story is based on Wentworth, *America's Sheep Trails*, 352–53, and on transcribed interviews with WD Farr. The details vary, but the essence of the event is clear.

32. *America's Sheep Trails*, 360, 370. By the end of 1925, Colorado's share of the nation's lamb feeding industry was just shy of 40 percent.

33. As quoted in Wentworth, *America's Sheep Trails*, 357, the *Daily Drovers' Journal* in Chicago reported an increasing gap between prices paid for lambs and sheep (wethers), from fifty cents in 1885 to eight dollars in 1945.

34. Buffum and Griffith, "Swine Feeding in Colorado," 4. In the Cache la Poudre, Big Thompson, St. Vrain, and South Platte river valleys, the principal crop in 1902 was alfalfa, followed by wheat, oats, and potatoes. However, the Colorado Agricultural Experiment Station, which was promoting cultivation of sugar beets, predicted that sugar beets "may eclipse some of the former products in acreage and importance."

35. "Beet Tops for Feed," *Greeley (Colo.) Tribune*, January 29, 1903.

36. Ubbelohde et al., *Colorado History*, 271.

37. Obituary of William H. Farr, *Weld County News*, September 29, 1932.

38. Weld County Court, affidavit dated July 19, 1886, petition no. P-10, Colorado State Archives, Denver. Brother Walter was granted citizenship March 12, 1892 (petition no. P-30), and Thomas was granted citizenship January 15, 1895 (petition no. P-53). Charles was granted citizenship by the District Court, August 29, 1908 (petition no. P-104). These records are available on line at www.colorado.gov/dpa/doit/archives/final.gif.

39. Navajo–Churro sheep are descended from an ancient Iberian breed that was brought to the Americas by Spaniards who used them for food and clothing. Prized for their remarkable hardiness and fine-textured wool, the churros became the mainstay for Spanish and Mexican ranches in the Southwest. When Native Americans engaged in raids on Hispanic communities, they stole livestock. Navajo weaving specialized in wool from these churros. El Rancho de las Golondrinas, a restored eighteenth-century *estancia* in Santa Fe, New Mexico, has studied the origins of the churro and presently serves as home for pure bloods of this breed. The author is indebted to staff at the Rancho for the above information.

40. Wentworth, *America's Sheep Trails*, 363.

41. "All Bound Over: Three Sheepherders Held to District Court," *Greeley (Colo.) Tribune*, July 11, 1901; and "Given One Dollar," *Greeley (Colo.) Tribune*, January 29, 1903.

42. *Greeley (Colo.) Tribune,* June 2, 1898.

43. *Greeley (Colo.) Tribune,* January 7, 1904.

44. Hartman, *Century of Remarkable Progress,* 12–13. At a later time, this ditch became an integral component of WD's plans to stabilize and expand Greeley's water system.

45. No record has been found of the stage driver's name, and the stories printed in the July 12, 1900, *Greeley (Colo.) Tribune* provide no clarification. Nevertheless, Harry Watson arrived in Greeley on May 1, 1870. According to his great grandson, John Watson, Harry hauled logs from the Poudre River for railroad ties in the 1870s. Conceivably, Billy Farr could have hitched a ride with Harry on a log wagon. But the truth is illusive. Because WD often repeated the story of his grandfather's repayment of this debt, it is included here with as much verification as has been available through research and to illustrate the importance to WD of honor and business integrity.

46. The *Tartar Prince* belonged to the Prince Line out of Newcastle, England. Built in 1895, it was considered one of the company's fastest and most reliable vessels until it tragically caught fire in the Azores and sank. See *New York Times,* December 8, 1902.

47. *Greeley (Colo.) Tribune,* July 12, 1900.

48. Ibid.

49. *Greeley (Colo.) Tribune,* March 11, 1897.

50. I am grateful to Peggy Ford for this observation. In a note to the author dated December 31, 2007, she commented that on occasion she had jokingly referred to the history of Greeley's families as "incestuous." But as viewed by Greeley attorney William R. Kelly, the five families and their businesses were generally appreciated by Weld County citizens, because they supported innovative farming, a developed transportation infrastructure, and better access to capital. Consequently, their actions brought improved credit and a reputation of business integrity to the entire community. See "The High Five" (unpublished article), 1968, William R. Kelly Papers, 94.49.10, Greeley Museum Archive, Greeley, Colo.

51. *Greeley (Colo.) Tribune,* August 14, 1902. The paper noted, "The potato is king."

52. Farr and Taylor separated by mutual consent, with Taylor continuing to run the blacksmith shop. *Greeley (Colo.) Tribune,* April 7 and 14, 1892.

53. One cfs is equal to 449 gallons of water per minute, or one cubic foot of water passing a given point in one second.

54. Within days of the Water Works Committee's vote to approve the purchase of W. R. Adams's 6.89 cfs from the Big Thompson River, a group from Fort Collins reportedly met with Greeley mayor H. G. Watson "between trains" to discuss the prospect of piping water from the Cache la Poudre River, a proposal that supposedly had support from Greeley's municipal board. There was also discussion of bringing water to Greeley through a longer pipeline from a chain of lakes near Mt. Clark in the Rawah Mountains west of Chambers Lake. See *Greeley (Colo.) Tribune,* December 11, 1902.

55. The bitterness of a feud that erupted in 1874 between Fort Collins and Greeley was still on the minds of many. During a very dry summer, Greeley found that its ditches were not getting water because of upstream diversions by Fort Collins. A lively debate ensued, with Fort Collins unwilling to recognize Greeley's priority rights. Fortunately, the matter was resolved when the rains returned, but the contentious nature of the quarrel inspired the Colorado constitutional convention to spell out the meaning of "priority" in the 1876 constitution. See Dunbar, "Water Conflicts and Controls in Colorado." In 1905, Larimer County farmers were concerned that Greeley would be getting a significant amount of water with an early priority of August 3, 1862.

56. The pipeline was made of 4 x 4 tongue and groove oak, wrapped with steel bands.

57. *Greeley (Colo.) Tribune*, May 5, 1905.

58. *Greeley (Colo.) Tribune*, May 11, 1905.

59. WD Farr, "Family History," Farr Papers, Water Resources Archive, CSU. See also Greeley *Tribune*, January 16, 1896.

60. *Greeley (Colo.) Tribune*, August 17, 1899.

61. *Greeley (Colo.) Tribune*, March 23, 1895.

62. *Fort Collins (Colo.) Weekly Courier*, March 3, 1909.

63. L. G. Norris, "Conversation with William R. Kelly," 427–30.

64. *Greeley (Colo.) Tribune*, January 1, 1910.

65. The U.S. Reclamation Service became the U.S. Bureau of Reclamation in 1923.

66. *Greeley (Colo.) Tribune*, June 16, 1909.

67. Speech by Delphus E. Carpenter, June 10, 1910, Box 57, Delphus Carpenter Papers, Water Resources Archive, CSU. I am indebted to Nicolai Kryloff for sharing his understanding of this occasion with me.

CHAPTER 2

1. WD Farr, interview by Sally Mier, December 21, 1999.

2. Noel Letters on Genealogy of the Noel Lines, http://www.mcn.org; and Family Group Record of Peter Daven, http://www.familysearch.org.

3. Formed in 1890, this club was named for a character in William Dean Howell's novel, *Lady of the Aroostook*, who went about saying, "But, I want to know." Members were required to wear a hat and gloves and were expected to make twenty-minute presentations on subjects of interest to the membership. I am indebted to Peggy Ford of the Greeley Museum for bringing this club to my attention and to Betty Henshaw for her research on this subject.

4. The health complications that prevented WD from completing his university training are detailed later in this chapter.

5. WD Farr, interview by Gregory M. Silkensen, August 4, 1997.

6. WD Farr, interview by Sally Mier, December 21, 1999.

7. As told to Betty Jo Geiger and published in "W. D. Farr: Recollections of a Pioneer Cattle Feeder" in *Calf News Cattle Feeder* (April 1991), p. 15, the last of a fourteen-part series of interviews between Geiger and WD. By 2009, WD's oldest son, John, was living in a house he built in Encampment, Wyoming.

8. Grade Reports, Grades 1–7, Personal Papers, Farr Papers, Water Resources Archive, CSU.

9. WD Farr, interview by Sally Mier, December 21, 1999.

10. Ibid.

11. "Greeley High School Yearbooks," Greeley Museum Archive, Greeley, Colo.

12. Montgomery, "Commercial Feeder of the Year," 13.

13. According to Pamela C. Whitenack, director of Hershey Community Activities, the company imprinted this slogan on its chocolate candy bars from 1906 to 1926. The slogan was based on comparing one pound of chocolate to one pound of beef. As she noted in an e-mail message to the author on March 31, 2008, "in the era when calories were a good thing and a major indicator for nutritional value, milk chocolate offered more than meat."

14. L. G. Norris, *Conversation with William R. Kelly.*

15. *Greeley (Colo.) Tribune,* February 22, 1930.

16. William R. Kelly Papers, no. 94.4919, Greeley Museum Archive, Greeley, Colo. Kelly noted that Harry Farr was considered a "ditch man," always searching for new sources of water and reservoir sites.

17. Ibid.

18. Robert D. Carey was the son of Joseph M. Carey, Wyoming Territory's first U.S. attorney general. He was also a U.S. senator from 1890 to 1895, during which time he sponsored an act that ceded federal lands in arid and semi-arid areas to the states with the understanding that private citizens could become landowners for a small fee, provided they brought water to their property. The Carey Act failed as an attempt at reclamation in western states, because private capital was insufficient to finance the vast enterprises needed to control water in the West. Not until the Newlands Act of 1902 did Congress demonstrate an understanding of this concept. Joseph Carey was a successful cattleman who was also known for outstanding crops produced through irrigation. His main ranch was located just east of Casper, Wyoming, at Careyhurst. For additional information, see the Joseph M. Carey Family Papers, 1869–1978, Collection no. 01212, American Heritage Center, University of Wyoming, Laramie, Wyo.

19. The Carey Ranch of Wyoming was also known as the Reverse Four Ranch. The ranch's owners had built a headquarters in the little town of Hayden sometime in the 1880s, where they also had a store and post office. After World War I, when cattle prices bottomed, the ranch was purchased by two Denver men, but it was still known as the Carey Ranch. WD Farr to Kimberley Vogel, district ranger,

Hahns Peak/Bears Ears Ranger District, U.S. Forest Service, February 26, 2004, Farr Papers, Water Resources Archive, CSU.

20. Descriptions of WD's California Park experience are drawn from several interviews with WD Farr (Mier, Silkensen, and Tyler).

21. Alan Dumas, "Citizen of the West W. D. Farr: Farr-Sighted Greeley Rancher Helped Bring Water to Front Range," *Rocky Mountain News*, January 10, 1999.

22. Kleinheinz, *Sheep Management Breeds and Judging*. Kleinheinz had no university education himself, but the University of Wisconsin hired him in 1889 because he knew sheep. For the next thirty-nine years, he was known for the prize-winning flocks he took to the Chicago Fat Stock Show and the International Livestock Exposition. See "Prof. Frank Kleinheinz," *Wisconsin Country Magazine* 22, no. 2 (November 1928), 23.

23. Table Showing the Average Scholarship Grades of Members and Pledges of Beta Theta Pi Fraternity at the University of Wisconsin, First Semester, 1928–1929, sent to the author by David Null, Director, University Archives, University of Wisconsin. See also www.betathetapi.org/index.php?option=com_content&task. The first Beta Theta Pi fraternity was organized at Miami University, Oxford, Ohio, in 1839.

24. Rotary's motto, "Service above Self," was followed by an action test: "Is it the truth? Is it fair to all concerned? Will it build good will and friendships? Will it be beneficial to all concerned?"

25. WD Farr, interview with Gregory M. Silkensen, August 4, 1997.

26. Announced in the *Greeley (Colo.) Tribune*, July 19, 1934.

27. WD Farr, interview with Gregory M. Silkensen, August 4, 1997. WD had to have two more operations on his sinus cavities. Throughout his life allergy attacks caused considerable suffering.

28. WD Farr, interview with Sally Mier, December 28, 1999.

29. Best known for inventing a flume that would measure the flow of water adjusted for depth, Parshall joined the Colorado Agricultural College faculty in 1907. After six years, he was hired by the U.S. Department of Agriculture, but he continued to use the laboratories of the college and became known as a pioneer in civil engineering and hydrology. See http://lib.colostate.edu/archives/water /Parshall/faculty.html.

30. WD Farr, interview with Gregory M. Silkensen, August 4, 1997.

31. According to information collected by the U.S. Bureau of Agricultural Economics and published in *Agricultural Outlook for 1934*, between 1923 and 1931 the number of sheep in the United States increased by 17 million. See "Sheep and Cattle Estimates," 19.

32. Montgomery, "Commercial Feeder of the Year," 13.

33. See *Greeley (Colo.) Tribune*, August 19, 1929.

34. Colorado Cooperative Crop Reporting Service and U.S. Department of Agriculture, *Agricultural Statistics*, 10; and Mehls and Mehls, *Weld County Colorado Historic*, 22–29.

35. *Fort Collins (Colo.) Courier*, October 27, 1921.

36. According to the *Weld County (Colo.) News*, June 26, 1930, the Colorado Cooperative Crop Reporting Service reported a total crop worth for Colorado of $21.8 million for 1929, of which the largest amount of money by far came from sugar beets ($7.1 million), followed by hay ($4.0 million), potatoes ($2.6 million), wheat ($2.25 million), corn ($1.25 million), and beans ($1.1 million).

37. H. H. Simpson, "Annual Report, Weld County Extension Service, 1930," Colorado Agricultural Archive, CSU. See also *Weld County News*, April 3, 1930, Greeley Museum Archive.

38. *Weld County (Colo.) News*, March 12, 1931.

39. This act, formally known as the U.S. Tariff Act of 1930, was signed by President Hoover on June 17, 1930. It raised import duties to protect American industries and farmers, bringing American protectionism to the highest level ever. Results were disastrous. Although lamb, beef, mutton, live cattle, sheep, wool, and sugar prices spiked briefly, the tariff resulted in retaliation by America's trading partners and hastened the economy's sharp decline.

40. As quoted in the *Greeley (Colo.) Tribune*, October 31, 1930.

41. Leonard, *Trials and Triumphs*, 20.

42. *Weld County (Colo.) News*, May 8, 1930.

43. *The Home Gas and Electric Company: The Story of Its Development through Forty-Five Years 1902–1947*, p. 12.

44. Minute books, Home Gas and Electric Co. of Greeley, archival holdings of Property Services, Records Department, Xcel Energy, Denver, Colo. (also available at Greeley Municipal Archives, Greeley, Colo., ID #1972.30.0021). It is not clear whether the company was ever in the gas business. It did well with what John Farr referred to as a "balanced electrical load," providing electricity to homes in the winter and to irrigation pumps in the summer. The Greeley Gas Company provided most of the gas. John Farr, communication to the author, April 28, 2008.

45. *Home Gas and Electric Company*, 55, 57.

46. Minutes books, Home Gas and Electric Co. of Greeley for 1928 show that Harry held 406 shares of stock, and his mother, Jenny Farr, held 250 shares. In 1929, the company had 40,000 shares outstanding, and some evidence points to share values as high as $50. One can only speculate how much Harry actually received when the company was sold, but as Nicolai Kryloff (one of the author's research assistants) astutely observed, the cash may have been a major factor in helping the Farrs get through the Depression.

47. *Home Gas and Electric Company*, 57.

48. Between 1929 and 1932, the number of employed households in Denver fell from 87 to 68 percent. "By 1933 one in four Coloradans was out of work" (Leonard and Noel, *Denver*, 204).

49. Wickens, "New Deal in Colorado," 283.

50. Ibid., 205–206.

51. *Weld County (Colo.) News,* July 9, 1931.

52. *Weld County (Colo.) News,* September 24, 1931.

53. "Annual Report, Weld County Extension Service, 1931," Colorado Agricultural Archive, CSU.

54. Leonard, *Trials and Triumphs,* 21–23.

55. Wolfenbarger, "Depression, Drought and Dust," 3–5.

56. WD told this same story in most interviews. He also wrote about it in letters, reminiscences, and published articles. See, for example, his letter to Susannah S. Borg, February 12, 1997, WDF—Editorial Board, Farr Papers, Water Resources Archive, CSU.

57. Creeps were small tables built low to the ground (i.e., self-feeders), around which an enclosure was built to keep out mother cows. Calves were started on shelled corn and oats. When wheat became available, it was substituted because of price. See "Report of Calf Creep Feeding Demonstration, F. L. Cuykendall Ranch, Roggen, Colorado, 1931–1932, Weld County Extension Service," Colorado Agricultural Archive, CSU.

58. First evidence appears in the *Greeley (Colo.) Tribune,* May 24, 1916.

59. Weld County Credit Association, as reported in the "Annual Report of the Weld County Extension Service, 1938," Agricultural Archive, CSU.

60. WD Farr, "Farr Family Early Years," manuscript in the Farr Papers, Water Resources Archive, CSU.

61. WD Farr, interview by Sherm Ewing, January 21, 1987, Farr Papers, Water Resources Archive, CSU.

62. *Weld County (Colo.) News,* October 8, 1931.

63. Wickens, "New Deal in Colorado," 277–78.

64. Ibid. See also Wickens, *Colorado in the Great Depression,* 22.

65. Ubbelhode et al, *Colorado History,* 312; and Lamm and Smith, *Pioneers and Politicians,* 129–131.

66. "Annual Report, Weld County Extension Service, 1934," Colorado Agricultural Archive, CSU.

67. Ben H. King, Editorial, *Weld County (Colo.) News,* February 6, 1930. King, assistant director of markets for the Federal Farm Bureau, wrote six guest editorials for the *Weld County (Colo.) News* in support of the Federal Farm Board as created by the Agricultural Marketing Act, signed by Herbert Hoover on June 15, 1929. King's third article is cited above.

68. Papers of William Kelly, no. 94.49.10, Greeley Museum Archive, Greeley, Colo.

69. Geiger, "W. D. Farr: Recollections of a Pioneer Cattle Feeder,"(April, 1991): 12.

CHAPTER 3

1. Consideration of the causes and role of myths abounds in scholarship dealing with the American West. Readers might consult Murdoch, *American West*; Wrobel, *End of American Exceptionalism*; R. White, *It's Your Misfortune*; Athearn, *Mythic West in Twentieth-Century America*; and Limerick, *Legacy of Conquest*.

2. Because of the confusion resulting from frequent use of her last name as a first name, "Judy" replaced "Gladell" as the name by which she was referred. Because she was also something of a tomboy, she referred to herself as "Bill" in family correspondence and insisted that her family call her "Bill" at home.

3. The *Greeley (Colo.) Tribune*, February 20, 1997, gives "Pinuker" as Amelia's maiden name. Other sources use "Pindergrass" (see http://trees.ancestry.com/pt /person.) and "Pinneker." See "South Dakota Marriages, 1905–1949," at http://search. ancestry.com/cgi-bin/sse.dll?rank.. Most probably, she had German and Russian roots.

4. WD Farr, interview with the author, December 22, 2006.

5. John Farr recounted this story in a communication to the author dated February 2, 2007. He noted that when a Farr family member became long-winded, someone would shout "caboose," and the monologue would end. John also reported that WD loved to attend Denver Bronco football games, but if he was driving and talking at the same time, the car would start slowing down and WD would have to be reminded of the game's starting time.

6. WD Farr, interview with the author, December 22, 2006.

7. Ibid.

8. WD Farr, interview with Sally Mier, February 15, 2000.

9. Jim Kehl, "Built to Last," *Greeley (Colo.) Tribune*, July 7, 2002.

10. *Greeley (Colo.) Tribune*, January 1, 1938; and June 19, 1939.

11. Leonard and Noel, *Denver*, 204–205.

12. U.S. Bureau of the Census, "Population, Internal Migration 1935 to 1940," 3, 17, 45, 69, 92, 115. Some evidence suggests that the slaughter of farm animals may have contributed to the ultimate failure of the Agricultural Adjustment Act. Whether or not this is true, according to U.S. Bureau of the Census figures, 110,000 people left Colorado in the 1930s (not all of whom were in agriculture), about one-half of whom moved to California and the Northwest. See also *Colorado Year Book, 1959–1961*, 497, as cited in Wickens, "New Deal in Colorado," 288, n. 49.

13. WD Farr, interview by Michael Welsh, October 16, 2002.

14. Leonard and Noel, *Denver*, 216. Leonard and Noel cite James Wickens's *Colorado in the Great Depression*, which notes that after initial suspicion of the Agricultural Adjustment Act, 11,000 sugar farmers eventually enrolled in the program.

15. Wickens, "New Deal in Colorado," 288. The Agricultural Adjustment Act was designed to raise prices of eight major commodities to levels equal to the buying power of the period from 1909 to 1914. It was based on voluntary production controls, with farmer committees working with the Department of Agriculture

to determine the amount of acreage to be fallowed. It remained in effect twenty-eight months (May 1933 to January 1936), when the U.S. Supreme Court found unconstitutional a provision in the law that it be funded by taxing those who processed the agricultural commodities.

16. Hofstadter, *Age of Reform*, 300–301; Degler, *Out of Our Past*, 416; and Leuchtenburg, *Roosevelt and the New Deal*, 326, 338–344, as cited in Wickens, "New Deal in Colorado," 291, n. 58.

17. In 1940 Colorado voted overwhelmingly for Republican Wendell Willkie against FDR, following the lead of Democrats Ed Johnson, Ralph Carr, Alva Adams, and others.

18. Wickens, "New Deal in Colorado," 291.

19. *Rocky Mountain News*, October 23, 1944, as cited in Wickens, "New Deal in Colorado," 291, n. 60.

20. *Greeley (Colo.) Tribune*, October 5, 1936. They were playing either bridge or rummy. Bridge requires the commitment of two players to a contract at the close of bidding.

21. *Greeley (Colo.) Tribune*, April 18, 1935.

22. "Weld County Colorado Extension Agent Annual Reports, 1936, 1937," Colorado Agricultural Archive, Fort Collins, CSU.

23. *Greeley (Colo.) Tribune*, September 12, 1935; May 19, 1936; December 16, 1937; and July 6, 1938.

24. *Greeley (Colo.) Tribune*, January 15, 1937. According to an article in *Feedlot* (Montgomery, "Commercial Feeder of the Year"), Harry's lamb feeding peaked in 1935 when he fed 100,000 lambs. His recognition of the newly organized chain stores as a factor in determining the future of meat production trends was visionary. Twenty years later, the *New York Times* noted that instead of cooperating, the large packing companies and chain stores were in conflict and a "revolution" was in the making. William M. Blair, "Packers Battle Chain Stores in Marketing 'Revolution,'" *New York Times*, March 24, 1958.

25. *Greeley (Colo.) Tribune*, May 25, 1936; and August 21, 1936.

26. *Greeley (Colo.) Tribune*, January 7, 1937.

27. *Greeley (Colo.) Tribune*, May 18, 1938.

28. *Greeley (Colo.) Tribune*, August 26, 1936.

29. *Greeley (Colo.) Tribune*, May 1, 1936; and July 3, 1936.

30. *Greeley (Colo.) Tribune*, February 9, 1935; and September 29, 1937.

31. The act prohibited packers from engaging in unfair and deceptive practices, giving undue preferences to persons or localities, apportioning supplies in restraint of commerce, manipulating prices, creating monopolies, or conspiring to aid in unlawful acts. The packers challenged the act, but the Supreme Court concluded it was legal under the Commerce Clause of the U.S. Constitution.

32. "Farr Family History," edited by Cattlemen's Communications, Farr Papers, Water Resources Archive, CSU.

33. WD Farr to M. E. Ensminger, May 30, 1996, Agriservices Foundation, Farr Papers, Water Resources Archive, CSU. See also Lenthe, "W.D. Farr, Statesman."

34. Geiger, "W. D. Farr: Recollections of a Pioneer Cattle Feeder," (April, 1991): 15.

35. For the early history of meat grading, see J. J. Harris, H. R. Cross, and J. W. Savell, "History of Meat Grading in the United States," at http://meat.tamu.edu/history.html.

36. WD Farr, interview by Sherm Ewing, January 21, 1987, p. 10, Farr Papers, Water Resources Archive, CSU.

37. WD Farr to Don Butler, July 26, 1996, National Cattlemen's Foundation, Farr Papers, Water Resources Archive, CSU.

38. Curran, "Pioneer of Farr West," 11A. Commission men represented livestock owners and communicated to packers what was available for purchase. "Stockers" were 300–500 pound animals that had been weaned and were ready to be fed for slaughter.

39. Sales brochure, "L.F. Ranch and Seventy Ranch," printed by Previews, Inc., 1984, Farr Papers, Water Resources Archive, CSU. The ranch is now owned by Arthur Gutterson, who has continued to run cattle while investing in numerous gas wells on the ranch that have proven productive. Dick Farr kindly toured me all over the LF Ranch while reminiscing about the years he spent there as a cowboy.

40. Colorado Agricultural College was established in 1870 as a land grant institution. In 1935, the college became known officially as Colorado State College of Agriculture and Mechanic Arts; in 1957 it became Colorado State University.

41. Montgomery, "Commercial Feeder of the Year," 13.

42. "Farr Family History," Farr Papers, Water Resources Archive, CSU.

43. Hart, *Changing Scale of American Agriculture*, 44.

44. James, "T-Bones and Talk," 32–33.

45. Geiger, "W. D. Farr: Recollections of a Pioneer Cattle Feeder," (May 1990): 17.

46. Phil Patterson, "Pass the T-Bone Steak," *Greeley (Colo.) Tribune*, n.d., ca. 1948. See "T-Bone Club Articles of Association," Farr Papers, Water Resources Archive, CSU.

47. Farr Family History, Farr Papers, Water Resources Archive, CSU.

48. C. E. Ball, *Building the Beef Industry*, 90. Steeped in the tradition of independence, cattlemen were divided to the point of inaction on the matter of accepting assistance from the federal government. When cattle were finally designated a "basic commodity" under the 1934 Jones–Connally Act, the USDA was authorized to subsidize ranchers for reducing their herds.

49. Ibid., 94, 95.

50. WD Farr, interview by Michael Welsh, October 16, 2002.

51. Leonard, *Trials and Triumphs*, 70–80.

52. WD Farr, interview by Sally Mier, December 28, 1999.

53. D. Tyler, *Last Water Hole in the West*, 13–16.

54. Taylor was a powerful congressman. He was the principal author of the 1934 Taylor Grazing Act, which removed a vast acreage of western land from homesteading and placed these lands under the jurisdiction of what is now called the Bureau of Land Management.

55. WD Farr, interview by Sally Mier, December 30, 1999.

56. In general terms, the following were the counties to which C-BT water could be delivered for first use and/or return flows in the South Platte River basin: Boulder, Larimer, Weld, Morgan, Washington, Logan, and Sedgwick.

57. WD Farr, interview by Gregory M. Silkensen, August 28, 1997.

58. WD Farr, interview by Sally Mier, December 28, 1999.

59. WD Farr, interview by Gregory M. Silkensen, August 28, 1997.

60. *Greeley (Colo.) Tribune*, February 5, 1938. Harry's endorsement of the C-BT, so important to the success of the project, seems to have been given with little concern about the future impact of a system that would be controlled, at least partially, by the Department of Interior. Harry did not like the idea of federal government control of western resources, but the drought was powerful, and he knew they were all fighting for survival. Political biases were malleable under such circumstances.

61. Minutes, NCWCD, July 5, 1938, NCWCD headquarters, Berthoud, Colo.

62. WD was appointed to the NCWCD board of directors in 1955. He remained an active director until 1995, when he was designated a board member emeritus.

63. Gropman, *Big 'L'*, 156; and *Greeley (Colo.) Tribune*, July 24, 1942.

64. "Farr Family History," Farr Papers, Water Resources Archive, CSU.

65. Ibid.

66. *Greeley (Colo.) Tribune*, September 19, 1941.

67. *Greeley (Colo.) Tribune*, April 10, 1943.

68. *Greeley (Colo.) Tribune*, September 13, 1943.

CHAPTER 4

1. WD Farr to Mr. and Mrs. Jack Harrison, March 26, 1984, Farr Papers, Water Resources Archive, CSU. At WD's "Celebration" in Greeley on August 23, 2007, Linda Mitchell Davis of Cimarron, New Mexico, noted that Judy could outshoot anyone in the Farr family.

2. The Crystal River Ranch name was registered by Harry and WD Farr on April 16, 1943. Previously, the land had been known as Sweet's Seed Farm, or the Metropolitan Ranch. See Affidavit for Registering Name of Ranch, Item 148988, Clerk and Recorder, Garfield County, Glenwood Springs, Colo.

3. John Farr, communication to the author, August 8, 2008.

4. Grubb and Guilford, *Potato*. See the sections on Colorado, especially p. 373.

5. Louis D. Sweet was president of the Potato Association of America from 1916 to 1918.

6. Edna D. Sweet [Frank E. Sweet's wife], *Carbondale Pioneers, 1879–1890*, 56–61; and Len Shoemaker, *Pioneers of the Roaring Fork*, 252–53.

7. Shoemaker, *Roaring Fork*, 165.

8. Petition of the Sweet–Jessup Canal for an adjudication of the Sweet–Jessup Canal, June 1, 1905, Case no. CA 1141, Garfield County District Court, Glenwood Springs, Colo. The request was approved for fifty cfs.

9. F. W. Jessup, "Crystal River Ranch," October 11, 1974, Crystal River Ranch file, Frontier Historical Society (FHS), Glenwood Springs, Colo. Patsy Stark, archivist at the FHS, called this item to my attention.

10. January 14, 1902, is the adjudicated priority date of the Sweet–Jessup Canal based on the beginning of construction. Additional water was appropriated in 1923 and 1943 for a total of 75 adjudicated cfs. Division of Water Resources, Division 5, Glenwood Springs, Colo.

11. According to the deed books located at the Glenwood Springs Clerk and Recorder's Office, the company purchased over 1,100 acres between April and August 1905. See Book 64, pp. 165, 197, 234, 237, and 239. I am indebted to Beverly Eberle, Garfield County Recording Clerk, for assisting me in locating this information.

12. Deed of Trust, February 14, 1920, between the Crystal River Land Company and the Garfield County Public Trustee, Item no. 70040, Garfield County Clerk and Recorder, Glenwood Springs, Colo.

13. Between 1920 and 1922, Sweet sent potato samples annually to Colorado State Agricultural College for analysis. He was told that he was "developing a potato drier year by year and richer in starch year by year." In his own promotional materials, Sweet noted the high marks he had received from experts at the college. See N. E. Goldthaite to Lou D. Sweet, February 28, 1923, Papers of Daniel W. Working, Colorado Agricultural Archive, CSU.

14. Glenn E. Rogers, second vice president, MetLife, memorandum, November 20, 1958, provided to the author by Daniel May, company archivist, Corporate Contributions, MetLife.

15. Ibid.

16. WD Farr, interview by the author, December 26, 2006.

17. Special Warranty Deed, No. 148941, Garfield County Clerk and Recorder, Glenwood Springs, Colo. Signing this document on behalf of the seller was MetLife's vice president, Glenn E. Rogers. Both Harry and WD signed as purchasers.

18. John Farr, communication to the author, March 16, 2008. Subsequent recollections from John Farr regarding his initial impressions of the Crystal River Ranch were written in the same message.

19. John Farr, communication to the author March 16, 2008. As a personal observation, I would add that this style of baler was being used in 1946 when my father bought the ranch. I recall the men sitting on the baler shoving wires back and forth, the cloud of hay dust that covered everyone, and the heavy bales I had

to align all day long so they could be picked up by an automatic loader attached to a flat-bed truck. The advent of string balers and bales weighing forty to fifty pounds was a celebratory moment for us all.

20. WD Farr, interview by the author, September 22, 2003. Some of these checks remain in the ditch after more than sixty years. According to the engineers (Applegate Group, Inc.) who have been working with Sue Anschutz Rodgers, present owner of the Crystal River Ranch, the only real security for the ranch's water supply was to put the main ditch in corrugated metal pipe from the headgate to the ranch. As of this writing (summer of 2008), 42 percent of the entire length of the ditch, on and off the ranch, has been replaced by pipe.

21. WD Farr, interview by the author, September 22, 2003, and December 23, 2006.

22. John Farr, communication with author, March 16, 2008.

23. WD Farr, interview by the author, September 22, 2003.

24. Ibid.

25. Ibid.

26. Sidney F. Tyler is my father. Unless otherwise noted, his experiences leading up to the purchase of the Crystal River Ranch come from his *A Joyful Odyssey*, vols. 2 and 3.

27. After a distinguished military career during both world wars, General Hubert Reilly Harmon was appointed the first superintendent of the U.S. Air Force Academy when it was first organized at Lowry Field in Denver, Colorado, in 1954 (www.usafa.af.mil/information/superintendents.asp).

28. WD Farr, interview by the author, September 22, 2003.

29. Ibid., December 23, 2006.

30. John Farr, interview by the author, September 6, 2007. Clinical trials of penicillin were performed in 1943. The drug was available in 1944 for troops during the Normandy invasion, and by 1946, the per-dose price for the public had declined from $20 to $0.55.

31. "National Affairs: Shakedown II."

32. Harry Farr appeared before the Senate Agriculture Committee on March 27, 1933, representing the Colorado–Nebraska Lamb Feeders Association. He was protesting the inclusion of sheep in a bill designed to provide farm relief. Harry testified to the voluntary efforts of sheep producers to reduce production, and he argued that the proposed legislation would only result in higher taxes and a larger federal bureaucracy. See *Greeley (Colo.) Tribune*, March 28, 1933. I am grateful to Peggy Ford for locating this item.

33. U.S. Senate Subcommittee of the Committee on Agriculture and Forestry, *Hearings on S. Res. 92*, 207–213. The OPA became operative in January 1942, with the objective of limiting prices and rationing scarce items during the war. It was officially abolished in May 1947.

34. Ibid.

35. U.S. Senate Committee on Banking and Currency, *Hearings on S. 2028*, 1344–49.

36. Ibid.

37. U.S. House Committee on Banking and Currency, *Hearings on H. R. 5270*, 740–45.

38. WD's testimony was directed at a "Bill to Amend the Emergency Price Control Act of 1942, as Amended, and the Stabilization Act of 1942, as Amended and for Other Purposes."

39. *Greeley (Colo.) Tribune*, June 12, 1947; and June 20, 1947.

40. *Greeley (Colo.) Tribune*, October 6, 1947.

41. *Greeley (Colo.) Tribune*, November 17; and December 4, 1947.

42. WR Farr, interview by the author, September 13, 2008.

43. In WD's words, "We did it just with my simple engineering, using a level and an old-fashioned four-wheeled McKormick Deering tractor with a horse-drawn fresno behind it that we jury rigged so the tractor operator could use it. . . . We found from experience [that] . . . the fields that consistently produced the most crops were the fields that had the same slope in every row." A rolling field would be staked "in hundred-foot squares. Then you would sit down and try to visualize how you would like to have it. . . . We increased our tonnage several times as we did that, but it was slow, tedious work." WD Farr, interview by Sally Mier, December 28, 1999.

44. Ibid. WR Farr recollected his father's involvement in developing a hydraulic apparatus to push heavy beet pulp off the bed of a truck into feed bins. Hurt built the mechanism and also designed a front-end loader that would lift pulp out of a pile, over the operator's head, and into a feed bin. He accomplished these innovations before Bud Harsh developed his popular tipping hoist and other products in 1948.

45. *Greeley (Colo.) Tribune*, December 7, 1947; and July 13, 1948.

46. C. E. Ball, *Building the Beef Industry*, 120.

47. When Greeley High School's football coach was unceremoniously fired after a championship season, WD ran for the school board. He was opposed by a fellow Rotarian, which was not considered appropriate in 1952. WD lost and never again aspired to political office.

48. I am grateful to John Farr for this assessment of WD's early leadership strengths.

49. WD Farr, interview by Sally Mier, January 13, 2000.

50. D. Tyler, *Last Water Hole*, 149–160.

51. WD Farr, interview by Sally Mier, January 13, 2000. In an interview with the author on July 8, 1988, WD stated, "You have never heard cheering equal to what was heard that day. No one, not even the fans of the Denver Broncos in more recent times, were as excited as those conservative businessmen and farmers when they saw that water." As CSU professor Robert Ward pointed out in a

review of this work, WD's comment is a classic statement of optimism consistent with most comments made during the first half of the 20th century. For him and for many others, more water was always good. It was later on before people in the West realized that population growth and environmental damage were consequences of the quest for unlimited water.

52. *Fort Collins Coloradoan,* June 24, 1947, as quoted in D. Tyler, *Last Water Hole,* 159.

53. C-BT construction was completed in 1957.

54. Described as the "analog approach," Krick's ideas were related to the National Weather Service's effort to develop predictability by looking at weather maps back into the late nineteenth century. Another weather expert known to WD was Jerome Namias of the Massachusetts Institute of Technology. As chief of the Extended Forecast Division of the National Weather Bureau from 1941 to 1971, Namias was primarily interested in the correlation between oceans and the atmosphere, especially the El Niño effect and its relevance to world climate. Arthur Douglas of Creighton University, a longtime friend of WD, shared these observations with me via telephone on August 19, 2008.

55. Mitchell managed the Bell Ranch from 1933 to 1947 and owned other New Mexico ranches. In addition to the bank connection, WD knew him as a member of the National Livestock and Meat Board and president of the ANLSA. Mitchell received many awards as a cattleman. He is also remembered for his role in establishing the Cowboy Hall of Fame and Western Heritage Center in Oklahoma City in 1975. See Boesen, *Storm,* chap. 8.

56. WD Farr, Interview by Gregory M. Silkensen, October 24, 1997.

57. *Greeley (Colo.) Tribune,* May 19, 1950.

58 *Greeley (Colo.) Tribune,* September 18, 1950.

59. *Greeley (Colo.) Tribune,* September 23, 1950.

60. *Greeley (Colo.) Tribune,* October 3, 1950.

61. *Greeley (Colo.) Tribune,* December 12, 1950.

62. *Greeley (Colo.) Tribune,* February 13, 1951.

63. *Greeley (Colo.) Tribune,* April 3, 1951.

64. *Greeley (Colo.) Tribune,* April 19, 1951.

65. *Greeley (Colo.) Tribune,* June 16, 22, and 27, 1951

66. WD Farr, interview by Gregory M. Silkensen, October 24, 1997.

67. The One Bar Eleven was purchased by John Rouse, one of WD's good friends, and the Big Creek Ranch, owned by Otto Gebhardt, was purchased by Wendell Anderson on the last day of an expiring option in April 1941. WD was heartbroken, because he had wanted to own a ranch on the North Platte River. John Farr, interview by the author, September 8, 2008, and e-mail communication of November 9, 2008.

68. Martinsdale was also the headquarters of Charles M. Bair, a successful sheep grower, who once shipped a record amount of wool to Boston for which

he received an untaxed $395,000. The Bair home is now a museum just west of Martinsdale.

69. Deed no. 53904, March 30, 1951, Book 60, pp. 346–48, Meagher County, Mont., Clerk and Recorder.

70. Descriptive List of Prisoner No. 9612, William Magelssen, April 13, 1930, Office of the Warden of the State Prison, RS 197, box 64, folder 2, Montana Historical Society Research Center, Helena, Mont.

71. Jeannette Rankin was the first woman elected to the House of Representatives. She was a pacifist who voted against U.S. participation in both world wars. Her brother, Wellington, a powerful lawyer and a major player in Montana politics, stood by his sister when she was maligned by Montanans for casting the only negative vote against the U.S. declaration of war against the Japanese in 1941.

72. John Farr, interview by the author, September 8, 2008.

73. See Keith, "Review of *Wellington Rankin*," 71.

74. Harvey R. Solberg, president of the Rocky Mountain Farmers' Union, statement presented at "A Clinic for Diagnosing the 'Economic Health' of Colorado," Colorado General Assembly, Denver, Colo., January 13, 1954, Farr Papers, Water Resources Archive, CSU.

75. Ibid. See also Emmett J. Dignan, vice president and manager, Livestock Loan Department, U.S. National Bank, "Agriculture in Colorado—1953," statement before the Colorado General Assembly, January 13, 1954. Available at www.cde.state.co.us/artemis/ga4/ga498internet.pdf.

76. See the history of the American National Cattlemen's Association at http://beefusa.org, and Goff and McCaffree, *Century in the Saddle*, 298.

77. WD Farr, untitled speech, 1952, WDF—Farr Cattle Talks, Farr Papers, Water Resources Archive, CSU.

78. Government grading of beef carcasses began before the Great Depression, but until price controls were established during World War II, participation by meat packers was voluntary. On August 1, 1950, the first day of the Korean conflict, WD was at a three-day meeting in Chicago attended by representatives from the Corn Belt, the USDA, packers, and cattle feeders. WD represented the ANLSA. Participants created new grades of prime, choice, and good, based on marbling and maturity. Because chain stores were beginning to buy choice grades in large quantities and to offer a money-back guarantee to consumers, WD argued that it was incumbent on feeders to know how their cattle would grade so they could meet the supermarkets' demand for choice beef. See *Greeley (Colo.) Tribune*, February 4, 1953; J. J. Harris, H. R. Cross, and J. W. Savell, "History of Meat Grading in the United States," at http://www.meat.tamu.edu/history.html; and WD Farr, interview by Sherm Ewing, January 21, 1987, Farr Papers, Water Resources Archives, CSU.

79. Quoted in H. P. White, "Fabulous Feeding Farrs," 46.

80. *Greeley (Colo.) Tribune*, February 23, 1952; June 7, 1952; and June 26, 1952. See also C. E. Ball, *Building the Beef Industry*.

81. WD Farr, interview with the author, July 10, 2007.

CHAPTER 5

1. Russell, "Ten Feet from a Killer Bear." Citation provided courtesy of the Archives and Library Reference Services, Whyte Museum of the Canadian Rockies, Banff, Alberta.

2. To the Farr family, the value of this connection with Andy Russell was measureless. In addition to the spiritual and philosophical enlightenment WD received as Russell's friend, other family members also benefitted from the relationship. John Farr worked with the Skyline Pack Train when he was in college. Judy Farr and John's siblings also enjoyed many years of hunting and steelhead fishing on the Dean River because of Russell's link to the Stewart family. John Farr, communication to the author, May 30, 2007.

3. All quotes in this paragraph are from WD Farr to Andy Russell, December 15, 1982, and December 31, 1986, Andy Russell Correspondence, Farr Papers, Water Resources Archive, CSU.

4. This classic admonition became a Farr family quote for many years.

5. Andy Russell to WD Farr, May 25, 1988, Andy Russell Correspondence, Farr Papers, Water Resources Archive, CSU.

6. WD Farr, telephone interview by the author, May 30, 2007.

7. In a review of Worster's *Passion for Nature*, Hirt notes that the Hetch–Hetchy battle served to create a false impression that Muir and Pinchot represented "incompatible archetypes." In fact, Hirt argues, Pinchot was not totally opposed to preservation and Muir was not opposed to wise use. See Hirt, Review of *Passion for Nature*, 73–74.

8. John Farr, communication to the author, May 30, 2007.

9. Andy Russell to WD Farr, May 25, 1988, Andy Russell Correspondence, Farr Papers, Water Resources Archive, CSU.

10. WD Farr, telephone interview by the author, May 30, 2007.

11. Andy Russell to WD Farr May 25, 1988, Andy Russell Correspondence, Farr Papers, Water Resources Archive, CSU.

12. This story is told in Russell, *Life of a River*. In his lifetime, Russell authored 13 books.

13. Andy Russell to WD Farr, March 15, 1988, Andy Russell Correspondence, Farr Papers, Water Resources Archive, CSU.

14. WD Farr to Andy Russell, April 20, 1988, in ibid.

15. For his work as a wilderness advocate and preservationist, Russell received the Order of Canada and was awarded honorary doctorate degrees by the University of Lethridge, the University of Calgary, and the University of Alberta.

16. Andy Russell to WD Farr, March 15, 1988, Andy Russell Correspondence, Farr Papers, Water Resources Archive, CSU.

17. WD Farr to Andy Russell, December 18, 1992, in ibid.

18. The Beebe Draw Gun Club, located near Greeley on Muskrat Lake, was organized by Greeley and Denver businessmen in the 1920s. Introduced to duck

hunting in 1920 when his father gave him a .410 shotgun, WD wrote about the club as "one of the greatest pleasures in life," especially in the early days when there were no limits, and the invention of storage batteries for automobiles made it possible to hunt all afternoon and drive home in the dark. When Weld County began producing hybrid corn that attracted more ducks and geese, the hunting became so good, he recalled, that one might leave Denver by train at 4:00 P.M. and shoot fifty ducks before dark. See WD Farr, The History of the Beebe Draw Gun Club, Beebe Draw Gun Club—1999, Farr Papers, Water Resources Archive, CSU.

19. Alan Dumas, "Citizen of the West W. D. Farr: Farr-Sighted Greeley Rancher Helped Bring Water to Front Range," *Rocky Mountain News*, January 10, 1999.

20. WD Farr to Andy Russell, February 28, 1985, Andy Russell Correspondence, Farr Papers, Water Resources Archive, CSU.

21. WD Farr, interview by Gregory M. Silkensen, August 28, 1997.

22. WD Farr, interview by Sally Mier, December 28, 1999.

23. WD Farr, interview by Gregory M. Silkensen, September 22, 1997.

24. The Blue River decrees of 1955 involved a struggle between the Denver Water Board and the NCWCD over Denver's plan to bring water from the Blue River to the South Platte. See D. Tyler, *Last Water Hole*, chap. 13.

25. WD Farr, interview by Gregory M. Silkensen, September 22, 1997.

26. All quotes from Eric Wilkinson, general manager of the NCWCD, are from an interview by the author, October 27, 2008.

27. Opinion of Robert R. Anderson, auditor, as mentioned in NCWCD minutes, February 13, 1959, NCWCD Archive, Berthoud, Colo.

28. The need for additional storage was first mentioned in the minutes by WD in the spring of 1961. He pursued the matter through 1963. See NCWCD minutes, March 10, 1961; January 11, 1963; September 13, 1963; and December 13, 1963, in ibid. By April 2, 1965, the USBR seems to have lost interest. The controversy over Poudre River storage continues today, with the NCWCD and fifteen cities supporting a $431 million dam on the lower Poudre River against a coalition of environmental organizations and other entities organized in opposition.

29. *Greeley (Colo.) Tribune*, February 21, 1956. According to figures released by the Colorado Department of Agriculture, Weld County was first in the state in beef cattle, dairy cattle, chickens, sugar beets, barley, alfalfa, total crop land, total farms, and irrigated farms.

30. Terah L. Smiley, *Denver Post*, January 2, 1963. Census data from 1960 exacerbated fears of a major water shortage. An article by University of Arizona professor Smiley, printed in the *Chicago Daily News* and reprinted by the *Post*, warned that if the present rate of migration to the West continued, "the desert dwellers, like desert animals, may need to eat certain foods that reduce the need for water." Professor Smiley, who was head of the Department of Geosciences at the University

of Arizona until his death in 1996, blamed the new passion for air conditioning as the major culprit in diminishing water resources.

31. Jon Monson, director, Greeley Water and Sewer Department, interview by the author, October 27, 2008.

32. Hartman, *Century of Remarkable Progress*, 43. Hartman received a doctorate in education and headed the journalism department at the University of Northern Colorado. He was active in the Greeley Social Science Circle and Rotary at the time of his death in 1993. See Obituary of Hartman, *Greeley (Colo.) Tribune*, August 17, 1993.

33. WD Farr, interview by Gregory M. Silkensen, October 24, 1997.

34. Ibid. Greeley's city council had to accept what the water board established as fees to run the system. If the city wanted more revenue, it was their responsibility to convince citizens.

35. Ibid.

36. Minutes, NCWCD, May 10, 1968, NCWCD Archive, Berthoud, Colo.

37. WD Farr, interview by Sally Mier, December 21, 1999.

38. *Greeley (Colo.) Tribune*, October 29, 1963.

39. WD Farr, interview by Gregory M. Silkensen, October 24, 1997.

40. *Fort Collins Coloradoan*, April 28, 1966.

41. In 1970 ANCA paid for a full-time lobbyist in Washington for the first time. That year was also WD's first year as president of the NCWCD Municipal Subdistrict, whose objective was planning and building the Windy Gap Project. When completed, Windy Gap would add approximately 50,000 acre-feet of water to the C-BT.

42. W. D. Farr, "Farr Reports on Washington Board," *Greeley (Colo.) Tribune*, April 24, 1972. WD's remarks were presented initially to the Greeley Social Science Circle.

43. Ibid.

44. WD Farr, interview by Gregory M. Silkensen, October 24, 1997.

45. Ibid., September 22, 1997; and WD Farr, interview by Sally Mier, January 20, 2000.

46. The seminal National Environmental Policy Act (NEPA), signed by President Richard Nixon on January 1, 1970, directed federal agencies to evaluate the impact of federal projects on the natural environment. The government demanded an environmental impact statement (EIS) and an environmental assessment (EA) to determine whether or not a proposed project fit within limits described by the act. The objective was to include the environment as an equal factor with economic motivation and technological feasibility when considering whether or not to go forward with a project that involved federal money or was related to existing federal systems.

47. WD Farr, interview by Gregory M. Silkensen, September 22 and October 24, 1997.

48. U.S. Department of the Interior, Bureau of Reclamation, *Reconnaissance Report on the West Slope Extension*, 2–3, as quoted in Silkensen, *Windy Gap*, 26.

49. *Fort Collins Coloradoan*, July 19, 1967. The amount was increased to 54,000 acre-feet, but the final decree was a compromise of 48,000 acre-feet.

50. WD Farr, interview by Gregory M. Silkensen, September 22, 1997.

51. John Sayre, telephone interview by the author, January 12, 2009.

52. Silkensen notes in *Windy Gap* that "Windy Gap was the first transmountain water diversion project to face the full brunt of these new legal, financial, and physical implications" (p. 58).

53. Ibid., 61.

54. WD Farr, interview by Sally Mier, December 28, 1999. The Six Cities Committee actually spent $100,000 for habitat manipulation and $450,000 over three years for field research and habitat evaluation. See Silkensen, *Windy Gap*, 87.

55. WD Farr, interview by Sally Mier, December 28, 1999.

56. 59 *Stat.* §1219, Treaty Series, 994 (1944). See also Silkensen, *Windy Gap*, 64–67.

57. Silkensen, *Windy Gap*, 73–75.

58. Ibid., 83.

59. John Sayre, telephone interview by the author, January 12, 2009.

60. Chris Jouflas, telephone interview by the author, January 12, 2009.

61. Wolford Mountain Reservoir on Muddy Creek just west of Kremmling, Colo., cost the subdistrict $10.2 million. When all the numbers were added, Windy Gap cost $107 million. The 1957 price tag was $8.4 million. See Silkensen, *Windy Gap*, 96.

62. Platte River Power Authority, located north of Fort Collins, is a coal-fired power plant that generates electricity for Estes Park, Fort Collins, Longmont, and Loveland. It acquired rights for all of Fort Collins's and half of Estes Park's and Loveland's Windy Gap water to cool its generators.

63. WD Farr, interview by Sally Mier, January 20, 2000.

64. Ibid., December 28, 1999.

65. *Greeley (Colo.) Tribune*, December 5, 1955.

66. Grading standards accepted by the USDA changed over the years. In 1960 the government ranked beef in descending order of quality: prime, choice, good, and commercial. WD learned early on as a cattle feeder that local packing plants were more inclined to buy animals graded choice, so he fed to that standard to achieve the consistency demanded by retailers.

67. WD claimed his biggest contribution to the cattle industry was uniform grading of beef. Appointed to ANCA's first beef-grading committee in 1956, WD was asked to study beef grading at the producer, feeder, packer, wholesaler, retailer, and consumer levels. See Radford Hall, executive secretary, ANCA, to WD Farr, January 18, 1956, folder 12, box 16, Executive Files, National Cattlemen's Association, American Heritage Center, University of Wyoming. WD served for twenty years on this committee and saw the packers' premium labels

gradually replaced by the yield grading system he favored. See Green, "W. D. Farr Shows Vision."

68. Silage, the entire corn plant chopped up, was harvested on the farms by Farr employees using Farr equipment. All loads of silage to the cattle were designed to be 25 percent dry matter and 75 percent moisture, and all materials in the lined trenches were supposed to be at 30 percent moisture or slightly above. Montgomery, "Commercial Feeder of the Year," 15.

69. ANCA news release, May 25, 1971, which includes Proxmire's charges and WD's response. See box 36, folder 28, Executive Files, National Cattlemen's Association, American Heritage Center, University of Wyoming.

70. C. E. Ball, *Building the Beef Industry*, 150–51.

71. WD Farr, "Farr Family History," Farr Papers, Water Resources Archive, CSU.

72. Barnhart, *Kenny's Shoes*, 42, 51–53.

73. Ibid., 103–104, 108–109, 111–12, 119, 142, 162–63.

74. "Farr Family History," p. 52, Farr Papers, Water Resources Archive, CSU.

75. Speech by WD to Nebraska Stockgrowers Association in Sidney, Nebraska, December 2, 1967, WDF—Speeches, Farr Papers, Water Resources Archive, CSU.

76. "Farr Family History," Farr Papers, Water Resources Archive, CSU.

77. Lemke, "Legend," 6–8, 10–11.

78. As described by McMillan in a December 20, 2008, telephone interview by the author, yield grading was designed to recognize cuts of meat with the least waste (Y-1) so the owner of such cattle would receive a premium price in contrast to animals with more fat, which would be graded Y-5. The owners of British breeds felt that if such a system was accepted across the industry, they would be penalized.

79. Quotes from Bill House are from a telephone interview by the author, December 18, 2008.

80. Burton Eller, telephone interview by the author, December 30, 2008. Eller was hired by House to work at the ANCA office in Denver to increase membership and generate revenue.

81. Bill House, telephone interview by the author, December 18, 2008. House claimed his biggest victory as ANCA president was persuading Congress to limit beef imports to 7.6 percent of domestic production. After his presidency, he continued to work on this matter, noting that Australians and New Zealanders attempted to eliminate import quotas by offering to buy more cars from automobile manufacturers and more tractors from John Deere and Caterpillar. See also WD Farr, interview by Sally Mier, December 30, 1999.

82. Bill House, telephone interview, December 18, 2008.

83. WD Farr, interview by the author, December 26, 2006.

84. Jim House, ANCA, speech to the Colorado Cattle Feeders Association, August 1973. Speeches—Farm, Farr Papers, Water Resources Archive, CSU.

85. Vickie Martin, "Greeley Man Named Citizen of the West," *Loveland (Colo.) Reporter–Herald*, October 5, 1998.

86. George S. Spencer, interview by the author, January 5, 2009.

87. Ibid.

88. John A. Rohlf, "Danger Flags for Beef," *Top Operator* (June 1970): 33–35, box 36, folder 28, Executive Files, National Cattlemen's Association, American Heritage Center, University of Wyoming.

89. WD, speech in draft form, n.d., ca. 1970–1972, Speeches by WD Farr, Farr Papers, Water Resources Archive, CSU. It is not possible to verify these percentages, but the gist of WD's assertion appears sound.

90. Harry and WD Farr were both members of the British Newcomen Society. Founded in London in 1920, it was organized as a learned society dedicated to sharing knowledge about engineering and technology. A branch was founded in the United States in 1943 at a time when fears of communism were reappearing. In North America, however, the society has been focused primarily on achievements of capitalism and the preservation of free enterprise. For cattlemen, who generally disdain government aid, a meeting of the Newcomen Society at the annual convention of ANCA was appropriate.

91. During WD's presidency of ANCA, 20 percent of all cattle on feed were represented by subscribers to Cattle-Fax. WD's goal was 50 percent. As of 2008, 53 percent of cattle on feed were represented by subscribers to Cattle-Fax.

92. Bill McMillan, interview by the author, December 20, 2008. See also C. E. Ball, *Building the Beef Industry*, 162–66.

93. The Capra–Volstead Act was passed when agricultural cooperatives persuaded Congress that farmers should be allowed to come together for the purpose of marketing their product without violating anti-trust laws in the process. The Justice Department investigated Cattle-Fax in the late 1970s but found no violation of the law.

94. Topper Thorpe was hired as an economist for Cattle-Fax soon after completing a master's degree in agricultural economics at New Mexico State University.

95. Topper Thorpe, interview by the author, January 7, 2009.

96. Ibid.

97. C. E. Ball, *Building the Beef Industry*, 166–67, 170–71.

98. George S. Spencer, telephone interview by the author, January 5, 2009.

99. George S. Spencer, interview by the author, January 7, 2009.

100. Bill McMillan, interview by the author, December 20, 2008.

101. Burton Eller, Jr., interview by the author, December 30, 2009. Eller was invited to Denver to meet with ANCA when WD was vice president of that association. Hired as a membership and revenue generator for ANCA, Eller served as a lobbyist and as deputy undersecretary in the USDA. He became head of the NCBA's Washington office in 2008.

102. Robert Josserand, interview by the author, January 7, 2009. Josserand resigned as chair of the National Cattlemen's Beef Association Foundation in 2009.

103. *Greeley (Colo.) Tribune*, April 12, 1981.

104. Lenthe, "W. D. Farr," 41.

105. Montgomery, "Commercial Feeder of the Year."

106. Gladwell, *Outliers*, 109, 115. Gladwell contends that "If you are someone whose father has made his way up in the business world, then you've seen first-hand, what it means to negotiate your way out of a tight spot." He concludes, "No one ever makes it alone."

CHAPTER 6

1. Gladwell, *Tipping Point*, 38.

2. Ibid., 48.

3. From the German *Welt* (world) and *Anschauung* (view), meaning a comprehensive conception or apprehension of the world, especially from a specific standpoint.

4. Gladwell, *Tipping Point*, 53.

5. Ibid, 258–59.

6. *Greeley (Colo.) Tribune*, October 3, 1969.

7. *Greeley (Colo.) Tribune*, January 20, 1972.

8. Gladwell, *Outliers*, 155, 246.

9. Oldfield, "Marion Eugene Ensminger." In his lifetime, Ensminger established schools in seventy countries, but his primary focus was on China, Russia, Cuba, and the Ukraine.

10. Preston, *Stetson, Pipe and Boots*, 322.

11. M. E. Ensminger, "I Was a Pilgrim and Stranger," address at the occasion of his being awarded the degree of doctor of humane letters, Iowa State University, May 10, 1996. Farr Papers, Water Resources Archive, CSU.

12. WD Farr, speech at the dedication of the Ensminger Room, Iowa State University, October 31, 1996, WDF—Dedication Ensminger Room, Farr Papers, Water Resources Archive, CSU.

13. WD Farr, speech to Greeley Rotary, June 7, 1967, WDF—Speeches by W. D. Farr, Farr Papers, Water Resources Archive, CSU.

14. WD Farr, speeches to the Greeley Social Science Club, January 7, 1969, and to the Maui Rotary Club, January 15, 1969, Farr Papers, Water Resources Archive, CSU.

15. WD Farr, interview by the author, December 26, 2007.

16. WD Farr, interview by Sally Mier interview, December 30, 1999.

17. Close ties between WD and Bill McMillan, ANCA representative in Washington, facilitated a deal with the USDA that resulted in a two-for-one match of funds by the USDA, provided the cattlemen could form a "cooperator organization to represent all red meat." Charter members of the USMEF, who met on February 20, 1976, represented producers of beef, pork, and sheep, along with packers and exporters. By 1995, USMEF had 177 organizational and corporate

members and a budget in excess of $25 million. WR Farr became chairman in 1990. See C. E. Ball, *Building the Beef Industry*, 188. Paul Clayton of USMEF Denver provided additional information via telephone, August 1, 2008.

18. Recollections of the trip to China are from WD Farr, interview by Sally Mier, December 21, 1999.

19. Ibid. See also WD Farr to Andy Russell, August 8, 1983, WDF—Andy Russell Correspondence, Farr Papers, Water Resources Archive, CSU.

20. WD Farr, interview by Sally Mier, December 21, 1999.

21. *Greeley (Colo.) Tribune*, February 6, 1975.

22. Ibid., December 16, 1978.

23. WD Farr, interview by Sally Mier, December 21, 1999.

24. *Greeley (Colo.) Tribune*, June 22, 1982.

25. WD Farr, interview by Sally Mier, December 26, 1999.

26. *Greeley (Colo.) Tribune*, October 3, 1969.

27. WD Farr, interview by the author, December 26, 2007.

28. Matsushima, *Journey Back*, 142. Professor Matsushima, a long-time member of the animal science department at CSU, worked with Farr Feeders and Monfort on nutritional aspects of feeding cattle. He also designed a mechanical feed mixer that Harsh International later patented. For a lifetime dedicated to animal science, education, and international relations, the Japanese government awarded the Emperor Citation to Matsushima in 2008.

29. Tom Norton, interview by the author, May 1, 2009. Norton graduated from CSU with a master's degree in agricultural engineering. His thesis on pollution control in feedlots prepared him to work effectively with WD, whom he described as having a clear concept of what "sustainable agricultural development" should look like, and whose level of knowledge made him appear to have the equivalent of a PhD in agricultural engineering.

30. *Greeley (Colo.) Tribune*, July 18, 1972; and WD Farr, interview by Sherm Ewing, January 21, 1987, Farr Papers, Water Resources Archive, CSU.

31. *Greeley (Colo.) Tribune*, July 18, 1972; and Farr Feeders brochure, n.d., Farr Papers, Water Resources Archive, CSU.

32. When consumers began to take a more active role in demanding cheaper and healthier food in the mid-1970s, criticism of growth implants increased. From a purely business point of view, however, the small pellets planted into feedlot animals increased weight gains anywhere from 6 percent to 30 percent. See http://osufacts.okstate.edu.

33. *Greeley (Colo.) Tribune*, March 4, 1974. Because of the size of the new feedlot, WD recognized the impracticality of insisting that all pens be supervised by inspectors on foot.

34. Dick Leffler, interview by the author, June 6, 2009.

35. I am indebted to Dick Farr for many insights into construction and operation of the new feedlot. His tenure at the lot lasted from 1972 to 1988, when it was sold to National Farms.

36. *Greeley (Colo.) Tribune,* June 28, 1974, italics added.

37. C. E. Ball, *Building the Beef Industry,* 150–51.

38. *Greeley (Colo.) Tribune,* February 20, 1973; and *Greeley (Colo.) Tribune,* April 14, 1973.

39. *Greeley (Colo.) Tribune,* April 14, 1973.

40. C. E. Ball, *Building the Beef Industry,* 179.

41. WR Farr was president of Farr Farms and Farr Feeders, Inc. Richard "Dick" Farr oversaw construction of the new feedlot and was responsible for managing it. After the feedlot was sold to National Farms in 1988, Dick continued as manager until his retirement. In an e-mail message to the author, April 9, 2009, WR noted that compared with the old feedlot, which was taking its lumps in this period, the new feedlot was able to withstand the economic difficulties of the mid-1970s because it operated on a cost-plus basis that passed on inflationary feed, transportation, and interest costs to cattle owners and investors.

42. *Greeley (Colo.) Tribune,* June 17, 1974.

43. C. E. Ball, *Building the Beef Industry,* 151, italics in the original. Some of the more imaginatively named organizations were FIT (Fight Inflation Together), STOP (Stop These Outrageous Prices), WASP (Women Against Soaring Prices), SCRIMP (Save Cash, Reduce Immediately Meat Prices), LAMP (Ladies Against Meat Prices), and UPD (Until Prices Drop).

44. Ibid., 181. See also Chuck Lambert, "Sorting It Out: Cattle Numbers, Beef Supplies and Demand," compiled for the National Cattlemen's Beef Association from data prepared by the National Agricultural Statistics and the Economics Research Service, USDA,

45. WD Farr, "The Beef Cattle Industry, Past, Present, and Future," speech to the National Livestock Grading and Marketing Association's annual conference, June 1982, WDF—Speeches W. D. Farr, Farr Papers, Water Resources Archive, CSU.

46. WD Farr, speech to the Nebraska Stock Growers Association, December 2, 1967, Farr Papers, Water Resources Archive, CSU.

47. WD Farr, unidentified speech, WDF—Speeches W. D. Farr, Farr Papers, Water Resources Archive, CSU. See also Lambert, "Sorting It Out," in note 44 above.

48. Farr, "What's Ahead?" 36.

49. A "beeferendum," designed to attain membership approval for a check-off fund to be used to promote beef, was attempted in 1973 and again in 1976. It failed both times to gain the required two-thirds vote in the National Cattlemen's Association and did not pass until 1986.

50. U.S. Select Committee on Nutrition and Human Needs, *Dietary Goals of the United States.*

51. Lambert, "Sorting It Out," cited in note 44 above.

52. C. E. Ball, *Building the Beef Industry,* 202,

53. WD Farr to Andy Russell, November 26, 1982, Andy Russell Correspondence, Farr Papers, Water Resources Archive, CSU.

54. WD Farr to Andy Russell, December 28, 1983, in ibid. See also *Denver Post,* January 20, 1984. In 1976, WD purchased a one-half ownership in the 70 Ranch with George Allard, who had sold the Allard Cattle Company in North Park to the federal government for use as a duck refuge. Allard and his brother, Martin, purchased the 70 Ranch and moved there in 1970 for his cattle operations. When Allard suffered a heart attack in 1979, he and WD sold the ranch to the Travelers Insurance Company for $4 million, but a year later, WD bought it back for $5 million and proceeded to improve the river bottom lands for hay production. In 1988, WD sold the ranch to National Farms, which established a controversial hog operation on the north end. *Greeley (Colo.) Tribune,* May 16, 2004. I am indebted to Peggy Ford of the Greeley Museum for sharing with me the contents of an interview she did with George Allard in May 2009.

55. Nick Kosmicki, interview by the author, April 20, 2009. Kosmicki was WD's tax accountant and auditor, but he was also a close friend. As others have noted, WD thought more about other people than about himself, and when the properties were sold, instead of lamenting his bad fortune, he wrote Kosmicki to say thanks for everything he had done for him, personally and professionally.

56. The name of the 70 Ranch came from its distance 70 miles from Denver, Estes Park, and Cheyenne. Its location along the South Platte River, with rich bottom lands and variety of game animals, gave it a reputation as one of the finest ranches in northern Colorado. During WD's eight-year ownership, James Michener's *Centennial* was filmed on the 70 Ranch. WD received a silver belt buckle from Universal Studios as a token of gratitude from the movie company.

57. Jack Kisling, "Farrs' For Sale Sign up on 38,000 Acres," *Denver Post,* January 29, 1984.

58. *Greeley (Colo.) Tribune,* November 26, 1986. The 70 Ranch sold in 1987 to the Traveler's Life Insurance Company.

59. *Greeley (Colo.) Tribune,* January 8, 1984.

60. WR Farr, interview by the author, April 20, 2009.

61. WD Farr, interview by Sally Mier, December 30, 1999. For additional assessments of WD's ability to deal with loss, I am indebted to Nick Kosmicki, Stow Witwer, Hank Brown, Eric Wilkinson, Rob Stewart, Greg Hobbs, Susi Seawald, Topper Thorpe, Burton Eller, and George Spencer.

62. WD Farr to Bruno Borhy, May 4, 1988, WD—Bruno Borhy, Farr Papers, Water Resources Archive, CSU.

63. Minutes of the CWRPDA, January 5, 1982, provided to the author in disk format by Daniel L. Law, executive director, CWRPDA.

64. Tom Sharp, CWRPDA authority board member and chair, responded to the author's questions, May 8, 2009. He noted that the $30 million was diverted from the construction fund of the CWCB, thus causing some tension between the CWRPDA and CWCB. These tensions were exacerbated when the CWRPDA seemed to be encroaching on the CWCB's territory when it began funding basin-wide water supply studies.

65. Daniel L. Law, communication to the author, May 12, 2009. Law noted that EPA wastewater grants to local governments had resulted in "gold-plated, i.e., over-designed" projects. This caused Congress in 1987 to convert the Construction Grants Program into a State Revolving Fund Program, allowing the EPA to give funds directly to the CWRPDA. Because the CWPRDA had to match each grant dollar with twenty cents, and the state had no funds available, the CWRPDA was authorized by the state legislature to use its bonding capability, which it developed—under WD's urging—to provide more money for projects while keeping interest rates low.

66. Ibid. See also WD Farr, interview by Sally Mier, December 28, 1999. Daniel Law credits WD with developing the Small Water Resources Projects Program, even though the legislature passed the appropriate law after he left the board.

67. When Goslin had to resign because of poor health, he was replaced by Uli Kappus, an equally talented executive director.

68. WD Farr, interview by Sally Mier, December 30, 1999. The Divide Water and Sanitation District defaulted on a $69,000 loan in the mid-1990s, but within a year or two, Teller County took over the wastewater system and paid off the loan. Daniel Law, communication to the author, May 12, 2009.

69. WD Farr, interview by Sally Mier, December 30, 1999.

70. WD Farr, "The Future Is Here: Are We Ready?" speech to the Colorado Water Congress, February 10, 1982, Water Talks by WD Farr, Farr Papers, Water Resources Archives, CSU. WD's management concept was a forerunner to the water roundtables held among Colorado's river basins today. Supported by state legislation, the nine roundtables (eight river basins plus a metropolitan Denver roundtable) are intended to facilitate discussions on water issues and encourage locally driven collaborative solutions.

71. WD Farr, interview by Sally Mier, December 28, 1999.

72. Hank Brown, interview with the author, February 1, 2009.

73. Ibid. See also Tyler, *Last Water Hole*, 440–42. The Poudre River was one of six rivers in Colorado studied for possible wild and scenic designation. It was the only one chosen.

74. Hank Brown, interview with the author, February 1, 2009.

75. WD Farr, interview by Gregory M. Silkensen, September 22, 1997.

76. WD Farr, "Challenge to Innovation," speech presented to a water workshop in Denver, November 29, 1977, WD Farr Speeches, Farr Papers, Water Resources Archives, CSU. See also WD Farr, interview by Gregory M. Silkensen, September 22, 1997.

77. WD Farr, interview by Gregory M. Silkensen, September 22, 1997.

78. WD Farr, interview by Sally Mier, December 30, 1999.

79. These organizations were coordinated by Jeanne W. Englert of Lafayette, Colo. Englert was a staunch opponent of the Animas–La Plata project and other water developments that she opposed for lack of citizen input. She was a crusader

against the appointment of conservancy district directors, but she was also a defender of those whose voices she believed were silenced by a powerful water oligarchy.

80. WD Farr, "New Directions for Colorado Water Conservancy Districts," keynote address for the Conservancy District Workshop, November 2, 1984; and speech to the Colorado Water Congress, November 15, 1994, Water Talks by WD Farr, Farr Papers, Water Resources Archive, CSU.

81. As a result of a 1962 amendment to the Colorado constitution, district judges were no longer elected, and it became apparent that those who supported TFRWP would claim that appointed judges should not be appointing conservancy district directors. In response to this potential bombshell, Fort Collins attorney Ward H. Fischer suggested that the four district judges who appointed directors to the NCWCD board should meet as a group (*en banc*) to make their appointments. The suggestion was incorporated into an amendment to the 1937 Conservancy District Act in 1963.

82. A conditional decree is a water right issued after a party applies for a decree but has not yet constructed the water works necessary to perfect the appropriative right. If the applicant develops the intended project within a reasonable time, the final water decree will bear the date of the conditional filing.

83. Luecke, "Two Forks Dam," 17–19

84. *Greeley (Colo.) Tribune*, April 10, 1986.

85. WD Farr to Governor Roy Romer, May 3, 1988, Water Management and Front Range Cities, Farr Papers, Water Resources Archive, CSU.

86. Tyler, *Last Water Hole*, 451.

87. Comanche, Barnes Meadow, Peterson, Hourglass, and Twin lakes had a total net decreed storage right of 7,314 acre feet, but in 1986, because of the deteriorated condition of the reservoirs, Greeley was allowed to store only 3,000 acre-feet.

88. WD Farr, untitled speech at Greeley City Council meeting, August 5, 1986, Water Talks by W.D. Farr, Farr Papers, Water Resources Archive, CSU.

89. WD Farr, interview by Gregory M. Silkensen, October 24, 1997.

90. The term *water buffalo* is a western reference to those—mostly lawyers, developers, and water managers—who are determined to harness free-flowing water at any cost.

91. A federal reserved water right was a claim—based on the Winters Doctrine, which was enunciated by the U.S. Supreme Court in the 1908 *Winters v. United States* decision—which affirmed water rights to Indian reservations based on their date of establishment and superior to subsequent water appropriations.

92. D. Tyler, *Last Water Hole*, 443, 445.

93. Unless otherwise noted, Four Party Agreement details are taken from May 12, 2009, communications between the author and Justice Gregory Hobbs of the Colorado Supreme Court, who served during this time, along with John Sayre, as counsel and environmental affairs specialist for the NCWCD and MSD.

94. The DWB wanted the right to use 28,000 acre-feet of water held in Dillon Reservoir, but they were prevented from doing this because of the requirement that they deliver this water to Green Mountain Reservoir downstream on the Blue River. What the DWB accomplished by joining in the Four Party Agreement was a water exchange, whereby the 28,000 acre-feet would be made available through Muddy Creek Reservoir.

95. Albert C. Yates, interview by the author, May 13, 2009. Dr. Yates was president of CSU for thirteen years.

96. WD Farr, "Wolford Mountain Dedication," September 23, 1995, NCWCD Archive, Berthoud, Colo.

CHAPTER 7

1. Lenthe, "W.D. Farr Statesman," 42.

2. Keith Schneider, "Billionaires in Duel Over Hog Farm," *New York Times*, November 28, 1989.

3. WD Farr to Bruno Borhy, May 4, 1988, WDF—Bruno Borhy, Farr Papers, Water Resources Archive, CSU.

4. John Farr, communication to the author, July 27, 2009.

5. WD Farr, "Should Voters Stiffen Controls on Hog Farm Waste?" *Greeley (Colo.) Tribune*, March 18, 1990.

6. Cindy Brovsky, "Decade of Prosperity a Possibility," *Greeley (Colo.) Tribune*, January 21, 1990.

7. Bill Jackson, interview by the author, July 28, 2009. The *Greeley (Colo.) Tribune* published an article titled "Pork Politics" by Dan England on June 18, 2000, in which Bill Haw was quoted as saying he sought out Phil Anschutz before hog farm construction began "to see how he could become a good neighbor." Anschutz told him, "You don't understand how powerful I am and I'm going to harass you for years and cost you millions." That, according to Haw, "was how we got started."

8. Theo Stein, "Hog Farm Closure Disputed: Company President Blasts State Officials," *Denver Post*, December 21, 2000.

9. In "Former Hog Farm is Big Mess for State" (*Rocky Mountain News*, February 21, 2006), author Todd Hartman noted that the former 70 Ranch was sold to several individuals: Todd Helton of the Colorado Rockies, with title to 4,500 acres; Bob Lembke, a neighboring rancher with title to 14,000 acres; and the State Land Board, with title to approximately 5,000 acres of land described as contaminated by liquefied hog manure. National Hog Farms' stock is owned by Mike Cervi, a rodeo stock producer. State regulators have declared that groundwater in test wells on the 70 Ranch shows ten times the level of acceptable nitrates. A cleanup of the area could cost more than $1 million. In a July 31, 2009, interview by the author, WD's grandson, RD Farr, who was living on the 70 Ranch during the early years of hog operations, noted that Haw managed irresponsibly and did not distribute the effluent on the grasslands as carefully as he might have.

10. RD stayed with the Bass Brothers after leaving the Greeley feedlot, managing their ranches and feedlots in Kansas and Oklahoma and then receiving a promotion to manage the farming and livestock operation of Lee Bass in Texas.

11. The Patagonian Express was made famous by Theroux in *The Old Patagonian Express*, in which he describes his journey in many trains from the Boston subway to Patagonia.

12. I am indebted to John Farr for sharing with me his recollections of the Argentina trip.

13. Sherman, "Farr Family Creates Weld Banking Dynasty," 5B.

14. WR was never as comfortable in cattle feeding as in banking. He first joined his father on the board of West Greeley National Bank in 1968. In 1979, he became a director of the Greeley National Bank and later vice president. In 1990, he was appointed president of Farmers National Bank in Ault and First Colorado Bank in Greeley. Farmers National had been part of the ABC holding company that was purchased by Banc One in 1993. In that year, WR became president of Centennial Bank Holdings, Inc., purchasing Eaton Bank and the Colorado Industrial Bank in Eaton. He and his partners also converted Colorado Industrial Bank to a state bank, using the "Farmers" name for the bank in Eaton and then branching into Ault. WR focused on small bank operations during his banking career. See Sherman, "Farr Family Creates Weld Banking Dynasty."

15. Leo Hill, first CEO of ABC and president of the Colorado Banker's Association, interview by the author, July 31, 2009.

16. *Greeley (Colo.) Tribune*, May 30, 1970. At that time, ABC was ranked the fourth largest bank holding company in Colorado, with the largest number of member banks.

17. Leo Hill, interview by the author, July 31, 2009.

18. *Greeley (Colo.) Tribune*, September 24, 1971.

19. Leo Hill, interview by the author, July 31, 2009.

20. By 1992, ABC had assets of $2.8 billion among twenty-seven banks. Banc One had assets of $46.2 billion, with offices in Indiana, Illinois, Kentucky, Michigan, Ohio, Texas, and Wisconsin. "Banc One to Acquire Affiliated Bankshares," *New York Times*, December 31, 1991.

21. John Farr, communication to the author, May 14, 2009.

22. Leslie Farr communication to the author, June 25, 2009.

23. Larry E. Scott, interview by the author, June 6, 2009.

24. The Judy Farr Alumni Center is located on the campus of the University of Northern Colorado, several blocks from the Farrs' home on 14th Avenue. The center is headquarters for the UNC Foundation, Inc.

25. Larry E. Scott, communication to the author, June 6, 2009.

26. Gene and Peggy Koplitz, interview by Carol Lucking, July 14, 2009.

27. Gilbert Hause, interview by the author, June 22, 2009. After receiving a master's degree from Colorado State Teachers College (UNC), Michener taught there from 1936 to1941 and returned in the 1970s to work on *Centennial.*

28. WD Farr, interview by Sally Mier, February 15, 2000.

29. WD Farr, interview by the author, December 26, 2006.

30. Judy joined the BE chapter of PEO in 1936. She was president in 1948 and delegate to the state convention in 1949. PEO was founded in 1869. It became an international women's organization focusing on providing educational opportunities for female students worldwide.

31. Larry E. Scott, interview by the author, June 6, 2009.

32. Tate Todd, interview by Carol Lucking, July 9, 2009.

33. Sharon Farr, interview by the author, July 13, 2009.

34. WD Farr, interview by Sally Mier, December 21, 1999.

35. Alfred R. Slighter, interview by the author, August 4, 2009.

36. Shirley Judy Lewis-Prater, interview by the author, July 22, 2009. Shirley, who also goes by Judy, mentioned the amazing caricatures her sister drew on the letters she wrote home from 1935 to 1938. Copies of these drawings can be found in WDF—Judy Farr Letters and Cartoons, Farr Papers, Water Resources Archive, CSU.

37. I have borrowed a few of the anecdotes recounted to me by Leslie and Sharon Farr and Greeley residents Gene and Peggy Koplitz.

38. Shirley Judy Lewis-Prater, interview by the author, July 18, 2009.

39. WD Farr, interview by the author, September 22, 2003; and D. Tyler, *Silver Fox of the Rockies.*

40. *Greeley (Colo.) Tribune,* June 21, 1991.

41. *Greeley (Colo.) Tribune,* October 30, 1991.

42. *Greeley (Colo.) Tribune,* September 15, 1991.

43. Unless otherwise noted, the details of the Dean River accident were provided by John and WR Farr.

44. John Farr, communication to the author, July 24, 2009.

45. WD Farr to Dr. Judith Vaughn, October 10, 1995, WDF—Letters Written to Friends After July 1995 Accident, Farr Papers, Water Resources Archive, CSU.

46. WD Farr to John and Bill Farr, September 7, 1995, WDF—1994 and 1995 Dean River, Farr Papers, Water Resources Archive, CSU.

47. WD Farr to Rob Stewart, September 13, 1995, in ibid.

48. WD Farr to Dick Blewett, January 24, 1996, in ibid.

49. WD Farr, interview by the author, December 26, 2006.

50. Rob Stewart, interview by the author, August 23, 2007.

51. WD Farr, speech at Wolford Mountain Reservoir Dedication, September 23, 1995, NCWCD Archives.

52. Farr, "Farewell from WD Farr," 2.

53. The others were Charles Lory, Ed Munroe, and Ben Nix.

54. Robert Barkley to WD Farr, November 8, 1995, Northern–Greeley Reception November 1995, Farr Papers, Water Resources Archive, CSU.

55. Rep. Wayne Allard of Colorado, *Congressional Record* 141, no. 180.

56. Ruth Wright, interview by the author, August 15, 2009.

57. These facilities are the Hansen Feeder Canal, Alva B. Adams Tunnel, Ed Munroe Canal, and the John Dille Tunnel.

58. Colorado Wilderness Act of 1993, August 13, 1993.

59. John M. Sayre to WD Farr, June 22, 1994, WDF—Farr Pumping Plant, Farr Papers, Water Resources Archive, CSU.

60. WD Farr to Honorable Hank Brown, June 21, 1994, in ibid.

61. See especially WD Farr to Lee Leachman of Billings, Montana, June 14, 1995, Lee Leachman, Farr Papers, Water Resources Archive, CSU.

62. C. E. Ball, *Building the Beef Industry*, 263. The beef check-off program became mandatory in 1988 when producers and importers were required to pay $1 per head each time an animal was sold. Fifty cents of each assessment was allocated to state beef councils, and fifty cents was invested by the Cattlemen's Beef Board, which represented all industries involved in beef production. The assessed monies were used to bring new products into stores and restaurants, help educate customers regarding the nutrient value of beef, promote beef abroad, develop safety standards, encourage research and development, and promote beef through advertising.

63. See NCBA Letters to Newspapers, Farr Papers, Water Resources Archive, CSU.

64. C. E. Ball, *Building the Beef Industry*, 263, italics in the original.

65. Wortham, "Historic Vote Creates NCBA," 1.

66. Robert G. Tointon, interview by the author, August 10, 2009.

67. WD Farr to Burton Eller, February 6, 1996, Letters and Replies, 1996, Leadership, Farr Papers, Water Resources Archive, CSU. Eller became executive vice president of the NCA in 1991. He resigned shortly after the NCBA was formed.

68. C. E. Ball, *Building the Beef Industry*, 265–66.

69. WD Farr to Paul Engler, WDF—1994 Business Hall of Fame, Farr Papers, Water Resources Archive, CSU.

70. "With prejudice" meant that the same matter could not be raised again in any court.

71. C. E. Ball, *Building the Beef Industry*, 266.

72. WD Farr to Susan Borg, project manager, July 3, 1996, WDF—Editorial Board, Farr Papers, Water Resources Archive, CSU.

73. Minutes of the Governing Board and Trustees, NCF, January 30, 1997, in ibid.

74. The American Meat Institute (AMI) describes itself as the representative of companies that produce 95 percent of the red meat and 70 percent of turkey produced in the United States. Headquartered in Washington, D.C., AMI keeps its finger on the legislative pulse. According to the organization's website, its primary focuses are on food safety, worker safety, international trade, economic trends, and animal welfare (www.meatami.com). But critics have charged AMI with opposing regulations designed to make the meat industry safer. In *Fast Food Nation*, for

example, Schlosser notes that AMI has opposed testing of ground beef for *E. coli* 0157:H7. The organization "routinely fought against any mandatory food safety measures proposed by the federal government"; AMI, in turn, accused Schlosser of using "anecdotal" evidence in his book. See Schlosser, *Fast Food Nation*, 207, 275–76.

75. WD Farr to Don Butler, chairman, NCF, July 26, 1996, WDF—National Cattle Foundation, Farr Papers, Water Resources Archive, CSU.

76. WD Farr to Susan Borg, July 5, 1996, Editorial Board, in ibid.

77. Susi Seawald, interview by Carol Lucking, August 25, 2009.

78. WD Farr, epilogue to C. E. Ball's, *Building the Beef Industry*, 280–81.

79. WD Farr to Susan Borg, September 9, 1996, WDF—Editorial Board, Farr Papers, Water Resources Archive, CSU.

80. Michener became associated with the Farrs through his experiences at UNC prior to World War II and during the years he spent writing *Centennial* in and around Greeley. WD did not know him well, but because Michener was a celebrated author with western connections, the editorial board felt he would be the perfect person to write the foreword.

81. *Greeley (Colo.) Tribune*, January 27 and June 18, 1997.

82. Comments of Jeannine Truswell, executive director of United Way of Weld County, as reported in the *Greeley (Colo.) Tribune*, May 17, 1997.

83. The Bravo award was presented by the Fort Collins Area Chamber of Commerce, the Fort Collins Economic Development Corporation, the Greeley/Weld Chamber of Commerce, the Loveland Chamber of Commerce, the Loveland Economic Development Council, and the Northern Colorado *Business Report*.

84. Justice Gregory J. Hobbs, National Western Citizen of the West Presentation, Westin Hotel, January 11, 1999, Farr Papers, Water Resources Archive, CSU.

85. John Farr, communication to the author, August 24, 2009.

86. Charles P. Schroeder to WD Farr, January 21, 1999, NCBA Growing Pains, Farr Papers, Water Resources Archive, CSU.

87. RJ Farr, communication to the author, August 25, 2009.

CHAPTER 8

1. *Greeley (Colo.) Tribune*, May 27, 2000.

2. *Greeley (Colo.) Tribune*, February 6, 2000.

3. WD Farr, address to Greeley City Council work session, April 25, 2000, Greeley—Thoughts on Water City of Greeley, Farr Papers, Water Resources Archive, CSU.

4. Ibid.

5. Harold Evans, Greeley Water Board member, communication to the author, September 4, 2009. Evans noted that "little Johnstown" seized on the opportunity "to go north and annex the southeast corner of I-25 and [Highway] 34. My feeling is that Mr. Farr was correct in 2000 and Greeley should have taken the opportunity when it was available."

6. Eric Wilkinson, interview by the author, October 29, 2008.

7. WD Farr, "Thoughts on Greeley's Future Water Supplies," n.d., Farr Papers, Water Resources Archive, CSU.

8. Eric Wilkinson, interview with the author, October 29, 2008.

9. John Farr, communication to the author, July 24, 2009.

10. WD Farr, interview by the author, December 26, 2006.

11. Ibid.

12. John Farr, communication to the author, July 24, 2009.

13. Susi Seawald, interview by the author, March 30, 2007. In addition to her duties with the Colorado Sugarbeet Growers Association, Seawald worked for WD for nineteen years.

14. WD Farr, interview by the author, December 26, 2006.

15. NCBA News, 2002, Swan Leadership Award (Colo.).

16. Allison Sherry, "Greeley Man Pioneered Efforts to Improve Water Use, Quality," *Greeley Tribune*, August 7, 2000. The reference to Cal Ripken, Jr., is appropriate. Ripken played baseball for the Baltimore Orioles for twenty years, during which time he remained in the lineup each day, even with injuries, eventually breaking Lou Gehrig's record for consecutive games played. He worked hard, overcame adversity, showed loyalty to Baltimore, and won the respect of players and fans. He was an outstanding leader.

17. Sample, *Contrarian's Guide to Leadership*, 17.

18. Ibid., 150–51. Linda Mitchell Davis, owner of the CS Ranch in Cimarron, New Mexico, pointed out that WD had the unique quality amongst cattlemen to put his visionary thoughts into words. "He remembered everything," she recalled, and "he was able to connect the dots in a way that listeners would understand." Telephone interview by the author, February 11, 2010.

19. Gardner, *On Leadership*, 18. Pete Morrell, Greeley city manager from 1973 to 1986, referred to this leadership talent as "constructive coaching." Interview by the author, September 25, 2009.

20. Darell Zimbelman, interview by the author, August 16, 2009. Zimbelman was chief engineer, associate general manager, and treasurer of the NCWCD when WD used to make periodic phone calls that began, "I've been thinking about . . ." For the most part, Zimbelman recalled, the ideas prompting those calls were timely, intellectually stimulating, and broadly conceived.

21. WD Farr's comments to John Farr on September 11, 2001, as relayed to the author by telephone, August 28, 2009. These same sentiments were expressed by John Gardner in his 1990 book *On Leadership*, p. 194.

22. Bennis, *Why Leaders Can't Lead*, 113–14, 117, 119.

23. WD Farr, "WD Farr Family History," edited by Cattlemen's Communications, n.d., pp. 64, 66, 69, 70, 74, 76, Farr Papers, Water Resources Archive, CSU.

24. WD Farr, interview by the author, September 22, 2003.

25. WD Farr, interview by Bob Holt, UNC, December 18, 1998. The video interview was shown to the "Citizen of the West" gathering in January 1999.

26. Ibid.

27. NISP calls for construction of Glade Reservoir along Highway 287 northwest of Fort Collins. Seven miles of the highway would have to be relocated. Glade would have a capacity of 170,000 acre-feet of water, which would be diverted from the Cache la Poudre River. Although the NCWCD is the primary organizer, fifteen Front Range water providers are participating in planning and funding the project at an estimated cost of $405 million. As of this writing, the project is going through a public comment period following a draft Environmental Impact Statement by the U.S. Army Corps of Engineers. Many Front Range residents expected to see this project develop after agreement was reached in 1986, designating parts of the Poudre River "wild and scenic," but stakeholders were exhausted after those negotiations.

28. Bill Jackson, interview by the author, July 28, 2009.

29. Larry Simpson, interview by the author, May 22, 2007.

30. WD Farr, "Farr Family History," p. 87, Farr Papers, Water Resources Archive, CSU.

31. WD Farr, interview by Sally Mier, December 28, 1999.

32. WD Farr, interview by the author, December 26, 2006.

33. Robert Jousserand, interview by the author, January 7, 2009.

34. Topper Thorpe, interview by the author, January 7, 2009.

35. Founded in New York in 1923, the Newcomen Society took its name from the British pioneer Thomas Newcomen, who invented the first practical atmospheric steam engine in 1712.

36. George S. Spencer, interview by the author, January 5, 2009.

37. Peggy Ford, research coordinator, Greeley Museum, communication to the author, June 8 and June 29, 2009.

38. Albert C. Yates, telephone conversation with the author, May 13, 2009.

39. Chris Jouflas, interview by the author, May 22, 2009.

40. Gregory Hobbs, interview by the author, June 15, 2007.

41. Burton Eller, interview by the author, December 30, 2008.

42. Bennis, "Revisionist Theory of Leadership," 27–28.

43. Ibid, 146–50.

44. John Farr, communication to the author, August 31, 2009.

45. Susi Seawald, interview by Carol Lucking, August 25, 2009. Unless otherwise noted, the information regarding WD's life at the office comes from this interview.

46. Gerald Nelson, interview by Carol Lucking, August 7, 2009.

47. Susan Wickham, interview by the author, August 16, 2009.

48. Butchart Gardens, located on fifty-five acres in Victoria, British Columbia, is one of the world's premier floral show gardens. Begun by Jennie Butchart in 1904, the gardens represent the aesthetic style prevalent in the Victorian era, when grand estates stood as singular representatives of aristocratic elegance. See http://www.butchantgardens.com.

49. Ibid.

50. WD Farr to Randy Farr, July 18, 1997, WDF—Randy Farr, Farr Papers, Water Resources Archive, CSU.

51. Charles P. Schroeder, communication to the author, April 11, 2007.

52. Charles P. Schroeder read these criteria to WD over the telephone on April 16, 2007, after the family decided he would be unable to travel to Oklahoma City to accept the award in person.

53. Charles P. Schroeder, communication to the author, April 11, 2007.

54. From the 1955 inception of the Hall of Great Westerners through 2007, approximately 265 individuals were chosen to have their portraits hung.

55. Craig, "Colorado's Cattle King," 42.

56. Joining WD in the first class of inductees was Paul Engler of Cactus Feeders, Amarillo, Texas.

57. WDF—Greeley National Bank History, Farr Papers, Water Resources Archive, CSU.

POSTSCRIPT

1. RD Farr, interview by the author, September 23, 2009. The author's perspective on RD's relationship to his grandfather comes from this interview.

Bibliography

ARCHIVAL COLLECTIONS

Colorado Cooperative Extension. Records. Colorado Agricultural Archive, Colorado State University Libraries.

Delph E. Carpenter Papers. Water Resources Archive, Colorado State University, Fort Collins, Colo.

Farr Family Papers. Water Resources Archive, Colorado State University, Fort Collins, Colo.

Hazel E. Johnson Research Center and Municipal Archives, Greeley, Colo.

Home Gas and Electric Company of Greeley. Minute books. Greeley, Colo.

Larimer and Weld Counties, Office of Clerk and Recorder. Larimer and Weld County, Colo.

National Cattlemen's Association Records, 1898–1990, and Joseph M. Carey Papers, 1869–1978. American Heritage Center, University of Wyoming, Laramie, Wyo.

Northern Colorado Water Conservancy District and Municipal Subdistrict. Minutes. Berthoud, Colo.

William R. Kelly Papers, Greeley Museum Archive, Greeley, Colo.

Xcel Energy, Property Services. Corporate records, Denver, Colo.

BOOKS, JOURNALS, AND OTHER SOURCES

Abbott, Carl, Stephen J. Leonard, and David McComb. *Colorado: A History of the Centennial State*. Niwot: University Press of Colorado, 1994.

The Agricultural Outlook for 1934. Washington, D.C.: U.S. Department of Agriculture, 1933.

Allard, Wayne. *Congressional Record*. 104th Cong., 1st sess., 1995. Vol. 141, no. 180.

Andreas, Carol. *Meatpackers and Beef Barons*. Niwot: University Press of Colorado, 1994.

Athearn, Robert G. *The Mythic West in Twentieth-Century America.* Lawrence: University Press of Kansas, 1986.

Ball, Charles E. *Building the Beef Industry. A Century of Commitment.* Englewood, Colo.: National Cattlemen's Foundation, 1998.

———. *The Finishing Touch: A History of the Texas Cattle Feeders Association and Cattle Feeding in the Southwest.* Amarillo: Texas Cattle Feeders Association, 1992.

Ball, Wilbur P. *The Last Roundup: A History of the Early Cattle Roundups in Northern Weld County, Colorado.* Eaton, Colo.: W. P. Ball, 1991.

Barnhart, Walt. *Kenny's Shoes: A Walk through the Storied Life of the Remarkable Kenneth W. Monfort.* West Conshohocken, Pa.: Infinity, 2008.

Bennis, Warren G. "Revisionist Theory of Leadership." *Harvard Business Review* 39 (1961): 26–28, 31, 34, 36, 146, 148, 150.

———. *Why Leaders Can't Lead: The Unconscious Conspiracy Continues.* San Francisco, Calif.: Jossey-Bass, 1989.

Boesen, Victor. *Storm: Irving Krick vs. the U.S. Weather Bureaucracy.* New York: G. P. Putnam's Sons, 1978.

Boyd, David. *A History: Greeley and the Union Colony of Colorado.* Greeley, Colo.: Greeley Tribune Press, 1890.

Brosnan, Kathleen A. *Uniting Mountain and Plain: Cities, Law, and Environmental Change along the Front Range.* Albuquerque: University of New Mexico Press, 2002.

Buffum, B. C., and Griffith, C. J. "Swine Feeding in Colorado." *Colorado Agricultural Experiment Station Bulletin* 74 (September 1902): 4.

Carpenter, Edward F. *America's First Grazier: The Biography of Farrington R. Carpenter.* Fort Collins, Colo.: Vestige Press, 2004.

Carpenter, Farrington R. *Confessions of a Maverick: An Autobiography.* Denver: State Historical Society, 1984.

A Church at the Bend of the River, 1845–1895. Port Stanley, Ontario: Anglican Church of Port Stanley, n.d.

Clay, John, and N. H. Sutherland. *The Story of a Carload.* Omaha, Nebr.: Clay, Robinson & Company, 1915.

Colorado Cooperative Crop Reporting Service and U.S. Department of Agriculture. *Agricultural Statistics, Crops and Livestock of the State of Colorado, 1942.* Denver: Colorado Cooperative Crop and Livestock Reporting Service, 1942.

Colorado Wilderness Act of 1993, Public Law 103-77 (H.R. 631), August 13, 1993.

Craig, Jim. "Colorado's Cattle King." *Colorado Business* 9 (November 1981): 38–42.

Cumming, Ross, ed. *Illustrated Historical Atlas of the County of Elgin, Ontario.* Toronto: H. R. Page and Company, 1877. Page references are to the 1972 reprint.

Curran, Dennis E. "Pioneer of Farr West Sees Hope in Far East." *The Northern Colorado Business Report* 4, no. 3 (December 1998): 11A.

Degler, Carl. *Out of Our Past: The Forces that Shaped Modern America*. 3rd ed. New York: Harper Perrenial, 1983.

Drache, Hiram M. *Creating Abundance: Visionary Entrepreneurs of Agriculture*. Danville, Ill.: Interstate, 2001.

Dunbar, Robert G. "Water Conflicts and Controls in Colorado." *Agricultural History*, XXII (July 1948), 180–86.

Ewing, Sherm. *The Ranch: A Modern History of the North American Cattle Industry*. Missoula, Mont.: Mountain Press, 1995.

———. *The Range*. Missoula, Mont.: Mountain Press, 1990.

"Examining the Transatlantic Voyage, Part 1." *Ancestry Magazine* 18, no. 6 (Nov. 1, 2000), pp. 1–4, http://anc.rootsweb.com/learn/library/article.aspx?article=3365.

Farr, W. D. "Farewell from WD Farr." *Waternews* 13, no. 3 (Fall 1995): 2, 7.

———. "What's Ahead?" (speech given at Beef Cattle Day, CSU). *Colorado Cattle Rancher and Farmer* (1979): 36. Available at Farr Family Papers, Water Resources Archive, CSU.

Ford, Peggy. "Greeley, Colorado: Agricultural Mecca of the West." Unpublished manuscript prepared for the Greeley Museum's Historical Preservation Plan, 1996. Greeley Museum Archive, Greeley, Colo.

Forman, Dorothy S., ed. *First Congregational Church: 100 Years of Service, 1870–1970*. Greeley, Colo.: First Congregational Church, 1969.

Gardner, John W. *Excellence: Can We Be Equal and Excellent Too?* New York: W. W. Norton, 1984.

———. *On Leadership*. New York: Free Press, 1990.

Geffs, Mary L. *Under Ten Flags: A History of Weld County, Colorado*. Greeley, Colo.: McVey, 1938.

Geiger, Betty Jo. "W. D. Farr: Recollections of a Pioneer Cattle Feeder." Pts. 1–14. *Calf News Cattle Feeder* (February 1990): 6, 8, 32; (March 1990): 8, 20, 24; (April 1990): 8, 9, 33; (May 1990): 16–17; (June 1990): 20–21; (July 1990): 20–21; (August 1990): 24, 25, 31; (September 1990): 34, 49; (October 1990): 24, 26; (November 1990): 3, 42; (December 1990): 14–15; (January 1991): 24–25; (February 1991): 10, 12; (April 1991): 14–15.

Gladwell, Malcolm. *Blink: The Power of Thinking Without Thinking*. New York: Little, Brown & Co., 2005.

———. *Outliers: The Story of Success*. New York: Little, Brown & Co., 2008.

———. *The Tipping Point: How Little Things Can Make a Big Difference*. New York: Little, Brown & Co., 2000.

Goff, Richard, and Robert H. McCaffree. *Century in the Saddle: The 100 Year Story of the Colorado Cattlemen's Association*. Denver: Colorado Cattlemen's Centennial Commission, 1967.

Green, Gibb. "W. D. Farr Shows Vision, Commitment." *Record Stockman* 7 (February 11, 1994).

Gropman, Alan L. *The Big 'L': American Logistics in World War II*. Washington, D.C.: National Defense University Press, 1997.

Grubb, Eugene H., and W. S. Guilford. *The Potato: A Compilation of Information from Every Available Source*. New York: Doubleday, Page and Company, 1912.

Hall, David John. *Economic Development in Elgin County: 1850–1880*. Petrolia, Ontario: Western District, 1972.

Hart, John Fraser. *The Changing Scale of American Agriculture*. Charlottesville, Va., and London, England: University of Virginia Press, 2003.

Hartman, Bill. *A Century of Remarkable Progress: The Greeley and Loveland Irrigation Company*. Greeley, Colo.: Greeley and Loveland Irrigation, 1981.

Hirt, Paul. Review of *A Passion for Nature: The Life of John Muir*, by Donald Worster (New York: Oxford University Press, 2008). *Montana: The Magazine of Western History* 59, no. 4 (Winter 2009): 73–74.

Hofstadter, Richard. *The Age of Reform*. New York: Knopf Doubleday, 1955.

"The Home Gas and Electric Company: The Story of Its Development through Forty-Five Years, 1902–1947." N.p., n.d. Available in the "Electric" file, Greeley Museum Archives, Greeley, Colo.

Hurt, R. Douglas. *The Dust Bowl: An Agricultural and Social History*. Chicago: Nelson-Hall, 1981.

James, Libby. "T-Bones and Talk." *Greeley Style* 2, no. 4 (Fall 1985): 32–34.

Keith, Edgerton. Review of *Wellington Rankin: His Family, Life and Times*, by Volney Steele (Bozeman, Mont.: Champions Publishing, 2002). *Montana: The Magazine of Western History* 53, no. 2 (Summer 2003): 71.

Kleinheinz, Frank. *Sheep Management Breeds and Judging: A Textbook for the Shepherd and Student*. 5th ed. Madison, Wisc.: published by the author, 1918.

Lamm, Richard, and Duane Smith. *Pioneers and Politicians: 10 Colorado Governors in Profile*. Boulder, Colo.: Pruett, 1984.

Lemke, Barbara. "Legend." *National Cattlemen* 10 (August 1995): 6–8, 10–11.

Lenthe, Sue. "W. D. Farr: Statesman in Worlds of Water Management, Agriculture and Business." *Today's Business* 4, no. 5 (May 1998): 41–44.

Leonard, Stephen. *Trials and Triumphs: A Colorado Portrait of the Great Depression, With FSA Photographs*. Niwot: University Press of Colorado, 1993.

Leonard, Stephen, and Thomas Noel. *Denver: Mining Camp to Metropolis*. Niwot: University Press of Colorado, 1990.

Leuchtenburg, William E. *Franklin D. Roosevelt and the New Deal*. New York: Harper Collins, 1963.

Limerick, Patricia Nelson. *The Legacy of Conquest: The Unbroken Past of the American West*. New York: W. W. Norton & Company, 1987.

Luecke, Daniel F. "Two Forks Dam and Endangered Species." *Colorado Water* 26, no. 2 (March/April 2009): 17–19.

Matsushima, John. *A Journey Back: A History of Cattle Feeding in Colorado and the United States*. Colorado Springs, Colo.: Cattlemen's Communications, 1995.

Mayer, Oscar G. *America's Meat Packing Industry.* Princeton, N.J.: Princeton University Press, 1939.

Mehls, Carol Drake, and Steven F. Mehls. *Weld County Colorado Historic Agricultural Context.* Lafayette, Colo.: Western Historical Studies, 1990.

Michener, James A. *Centennial.* New York: Random House, 1974.

Montgomery, George A. "Commercial Feeder of the Year." *Feedlot Magazine* 11, no. 2 (February 1969): 12–15, 37, 38.

Murdoch, David Hamilton. *The American West: The Invention of a Myth.* Reno: University of Nevada Press, 2001.

"National Affairs: Shakedown II." *Time,* April 22, 1946. www.time.com/time/magazine/article/0,9171,792759,00.html.

Noel, Thomas J. *Growing through History with Colorado: The Colorado National Banks, the First 125 Years, 1862–1987.* Denver: Colorado National Banks and the Colorado Studies Center, University of Colorado at Denver, 1987.

Norris, Jane E. *Written in Water: The Life of Benjamin Harrison Eaton.* Athens, Ohio: Swallow Press/Ohio University Press, 1990.

Norris, Lee G. "A Conversation with William R. Kelly, Esquire." N.p., n.d. Available at Greeley Museum Archives, Greeley, Colo.

Oldfield, J. E. "Marion Eugene Ensminger: 1908–1998. A Brief Biography." *Journal of American Science* 77 (1999): 2325–26.

Preston, R. L. *Stetson, Pipe and Boots—Cattleman Governor. A Biography about Dan Thornton.* Victoria, B. C.: Trafford, 2006.

"Prof. Frank Kleinheinz" (obituary). *Wisconsin Country Magazine* 22, no. 2 (November 1928): 23.

Rayburn, Alan. *Place Names of Ontario.* Toronto: University of Toronto Press, 1997.

Russell, Andy. *The Life of a River.* Toronto, Ontario: McClelland and Stewart, 1987.

———. "Ten Feet from a Killer Bear: An Alberta Rancher Gets That Cattle-Slaying Blackie—And a Gray Hair or Two." *Outdoor Life* 97, no. 3 (March 1946): 52, 103–104.

Sample, Steven B. *The Contrarian's Guide to Leadership.* San Francisco: Jossey-Bass, 2001.

Schlosser, Eric. *Fast Food Nation: The Dark Side of the All-American Meal.* New York: Houghton Mifflin, 2001.

"Sheep and Cattle Estimates." *Through the Leaves* 22 (January 1934): 19.

Sherman, Diana. "Farr Family Creates Weld Banking Dynasty." *Northern Colorado Business Report* (April 1996): 1B, 5B.

Shoemaker, Len. *Pioneers of the Roaring Fork.* Thousand Oaks, Calif.: Sage Books, 1965.

Silkenson, Gregory M. *Windy Gap: Transmountain Water Diversion and the Environmental Movement.* Technical Report No. 61. Fort Collins, Colo.: Colorado Water Resources Research Institute, 1994.

Sims, Hugh Joffre. *Sims' History of Elgin County.* 3 vols. Edited by Irene Golas. St. Thomas, Ontario: Elgin County Library, 1984.

Smith, Barbara. *1870–1970: The First Hundred Years, Greeley, Colorado.* Greeley, Colo.: Greater Greeley Centennial Commission, 1970.

Sonnichsen, C. L. *Cowboys and Cattle Kings.* Westport, Conn.: Greenwood Press, 1980. First published 1950 by University of Oklahoma Press.

Sprague, Marshall. *Colorado: A Bicentennial History.* New York: W. W. Norton & Co., 1976.

Sweet, Edna D. *Carbondale Pioneers, 1879–1890.* Carbondale, Colo., Privately printed, 1947.

Theroux, Paul. *The Old Patagonian Express: By Train through the Americas.* Boston: Houghton Mifflin, 1979.

Tyler, Alice Felt. *Freedom's Ferment—Phases of American Social History to 1860.* New York: Harper & Row, 1944.

Tyler, Daniel. *The Last Water Hole in the West: The Colorado–Big Thompson Project and the Northern Colorado Water Conservancy District.* Niwot: University Press of Colorado, 1993.

———. *Silver Fox of the Rockies: Delphus E. Carpenter and Western Water Compacts.* Norman: University of Oklahoma Press, 2003.

Tyler, Sidney F. *A Joyful Odyssey.* 3 vols. Tucson, Ariz.: Sunset Press, 1990, 1991, 1993.

Ubbelhode, Carl, Maxine Benson, and Duane A. Smith. *A Colorado History.* 6th ed. Boulder, Colo.: Pruett, 1988.

U.S. Bureau of the Census. "Population, Internal Migration 1935 to 1940" in *Sixteenth Census of the United States: 1940.* Washington, D.C.: GPO, 1943.

U.S. Congress. House. Committee on Banking and Currency. *Hearings on H. R. 5270.* 79th Congress, 2nd sess., February 1946. Washington: GPO, 1946.

U.S. Congress. Senate. Committee on Agriculture and Forestry. *Hearing before Subcommittee on S. Res. 92.* 79th Cong., 2nd sess., April 1946. Washington: GPO, 1946.

U.S. Congress. Senate. Committee on Banking and Currency. *Hearing on S. 2028.* 79th Congress, 2nd sess., May 1946. Washington: GPO, 1946.

U.S. Department of the Interior, Bureau of Reclamation. *Reconnaissance Report on the West Slope Extension, Colorado–Big Thompson Project, Colorado.* Denver: Bureau of Reclamation, Region 7, December 1956.

U.S. Select Committee on Nutrition and Human Needs. *Dietary Goals of the United States* (report prepared by select committee staff, chaired by George S. McGovern, 95th Cong., 1st sess.). Washington, D.C.: GPO, 1977.

Webb, Walter Prescott. *The Great Plains.* Boston: Ginn & Co., 1931.

Wentworth, Edward Norris. *America's Sheep Trails.* Ames: Iowa State College Press, 1948.

Wharton, Edith. *A Backward Glance.* New York: Charles Scribner's Sons, 1993.

White, H. P. "The Fabulous Feeding Farrs." *Western Live Stock* 39, no. 1 (August 1953): 32–33, 44, 46.

White, Richard. *It's Your Misfortune and None of My Own.* Norman: University of Oklahoma Press, 1991.

Wickens, James F. *Colorado in the Great Depression.* New York: Garland, 1979.
———. "The New Deal in Colorado." *The Pacific Historical Review* 38, no. 3 (August, 1969): 275–91.
Wolfenbarger, Deon. "Depression, Drought and Dust: A New Deal for Colorado." *Colorado Preservationist* 18, no. 4 (Winter 2004–2005): 1–24.
Worster, Donald. *Dust Bowl: The Southern Plains in the 1930s.* New York: Oxford University Press, 1979.
Wortham, Fred. "Historic Vote Creates NCBA." *Western Livestock Journal* 75, no. 15 (February 5, 1996): 1, 5.
Wrobel, David. *The End of American Exceptionalism: Frontier Anxiety from the Old West to the New Deal.* Lawrence: University Press of Kansas, 1996.

Index